Daughter of Derry

Daughter of Derry

THE STORY OF BRIGID SHEILS MAKOWSKI

Margie Bernard

PLUTO  PRESS

First published 1989 by Pluto Press
11–21 Northdown Street, London N1 9BN

Distributed in the USA by Unwin Hyman Inc
8 Winchester Place, Winchester
MA 01890, USA

Lasersetting: Ponting–Green Publishing Services
London

Printed in Great Britain by
Billing & Sons Ltd, Worcester

British Library Cataloguing in Publication Data

Bernard, Margie
  Daughter of Derry
  1. Ireland——Politics and government——1949-
  I. Title   II. Makowski, Brigid Sheils
  941.50824'092'4   DA963

ISBN 0–7453–0210–6

For Donald and Mark – the dearest and most understanding friends a mother could desire. And for Janet, Mark Bryan and Christopher Robin – the newest addition to our family.

But especially for T.T.T. – Venceremos! – there will be a better day!

Contents

Acknowledgements

The following represents the final and delightful aspect of writing this book – thanking some of the many people who helped me to bring *Daughter of Derry* to fruition.

First and foremost is Brigid who trusted my ability to present an accurate account of her personal and political involvement in the revolutionary movement to establish an Irish democratic socialist republic. And I speak for the both of us in jointly thanking the following people who allowed us formally to interview them and gain their insights of certain time periods and significant events: Jerry 'The Bird' Doherty; Stella Makowski Fean; Harry Flynn; Pauline Gillespie; Peggy Mellon; Terry Robson; Johnny White. Informally, additional information was provided by: Mary Sheils Baggerly; Naomi Brennan; Eileen Sheils Collins; Jim Collins; Jim Og Collins; Patrick Collins; Eilis Flynn; John Lyons; Marion Lyons; Tom McGuigan; Patsy Moore; Teresa Sheils Moore; Eamon Sheils; Sean Sheils.

Finally, I want to thank the following people who contributed to my knowledge during our conversations: Tony Gregory; Breige Makowski Healy; Liam Healy; Bernadette Devlin McAliskey; Tommy McCourt; Mary McGlinchey; Brian Makowski; Leo Makowski; Leo Patrick Makowski; Margaret Makowski Molloy; Jack O'Brien; Tony O'Hara; Margaret Powers; Mrs Patrick Sheils.

I also want to thank all those who contributed to the process of *Daughter of Derry* becoming a published reality: Neil Middleton, my original editor at Pluto Press, for accepting the work of an unknown author; Roger van Zwanenberg, my publisher, who had the wisdom to revive Pluto Press after it went into liquidation; Anne Beech, my current editor, for her patience and prompt replies to all my enquiries; and Sarah Stewart, my copy editor, for providing clarity without changing content. I would also like to thank Thomas Kinsella for permission to quote from *Butcher's Dozen*, first published by Pepper-canister, Dublin, 1972, and Donal Fean, who drew the maps.

But above all I offer a special tribute to Mrs Patrick 'Ma' Sheils, the indomitable matriarch of the Sheils Clan, for her strength, endurance, commitment and life-long dedication to the goal of a united Ireland. She opened her heart to me, warmly welcomed me as a frequent guest in her Bogside flat and on several occasions allowed me the use of her cottage on the shore of Lough Swilly in County Donegal.

And finally, my thanks to my ex-husband, Burton Bernard, for his love, encouragement, and support during all the good years we shared which provided the foundation upon which I have built my present.

Abbreviations

AFNICRA	American Friends of the Northern Ireland Civil Rights Association
AI	Amnesty International
APL	Anti-Partition League
ASU	Active Service Unit
BJU	Bob Jones University (USA)
B-Specials	Ulster Special Constabulary
CIA	Central Intelligence Agency (USA)
CSJ	Campaign for Social Justice
DCAC	Derry Citizens' Action Committee
DCDC	Derry Citizens' Defence Committee
DHAC	Derry Housing Action Committee
DPP	Department of Public Prosecutions
ECHR	European Commission on Human Rights
EEC	European Economic Community
FMOA	Forensic Medical Officers Association
GHQ	General Headquarters
ICJP	Irish Commission for Justice and Peace
INLA	Irish National Liberation Army
IRA	Irish Republican Army
IRB	Irish Republican Brotherhood
IRSP	Irish Republican Socialist Party
ISRP	Irish Socialist Republican Party
ITGWU	Irish Transport and General Workers Union
MP	Member of British Parliament
MRF	Mobile Reconnaissance Force (British Army)
NATO	North Atlantic Treaty Organisation
NI	Northern Ireland
NICRA	Northern Ireland Civil Rights Association
NORAID	Northern Irish Aid (USA)
OC	Officer Commanding
PD	People's Democracy
PLA	People's Liberation Army

RI	Republic of Ireland
RTE	Radio Telefis Eireann (RI State-operated Radio and Television Broadcasting Service)
RUC	Royal Ulster Constabulary
SAS	Special Air Sevice Regiment (British Army)
SDLP	Social Democratic and Labour Party
SFADCo	Shannon Free Airport Development Company
SNCC	Student Nonviolent Coordinating Committee
TD	Member of Dail Eireann (RI Parliament)
UDA	Ulster Defence Association
UDR	Ulster Defence Regiment (formerly B-Specials)
UFF	Ulster Freedom Fighters
UPV	Ulster Protestant Volunteers
UVF	Ulster Volunteer Force

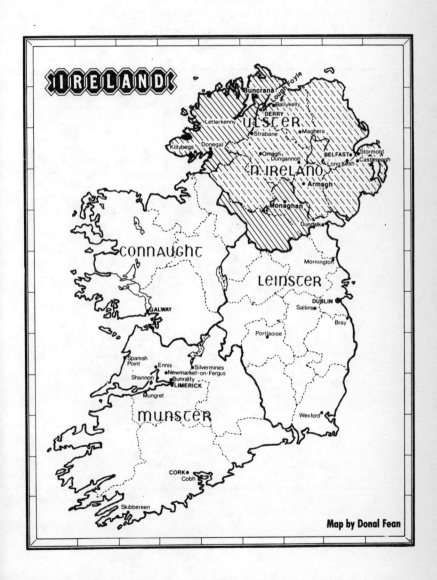

IRELAND

Buncrana
Lough Foyle
Ballykelly
DERRY
Letterkenny
ULSTER
Strabane
Maghera
Killybegs
Donegal
Omagh
Dungannon
BELFAST
Stormont
Long Kesh
Castlereagh
N.IRELAND
Armagh
Monaghan
Dundalk

CONNAUGHT
Mornington

LEINSTER
GALWAY
DUBLIN
Sallins
Bray
Portlaoise

Spanish Point
Ennis
Silvermines
Newmarket-on-Fergus
Shannon
Bunratty
LIMERICK
Mungret

MUNSTER
Wexford

CORK
Cobh

Skibbereen

Map by Donal Fean

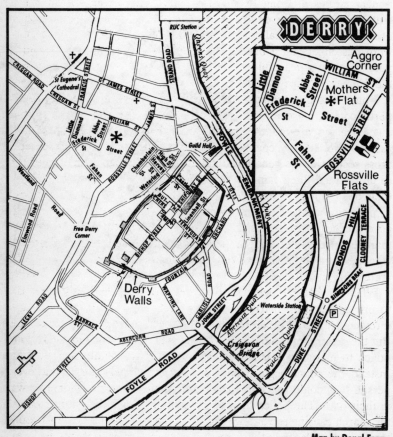

DERRY

Aggro Corner

Little Diamond
Frederick St
Abbey Street
WILLIAM St
Mothers *Flat
Street
Fahan St
ROSSVILLE STREET
Rossville Flats

RUC Station

St Eugene's Cathedral
CREGGAN ROAD
FRANCIS STREET
CREGGAN ST
Ct JAMES STREET
STRAND ROAD
Queens Quay
FOYLE

Little Diamond
Frederick St
Abbey Street
WILLIAM ST
JAMES STREET
*Street
Westland
Fahan St
ROSSVILLE STREET
Chamberlain St
High St
Harvey St
Waterloo St
Guild Hall
EMBANKMENT

Elmwood Road
Road
Free Derry Corner
BUTCHER'S GATE
London St
FERRYQUAY St
Linenhall St
ORCHARD ST
FOYLE

LECKY ROAD
BISHOP STREET
FOUNTAIN
WAPPING LANE
CARLISLE ROAD
JOHN STREET
Abercorn Quay
Waterside Station
BONDS HILL
SIMPSONS BRAE
CLOONEY TERRACE

Derry Walls

BARRACK STREET
ABERCORN ROAD
Craigavon Bridge
Waterside Quay
DUKE STREET
STREET
P

BISHOP
STREET
FOYLE ROAD

Map by Donal Fean

Introduction

I first met Brigid on 18 July 1981 during the tumultuous period of the hunger strikes at Long Kesh Prison in Northern Ireland which ultimately resulted in the deaths of ten young Irish freedom fighters, three of whom were political comrades of hers. On that Saturday she and I were passengers on a bus taking people from Shannon to Dublin to participate in a peaceful march that later would come to be known as the 'Embassy Police Riot'.

I have a long-standing resolve, which borders on a phobia, to not participate in marches – this was a rare exception and before starting out I walked around the crowd (officially estimated as 15,000), to assess its mood. My conclusion was that those present represented a cross section of the general population, from former cabinet ministers to farmers and their families, who had come to Dublin to demonstrate their deep anguish over the deaths of the first six hunger strikers and to petition their government to put diplomatic pressure on the British government to resolve the crisis before more lives were sacrificed. The marchers were met with a police assault reminiscent of those I'd witnessed on television during civil rights and anti-Vietnam War marches in the United States.

When the police blockaded the street in front of the British Embassy to prevent the crowd from marching past, some young people began throwing stones and then overturned three cars which they set on fire. But the general mood of the crowd remained peaceful and the ratio of police to marchers was more than sufficient to contain the situation. Instead, the police begin striking out indiscriminately at each and every person they could reach as their batons came down on whomever was in their path. The police then began charging down the entire route of the march causing terror and pandemonium among the demonstrators, most of whom froze in their tracks in disbelief, making themselves easy targets for police batons. The people of the Republic of Ireland had received an answer from their government – it would not condone peaceful protest when the impetus of that protest was to call upon the government to deliver a formal complaint to the British.

Our return trip to Shannon was delayed as we waited for Brigid. She had been taken to hospital for treatment of injuries sustained after she was batoned by the police.

I was puzzled when I learned from newspaper accounts the following day that the police had made no arrests. My puzzlement ended several months later when twenty people were arrested and charged with 'preventing the police from carrying out their duties' at the march. All twenty were prominent members of either the Irish Republican Socialist Party (IRSP) or Provisional Sinn Fein. At their trial before the three-judge, no-jury Special Criminal Court in Dublin all were convicted, with the major evidence against them being the word of police who testified that the defendants had been on the march. At their sentencing, all but two of the defendants were released when they agreed to pay fines which were to be contributed to the Gardi (Police) Benevolent Association. The two who chose to serve time in Portlaoise Prison rather than pay the fines were IRSP members, Harry Flynn and Gerry Roche. Roche was given an additional sentence when he announced that he considered it an honour to be sentenced by the same judge who had sentenced Nicky Kelly (see Chapter 18).

The next time Brigid and I met was a few weeks later and under more pleasant circumstances. We were dinner guests of Anne and Davoc Rynne at their Spanish Point home overlooking the Atlantic Ocean near Miltown Malbay, County Clare. After dinner, while drinking copious pots of tea, we began to talk about events in Ireland since the Derry Civil Rights March in October 1968. What emerged from our conversation was the extent of Brigid's participation in events which had shaped history during that time. At the end of the evening I enthusiastically agreed with Davoc's suggestion that writing a book based on Brigid's experiences would be a worthwhile undertaking; Brigid, somewhat taken aback, hesitantly acquiesced. The next afternoon we began what was to become hours of taping sessions over the next several years.

On 18 September 1981 I made my first trip with Brigid to her native city of Derry where I began a love affair with a town and its people which has intensified with every subsequent visit. On that day I also realised I had entered a war zone where armed British troops patrolled the streets in their jungle camouflage uniforms which contrasted sharply with the grey city streets, grey housing estates and grey, misty weather. There was no way to enter the main downtown area from the Bogside without being under constant surveillance by British soldiers stationed on top of the Rossville flats.

On the sixth day of our visit I agreed to drive Brigid and some of her friends to Buncrana across the border in County Donegal. We had barely gone three blocks when we were stopped at a police checkpoint and the names of everyone in the car taken, but it was clear that I was the only person they didn't already know. We crossed the border checkpoint with no further trouble. However, upon our return to Derry several hours later, I could feel tension mounting in the car as we once again neared the border crossing.

When we reached the hut at the checkpoint I stopped the car and produced my US passport for the soldier on duty. A buzzer went off inside the hut and I was told to pull the car over and wait for an escort to take us to the Fort George Interrogation Centre.

After about half-an-hour, two British army jeeps arrived. Brigid was put into one, the three men into the other and a young soldier with a rifle got into the back seat of my car and instructed me to follow them. I felt quite calm: I instinctively knew that nothing of a compromising nature would be found on any of my passengers or in the car itself.

We were held for about an hour while the car was given a thorough search, and then released. As a novice to the situation I didn't realise, as did my companions from their years of experience, that this exercise was just routine harassment and not a serious attempt to gather intelligence.

I returned to the US in November but managed to save money for another trip to Ireland in January 1982 which allowed me to stay through the first week of April. On this visit I was to experience the harassment of the Task Force (Political Police) in the Republic of Ireland. Shortly after my return to Ireland I decided to rent a car for another trip to Derry. When I arrived at Brigid's house I learned that her youngest daughter, Breige, was getting ready to walk to a job interview, so I volunteered to drive her. As we walked out the back door, Breige spotted a parked car with two men inside and muttered 'That's the Task Force, they're going to stop us if we take the car.' We walked down the pathway as though we were going to the local shop, waited out of sight for about ten minutes then went back to the car. The men had gone.

We began driving to the town centre but as we turned the corner we saw their car parked at the curb. As we drove past them they pulled in behind and followed us, then sped ahead and pulled in front of us, forcing me to slam on the brakes. The two came over and asked me for identification. One of them then asked me to open the trunk of the car, and grabbed a bag containing my notes for the book and my address book and told me I could pick them up at the police station the next day. When I questioned his right to take my personal belongings, he looked at me with a sneer saying, 'I could also arrest you under Section 30 [of the Offences Against the State Act] if I choose to do so.' I knew he had that right (which allowed me to be held for up to 48 hours without any charge), but added that if he was going to confiscate my personal property, I wanted a written receipt for everything he was taking. At that point he said, 'Wait here. Perhaps I won't have to take these after all.' Taking my bag, he walked to his car and got in while his partner stood watch over me.

Breige went over to the car and watched him go through my address book taking down the name of every person who had an address in Ireland. When finished, he returned my things telling me we were free to leave. When I said that Breige had now missed a job interview, he replied 'Don't worry she wouldn't have gotten the job anyway', and walked off. I was shaking with anger at his arrogance but I also knew I was powerless. When we told Brigid, she insisted on driving to the police station where she went through the empty formality of lodging a complaint against the two officers for harassing me.

In the Summer of 1984 I was able to return to Ireland where I lived as a resident alien until November 1986. In the interim, I steeped myself in Irish history, culture, economics and politics.

During that background reading, I came to realise how little I knew about the true nature of the situation in Ireland – and how much this is the case for many people, including those who regard themselves as being politically astute about international affairs. This is not too surprising when one realises that the major newspapers cover events in Ireland from their London offices and most of the information supplied to their staff about the situation there is, in general, provided by the British Information Service. But newspapers are not the only media sources to be faulted in this regard – no US wire service, for example, no news magazine, radio or television news-gathering agency has a full-time reporter covering Ireland. It is hardly surprising that the news about events in that country, both north and south, contains a pro-

British slant – with the rare exceptions proving the rule. This lack of unbiased reporting results in a skewed view of the historical and contemporary reality of Ireland – a country that some regard as England's Vietnam while others fear it may become Britain's Cuba.

One reality difficult to grasp is the fact that Ireland was the only colonised country in Europe. As a result, the island has suffered the same inequities as other colonised countries: near destruction of the Irish language and culture; the undermining of national self-esteem as the result of British racism; plunder of national resources; economic policies that have left Ireland underdeveloped and plunged the country into a downward cycle of undevelopment. In contemporary economic terms its former colonial status has left the Republic of Ireland as the second poorest country in the European Economic Community, only slightly ahead of newly admitted Spain. The national debt per person in the Republic is among the highest in the world. (As one wag in Dublin recently quipped, 'The only reason Ireland isn't a Third World Country is because it doesn't have the right climate!') With the decline of shipbuilding, the linen trade and clothing manufacture in Northern Ireland, its economy is also in serious decline and currently subsidised by the British government at the rate of £1.8 billion per year. Employment discrimination has always produced astronomically high un-employment for the Nationalist population in Northern Ireland but with the sagging economy, Loyalists, for the first time, are also beginning to experience high levels of unemployment. And the major source of industrial employment, in both Northern Ireland and the Republic, is in multinational companies, a significant number of which are US owned.

While the 26 counties of the Republic of Ireland represent its neo-colonial present, the six of the former nine counties of the Province of Ulster still under British control serve as a constant, galling reminder of Ireland's colonial past. For the majority of Irish citizens, and those of the Irish Diaspora in other countries (43 million in the US), the anguish of that past lives on in their collective unconscious, always ready to surface in anger and outrage whenever the British government acts with total disregard for the human, civil and legal rights of the Irish who reside in England or Northern Ireland. It is against this background that Brigid recounts her childhood and youth while growing up in the Bogside of Derry, the years spent in Philadelphia after her marriage to a Polish American, culminating with the past seventeen years spent in Shannon after she and her family moved there in 1971.

Daughter of Derry is based on Brigid's personal/political experiences as a Republican Socialist actively engaged in the perennial effort to achieve self-determination for all Irish citizens in a united Ireland freed from British control. I have provided the historical background to events she related to me in our collective effort to provide some clarity to what has transpired in Ireland, both north and south, during the strife of the past twenty years.

Margie Bernard
Washington, 1988

A Rebel Heart (Traditional)

From rebel veins my life I drew
In rebel arms I lay
And rebel were my mother's eyes
That watched me night and day.

I was rocked to rest on a rebel breast
I was nursed on a rebel knee
Then there awoke and grew
This rebel heart in me.

My thoughts are among the Derry hills
Where still some hearts are brave
And the murmur of each streamlet there
Forbids me to live like a slave.

I ponder still my bosom thrill
Though dark in death I lie
Never sink or quail or try to fail
This rebel heart in me.

Forces of Occupation

The weather forecast for Monday 13 July 1970 predicted another hot, humid day in Philadelphia. I had slept fitfully but when the alarm clock rang at 6:30 am I was instantly awake, anticipating the day. My plan was to attempt a sit-in at the British Consulate to protest the actions of the British army in Belfast during the past ten days.

Only three weeks earlier, the Conservative Party in the UK had been voted back into power. Northern Ireland had hardly figured in the election campaign, but the change in government had resulted in an immediate change in policy regarding the role of the British army stationed there. When British soldiers were first sent to Derry in August 1969 by the Labour government, they were meant to be a peace-keeping force. With the 1970 election, this role was abandoned. Under the direction of the Army Command and Lt General Sir Ian Freeland, Commander-in-Chief for NI (Northern Ireland), British forces became an instrument of repression, openly siding with the Loyalists at the expense of the Nationalists.

The action which marked this change originated when the Orange Order[1] had been given permission by Freeland to march in Belfast on Saturday 27 June, despite a general ban on marches. The parade resulted in a rampaging riot by Loyalists who attacked Nationalists in the Ardoyne area of Belfast; the newly formed Provisional IRA sought to defend the area and three Loyalists were killed. A Loyalist mob trying to burn down a Catholic church, St Matthew's, in the Nationalist enclave of Short Strand, was stopped only when the Third Battalion of the Provisional IRA under the command of Billy McKee fought off the attack resulting in the deaths of four Loyalists and one Provisional IRA volunteer.

The Short Strand incident ended in a short-lived Nationalist victory. On 3 July, after having turned a blind eye for months while Nationalist communities were constantly invaded by armed Loyalists, the British army command decided to carry out a search for weapons – not in Loyalist areas but exclusively in the Nationalist Lower Falls section of Belfast.[2]

The 'Rape of the Falls', as it was later called, was responsible for my decision to stage a protest at the British Consulate in Philadelphia. Nationalists had resisted this invasion, and the British reacted strongly. General Freeland brought in troops to surround the area, imposed a 35-hour curfew, and ordered a house-to-house search. Four Nationalists and a London-based Polish photojournalist died; 60 civilians and 15 soldiers were injured; and hundreds of families, terrified and homeless, fled in a mass exodus across the border into the Republic of Ireland (RI). The only weapons the army found were 28 rifles, 2 carbines, 52 pistols and 24 shotguns, most of which were old and unusable.

Then, while residents of the Lower Falls were still in a state of shock, British army commanders drove two Unionist Party officials through the area to verify that the army was in control of the situation. This insensitive performance destroyed any lingering belief that the army was in NI to protect the rights of the Nationalist minority; and the number of volunteers who joined the Official and Provisional IRA soared.

The reports of the battle in the Falls brought back to me the sounds, smells and sights I had witnessed during the Battle of the Bogside almost a year before – the incessant sirens and thudding CS gas canisters, the eerie light through the smoke of burning buildings, the acrid clouds of CS gas which constricted throats and seared eyes, the maimed bodies of the injured. Although 3,000 miles away, I shared the frustration, terror and anger of the Nationalists in Belfast and I wanted to run through the streets of Philadelphia, grab every person I met, and get them to help stop this rampage by the British army.

On 11 July, I telephoned two political allies, Frank and Delma Houlihan, Maura Curran, a freelance journalist, and Hugh Logue, a Queen's University student who was in the US for the summer, told them I was planning a sit-in at the British Consulate on Monday morning and asked them to come to my house for a meeting. At the meeting I outlined my plan and they agreed to help. Everyone was assigned a task. Maura and Delma agreed to go to the consulate with me, and Frank and Hugh said they could contact people to picket outside.

Now Monday morning had arrived. My husband Leo had given me his full support, and I had decided to take our five children with me. I dressed hurriedly and made our breakfast. Then, after Leo left for work, I packed a change of clothes, diapers and baby food for eight-month-old Brian, and prepared a lunch for the rest of us. I explained to the four older children what we were going to do and made them promise to be on their best behaviour. Almost as an afterthought I packed a tape recorder and several tapes of Irish music.

Delma and Maura arrived on time. The temperature was nearing 100 degrees and we were sweltering as we drove downtown. For blocks ahead I could see 'PSFS' in red neon-lit letters marking the top of the Philadelphia Saving Fund Society building where the consulate was housed, and could feel my stomach becoming queasy as we approached our destination. We went over what we were to do once we arrived – Delma was to go into the consulate with me and the children, Maura would locate the nearest pay telephone and call the journalists on the press list we had compiled.

The temperature in the air-conditioned lobby of the building was a freezing contrast to the outside heat and I mentally cursed myself for not having thought to bring sweaters for everyone. I looked at my watch – it was 11 am. I put Brian in his pram and gave him a lollypop to ensure his silence and contentment. When the elevator arrived we crowded in and I pushed the button for the 23rd floor. Within seconds the elevator doors opened onto the quiet hallway and we went in search of the consulate. At the entrance Delma and I shook hands in silent commitment. I took a deep breath and opened the door.

The reception room had a bright green carpet and the woman behind the desk smiled and asked if she could help us. I answered by requesting to see Mr Barrett, the Acting Consul. Did I have an appointment? 'No', I replied, 'but would you please inform Mr Barrett that Brigid Makowski is here and I will not leave this office until the British government gets out of Northern Ireland.'

I set the tape recorder on her desk, told the children to sit down, and pushed the play button. 'The Belfast Brigade' blared out. Within seconds doors down the corridor began opening and people came out of their offices to investigate the commotion. A man walked over to me and announced, 'I am Keith Barrett, what is this all about?'

At that moment I was more concerned that Brian might put his lollypop on Barrett's impeccable suit than with giving a diplomatic answer. 'I've had it with what your troops are doing in Belfast. I'm taking this place over and I'm not leaving until the British government leaves Northern Ireland.'

'I want you out of here in 10 minutes. If you are not gone by then I will take action to have you removed.'

'I'm not leaving.'

Barrett turned and went back to his office and the others, following his lead, returned to theirs. We were left with the receptionist who tried to look busy while the music continued to fill the room.

Delma and I sat down beside the children. On the wall facing us were pictures of the British Royal Family. I recalled having read that Prince Charles was in the US on holiday and was to be honoured by President Nixon at a White House dinner on Friday. About twenty minutes passed and just as the last song on the tape ended, a man rushed in and announced to the receptionist he was Claude Lewis, a journalist from the *Philadelphia Bulletin*. Within minutes more reporters, some photographers and two television crews arrived.

For the next hour-and-a-half the office was complete mayhem while the press interviewed me and attempted to get a statement from Barrett. I explained why events in Belfast during the previous ten days had caused me to take a stand. One reporter asked how long I intended to stay and I replied, 'I've been looking around the room, and if the British government doesn't meet my demands to leave Northern Ireland before Christmas, I've decided that corner over there would do nicely for our Christmas tree!'

The journalists laughed, easing the tension. Inwardly I thanked my lucky stars that the press had arrived before Barrett had had a chance to call the police and have us removed. No matter what happened in the hours ahead I knew there would at least be some media coverage of our action.

When the reporters left, Delma and I gave the children their lunch and I rocked Brian to sleep in my arms. The receptionist was busy placing and taking calls and from what I could overhear I realised Barrett was relaying what had happened to the British Embassy in Washington, DC.

A little after four, two plain-clothes police officers arrived and announced to the receptionist that they were expected by Mr Barrett. As she ushered them into his office Delma leaned over and whispered, 'I wonder if they are going to arrest us?' We reassured the children that everything would be all right. The next thirty-five minutes seemed like thirty-five hours.

Barrett emerged from his office with the police officers in his wake and told me he wanted us to leave. I answered, 'I'm not leaving until I have an assurance that your government is leaving my country for good.'

'We are about to close the office for the day and I want you out before six.' Barrett and the officers went back into his office. The staff began leaving – the last to go was the receptionist.

At 6 on the dot, Barrett and the two officers came back into the room. He informed me he was leaving and once again asked us to go. When I told him we had no intention of doing so he said the officers would then stay to stand guard. I told him that wouldn't be necessary as we had no intention of doing any harm; contrary to the actions of his government in my country, this was a peaceful protest.

After a short conference with the police, Barrett departed with one of the officers. The other walked over and sat at the reception desk – we stared at each other without speaking. Ten minutes passed before he stood up, went out into the hall and closed the door. I was nervous. What were the police going to do?

The telephone rang. I answered and heard Leo's startled voice, 'Brigid? What the hell are you doing answering the telephone? When I got home I turned on Channel 10 to watch the news and there was a report about you, Delma and the children at the consulate and Frank Houlihan just called to say there was also a report on the Channel 3 news. What's happening? How are you and the children?'

'We're all fine. There are two men outside the office guarding the place but so far there's been no attempt to arrest us. I don't know what's going to happen. The children have been fantastic but they're starting to get restless and hungry. It would be great if you could buy a pizza and bring it down. I'm not sure if they will let you in but it's worth trying.'

'I can be there in about 45 minutes. Is there anything else you need?'

'Would you bring Brian's playpen and some diapers? Also grab sweaters for everyone, it's freezing in here.'

Neither of the police officers had come back in, so I took advantage of their absence to make telephone calls. One was to Walter Sullivan, a major figure in the Democratic Party in Philadelphia. Earlier in the year Sullivan had convinced me to run for the office of Democratic Committeewoman for the 45th Ward in the city and I had won the position in the Primary Election held on 19 May. Now I felt a call to Sullivan was in order.

Sullivan was most cordial, telling me he had already heard about the sit-in on the evening news. He assured me I had his support and promised he would contact others in the local party organisation to see what help they could provide. He made me promise to let him know if there were any further developments. 'That's not bad support to have', Delma said as I hung up.

'We'll see, so far most politicians I know haven't been interested in what's happening in Derry or Belfast. I wrote Bob Kennedy a letter a few years ago asking him to support our civil rights movement in NI and all I received back was a form letter saying he wouldn't involve himself in something he considered to be an internal British matter.'

Around 8 pm I heard Leo in the hall talking with the police officers so I opened the door. I confirmed he was my husband and asked if he might be allowed to bring in the food and other things he had with him. After they searched through the bags he was carrying they let him enter. I gave him a hug, 'Am I glad to see you!'

While we ate I told Leo about the day's events and said that unless we were arrested, we were going to spend the night. He was hesitant about the children staying but I assured him they would be okay adding, 'I have a sense that if the children remain the authorities will be less apt to take action against us.'

After some hesitation, Leo agreed they could stay but made me promise that if anything seemed about to happen I would call him. One of the officers opened the door and told Leo he would have to leave. Delma left with him, a little reluctantly, to let her husband Frank and the other picketers know what had happened so far.

After they had gone I changed Brian, put him in his playpen and gave him a bottle. Then Stella, Margaret and I put all the couches and chairs together, to make a huge bed for the children in the hope that they would feel safer sleeping all cuddled together. I got Breige and Leo Patrick bedded down and sat talking with the two other girls.

The telephone rang. It was the host of a local radio talk show who asked if I would be willing to talk to his audience and tell them why I was at the consulate. We chatted on the air for about 30 minutes; when I hung up the children were asleep. As I looked at them, so innocent and relaxed, I was struck with how magnificently they had behaved all day and tears formed in my eyes.

I called Leo to let him know everything was okay and told him I would ring him in the morning. After I hung up I realised I was too keyed up to sleep so sat staring out the window. I found pleasure in the realisation that I, Brigid Sheils Makowski from the Bogside in Derry, had managed to outfox the mighty British Empire – for a few hours at least. Thoughts of my father kept vigil with me as I waited for the dawn.

2

The Name of Freedom

Every year, on the anniversary of the Easter Rising, my father, Patrick 'Paddy' Sheils, would stand at a street corner in Derry known as the Little Diamond with ten or twelve people gathered around him. He would read out the Proclamation of the Provisional Government of the Republic of Ireland just as Patrick Pearse had done from the steps of the General Post Office in Dublin in 1916. Termed as Ireland's Magna Carta, the declaration stated Ireland's right to be a free and independent Republic.[1] My mother used to tell him he was wasting his time because no one was listening but he would say, 'No, it has to be done. Even if there is only one person listening, so long as there is one spark that can be fanned into a flame, I'll do it.'

My father was born in Derry, on St Patrick's Day 1877, the oldest son of John and Mary Hegarty Sheils. His father owned a spirit grocery[2] and several pieces of property which placed my grandparents among the rare Nationalist middle-class segment of small shop and pub owners in Derry.[3] My father graduated from St Columb's College, a Catholic preparatory school whose graduates often went to St Patrick's College at Maynooth to be educated as priests, solicitors or teachers. He wanted to become a teacher, but instead joined the Irish Republican Brotherhood (IRB) around the age of eighteen – a first step in what became his lifelong commitment to the liberation of Ireland. In 1898, he was selected as a member of an IRB delegation sent to raise funds from the Clan-na-Gael in the US for the centenary celebration of the 1798 Rebellion.[4]

In 1913 my father joined the newly organised Irish Volunteers and took its oath, pledging himself 'to secure and maintain the rights and liberties common to all people of Ireland without distinction of creed, class or politics'. The Irish Volunteers, established by the IRB, was a direct response to the formation of the paramilitary Ulster Volunteer Force (UVF) in 1912 by Loyalists. The UVF's purpose was to resist, by force of arms if necessary, a proposal in the British Parliament to grant Ireland home rule, but despite –or perhaps because of – the UVF's position, the British government turned a blind eye to their growing supply of armaments. If Ireland, the first colony, were granted home rule, the logic ran, then other colonies, India in particular, might demand the same right. In the end, the First World War resulted in the shelving of the Home Rule Bill, but the line dividing home rule proponents and Loyalists had already been drawn.

The war itself split the Irish Volunteers. Nationalists argued that joining the British army was the best way to ensure that Britain would grant independence to Ireland when the war ended. Republicans disagreed and, giving the counter argument that Britain's dilemma was Ireland's opportunity, refused to fight on behalf of a government which they felt could not be trusted on the issue of Irish self-determination. Families split on the issue as well and against the pleading of my father, my Uncle John joined the British army.

After the war, of course, things continued as before; independence looked further away than ever. Unbeknownst to Eoin MacNeill, Chief of Staff of the Irish Volunteers, a small but influential group of IRB members led by Patrick Pearse met in secret and planned a rebellion for the spring of 1916. As time for the rising neared the IRB leadership co-opted the socialist labour leader, James Connolly, into the planning group and Connolly pledged the support of his Irish Citizen's Army to the venture.[5] Under the guise of holding a practice drill by the Irish Volunteers, the rising was scheduled to begin on Easter Monday, 24 April 1916, and volunteers around the country were urged to come to Dublin. MacNeill learned of the plan and, angered by not having been consulted, attempted to stop the rising by placing a notice in the newspapers cancelling the exercise. My father and other volunteers in Derry, who were preparing to go to Dublin, changed their plans when they read the notice. When they learned they had been misinformed, they tried to join their comrades but were unable to reach Dublin; by then, the city had been cordoned off by British troops.

The failure of the Easter Rising led to mass arrests of Republicans. My father was interned, along with some 1,800 others, at Frongoch Internment Camp in Wales until the end of 1916. While at Frongoch my father learned of the execution by firing squad of his friend Patrick Pearse and 13 others. Another friend, Eamon de Valera, was spared because he was a citizen of the United States.

The executions of Pearse, Connolly and the others strengthened popular support for the IRA (as the Irish Volunteers came to be known after the Rising), and its political party Sinn Fein. Founded in 1905, Sinn Fein had had as its original goal the establishment of a dual monarchy between Ireland and Great Britain like that between Austria and Hungary, but with the Easter Rising it became committed to an Irish republic. In the December 1918 general election Sinn Fein candidates won 73 of the 105 Irish seats to the British Parliament, with Eoin MacNeill elected MP for Derry City.

Although 36 Sinn Fein MPs were in prison, the 37 who remained at liberty met in a public session in Dublin on 21 January 1919. Constituting themselves as members of Dail Eireann (Irish Parliament) they formed a cabinet, declared the Dail as the legitimate government of Ireland and passed a Declaration of Independence. On 10 September the British government responded by declaring Dail Eireann an illegal assembly and in November outlawed Sinn Fein as a political party. Dail Eireann continued to meet in secret.

In January 1920 local government elections were held in Ireland and, in an attempt to weaken Sinn Fein and Nationalist support, the procedure of proportional representation was adopted. However, in Derry City, which had a Nationalist majority, proportional voting resulted in a Nationalist controlled corporation and the election of a Nationalist mayor, Hugh O'Doherty. Loyalists, who had controlled Derry for 230 years, were furious that this city, the historic symbol of Loyalist resistance, had fallen into 'enemy' hands.

Although never formally declared, the Irish War of Independence began in the spring of 1920. During this period my father was arrested and interned at Mountjoy Jail in Dublin, along with about 100 other Republicans. None of them had been charged with any offence and when Bonar Law, Leader of the House of Commons, was questioned by other MPs as to why these men were being held without trial he replied:

> The Government consider it their duty, as had [sic] been done over and over again when Ireland had been in a similar condition, to arrest men on suspicion to prevent crime. We have done so and we feel it our duty to continue to do so.[6]

On 5 April 1920 my father joined other Republican prisoners at Mountjoy on hunger strike seeking release. Ten days later, following a General Strike by Irish workers which completely paralysed the country for 24 hours, their demand was granted. My father was the first man released. Hogan recounts the day the men knew they had won:

The first name was called. It was Patrick Shiels [sic] of Derry. To all
who heard it shouted in the strong voice of a warder, to all who
heard it come echoing through the prison shadows, it was the name
of freedom itself. If Patrick Shiels of Derry went out, then after him,
one by one we would go out, too, free again – men who had not
failed .... The name had dissolved in reverberations long before
warders came carrying the stretcher, taking their burden down the
iron stairs, along the central hall, through the great bars into the
circle as we watched with burning hearts silently .... It had all come to
pass, the abasement of the [British] Field Marshals and the Generals
... before Volunteer Patrick Shiels of Derry on a stretcher.[7]

On June 1920 a week of rioting broke out in Derry when the UVF
attacked Nationalist areas. When the UVF occupied the grounds of St
Columb's College and attempted to burn it down, my father, as commanding officer of the Derry IRA Battalion, led a charge which drove
them out of the college grounds and saved St Columb's from destruction. My father told me it was only then that the British army was
ordered into action – not to protect the school but to drive him and
his men out of St Columb's grounds! The army opened fire with
machine guns and several innocent by-standers were killed. He and his
men made it out of the school grounds safely just before the army
sealed off the area. He managed to elude the army when it conducted
a house-to-house search in the Bogside, but several of his men were
captured during the massive occupation of Derry.[8] When the final
count was taken, eighteen people had died during the riot and its
aftermath – fourteen Catholics and four Protestants and scores of
people were injured. Not one member of the UVF was arrested.

The Government of Ireland Act (1920) took effect in May 1921.
Nationalists were to have their Parliament at Dublin – Loyalists would
have theirs at Stormont. Neither side wanted home rule. Nationalists
wanted complete independence from Great Britain and Loyalists
wanted to remain part of the British Empire. Elections were held and
only after the Loyalists were firmly ensconced at Stormont did the
British seek a truce with the IRA. The Irish War of Independence
ended on 11 July 1921. My father was appointed liaison officer for the
IRA in Ulster while a treaty was being worked out between Ireland
and Britain.

The Sinn Fein-controlled Second Dail Eireann met in Dublin on 16
August 1921 and pledged themselves to resist partition. During treaty
negotiations, the Irish delegation, threatened by Lloyd George with

'immediate and horrible war' if they didn't accept a divided Ulster province and partition, signed the Articles of Agreement for a Treaty between Great Britain and Ireland on 6 December 1921. After a heated debate in the Dail, the treaty was narrowly accepted by a vote of 64–57 on 4 January 1922.

The only people pleased by the 250-mile border separating the 6 north-eastern counties from the remaining 26 were Loyalists who could feel they were still part of Britain. Republicans charged that Nationalists in the new political subdivision called Northern Ireland (NI) had been sold out in exchange for the creation of the Irish Free State. Nationalists believed partition was only a temporary measure that would eventually prove unworkable and set their hopes on the Boundary Commission which was to be established to resolve the partition dilemma. The commission failed to reach an agreement and the border remained intact.

Disagreement between Republicans and Nationalists over accept-ance of the Anglo-Irish Treaty led to civil war in the Irish Free State (1922–3) and the pro-treaty forces prevailed. My father and De Valera were to remain friends during this conflict as they both sup-ported the Republican anti-treaty side. However, they parted company in 1927 when De Valera side-stepped the Oath of Allegiance to the British Monarchy in order to take his seat in the Free State Dail as the leader of his newly created Fianna Fail Party. Fianna Fail won a majority in the 1932 general election and De Valera became Taoiseach (prime minister). My father regarded De Valera and other members of the Second Dail who became officials in the Free State government as traitors who had sold out their former comrades-in-arms by breaking their pledge to fight for a 32-County Irish Republic.

In 1937, the year I was born, voters in the Irish Free State approved a new constitution which defined its national territory as 'the whole of Ireland, its islands and the territorial seas', and changed the name of the Irish Free State to Eire (Ireland). Nationalists in Northern Ireland argued that although the constitution claimed the whole of Ireland, it in fact tacitly accepted partition. Furthermore, the new Constitution confirmed the worst fears of Loyalists (whose watchword was 'Home Rule means Rome Rule') by giving special privilege to the Catholic Church. Eire had become a sectarian state.

In 1947 a new political party, Clann na Poblachta, was founded by Sean MacBride and other disaffected Republicans in Eire who felt that Fianna Fail, under the leadership of De Valera, had become a bankrupt party which paid mere lip-service to the goal of a united

Ireland. Clann na Poblachta committed itself to achieving reunification of Ireland by constitutional means and the enactment of legislation to provide improved social welfare benefits. In an attempt to silence his critics, De Valera dissolved his government in 1948 and called for a general election.

After 16 years in power, De Valera and Fianna Fail were replaced by a coalition government consisting of Fine Gael, Labour and Clann na Poblachta with John A. Costello, Fine Gael, as prime minister. Under pressure from MacBride and Clann na Poblachta, Costello proposed legislation to end Ireland's membership in the British Commonwealth by establishing an independent Republic of Ireland. The Republic of Ireland Act became law in December 1948 and took effect on 18 April 1949, the 33rd anniversary of the 1916 Easter Rising.

Republicans, and a significant segment of Nationalists, objected that whereas the 1937 Constitution represented de facto recognition of partition, the Republic of Ireland Act gave partition de jure status. In response to this charge, Costello and De Valera submitted a joint proposition which passed as a Unanimous Declaration of Dail Eireann on 10 May 1949. This declaration reasserted the right of the Irish people to a united Ireland and the right to choose their own form of government. In addition the declaration rejected the claim of the British Parliament to legislate against those rights and pledged 'the determination of the Irish people to continue the struggle against the unjust and unnatural partition of our country until it is brought to a successful conclusion.'

In June 1949, the British Parliament enacted the Government of Ireland Act establishing its relationship with the newly created Republic of Ireland. In that section of the act which pertained to Northern Ireland it stated that:

... Northern Ireland remains part of His Majesty's Dominions and of the United Kingdom and ... in no event will Northern Ireland or any part thereof cease to be part of His Majesty's Dominions and of the United Kingdom without the consent of the Parliament of Northern Ireland.

The minority Nationalist population in NI, underrepresented at Stormont due to restricted voting qualifications and gerrymandered election districts, contended there was no legislative avenue open for them to seek reunification by constitutional means.

My father not only refused to recognise the legitimacy of either the

British or Irish government, he also refused to take their money. When the Free State government awarded a pension to IRA veterans of the War of Independence and Civil War my father refused to accept his. And, although he worked only occasionally as a turf accountant (bookie), he would not accept the dole from the British government. When De Valera came to Derry in 1956 to preside over the opening of a Gaelic League sponsored week of Irish games, he especially requested a meeting with my father who had been one of the founders of the League in Derry. My father politely turned down his invitation.

While I always had great respect and love for my father, it was only years later that I came to realise how much his principled life had meant to others:

There were men in [Derry] who embodied the tradition – Paddy Shiels [sic], Neil Gillespie, Sean Keenan, Old Republicans who had fought in the past and been jailed and whose suffering represented a continued contribution from our community to the age-old struggle. They were regarded with guilty pride by the great majority as living out too urgently the ideals to which, tacitly, we were all committed. When Paddy Shiels died everyone said that he was a 'Great Irishman'.[9]

3

Number Six Union Street

Although I grew up in a very Republican, very Catholic home where the rosary was said nightly and my father gave us frequent lessons in Irish history, ours was not a sectarian house. My father had fought alongside and been in prison with Protestants who shared his belief in a united Ireland. It was not my parents who kept me from knowing Protestant children when I was growing up, but the segregated housing and schools. Housing segregation was maintained by the Loyalist-controlled local housing authority, which assigned Derry Corporation houses and building permits for privately owned dwellings according to religion in order to prevent integrated neighbourhoods. This system maintained the gerrymandered election districts which preserved a Loyalist majority in a city where they were a minority of the population. As for education, the Catholic Church insisted that all Catholics send their children to church-run schools. There we were taught that the one true faith was Catholic, and that those who belonged to other religions would never make it to heaven; Jews were further vilified as being 'Christ killers'.

Any trace of sectarianism that crept into our house received the full wrath of my father, who once ordered me inside and gave me a stern lecture when he heard me singing a song with other children while jumping rope which went: 'St Patrick's Day will be jolly and gay/We'll kick all the Protestants out of the way/If that won't do, we'll tear them in two/And send them to Hell with their red, white and blue.' To expand my singing repertoire he gave me a book which contained songs of Irish resistance and rebellion. Thereafter, I tried to learn a new one every week and on Friday evenings would stand on a chair and sing the latest one. If I did well he would reward me with threepence.

I first saw the light of a Derry day on 6 January 1937 when I was born at home, number 6 Union Street, the Bogside.[1] I was to be the third of seven surviving children of the eleven born by my mother, Brigid Doherty Sheils.

My mother's parents were from a long line of peasant farmers who scraped their living from the inhospitable mountainous soil on the Inishowen Peninsula of County Donegal. When she was a young girl, my grandmother, Brigid McLaughlin, was sent by her parents to the hiring fair at Strabane, County Tyrone, where she was hired out for six months. She was not atypical: twice a year, in May and November, children as young as 10 were hired at these fairs by wealthy farmers or agents of British landlords. Their wages for the six months were only a few pounds but this often represented the only cash income for their families who were also spared the necessity of feeding the young person hired out.

My grandmother married Edward Doherty who, in the Irish need for genealogical identification, was referred to as part of the 'Scalper' Dohertys to distinguish his Doherty clan from the other Dohertys in the area. The Scalper Dohertys farmed land at the base of Scalp Hill near Burnfoot in County Donegal, hence the name.

Brigid and Edward Doherty had six children, three boys and three girls. The three sons (who did not survive infancy) and a daughter were born in County Donegal but because my grandfather couldn't make a living at farming, the family moved to Derry, where my mother and another daughter were born. When my grandfather learned he had tuberculosis the family moved back to County Donegal where it was hoped that rest and fresh air would cure him but he died a short time later. After his death, my grandmother took her three daughters back to Derry where she obtained work at one of the shirt factories to support them. My mother attended the local primary school, but because only well-to-do families could afford to send their children to secondary school, her formal education ended when she was around 11 and she joined the workforce of Derry women in the shirt factories.

My mother was a young girl when she first saw my father. She had gone shopping with my grandmother and they were standing outside a shop when a tall, good-looking man in handcuffs was led past them en route to the Derry Jail. They didn't meet until 1926 when he came out of Dalton's Pub one evening to find my mother talking to a mutual friend. About a week later they met again outside Dalton's and he asked if he could walk her home later that evening. She agreed, and he arranged to meet her at Watt's Distillery wall after the pub closed. Feeling too shy to be alone with him, my mother asked a girl friend to go with her. As they neared Watt's they could see my father waiting but when they were about half-a-block away they saw him start walking in the other direction. My mother, puzzled as to why he left, speculated with her friend on his strange behaviour. The next time she saw him he explained, 'I didn't wait the other night because when I saw you coming with your friend, I realised you didn't trust me. I hold you no harm and I assure you my intentions are honourable.' They married four years later when she was 27 and he 53.

As newlyweds they rented a room in the home of a Loyalist woman on Hawthorne Terrace in a middle-class section of Derry, but mother wasn't happy living away from her family and friends and persuaded my father to move to the Bogside. They rented a two-storey, two-bedroom house at 6 Union Street in what today would be regarded as an urban slum – to us it was home. Next door in number 8 was the Coyle family;[2] my grandmother, Brigid Doherty, lived in number 10; next door to her was my Aunt Sarah Ellen and around the corner lived my Aunt Mary Jane.

In the row of attached dwellings which lined the narrow cobblestone street, our house was identical to the others – small, dark and over-crowded. The main room was about 12ft # 12ft off which was a tiny entry hall at the front and a narrow kitchen at the side. There were two bedrooms upstairs; one for my parents and the other for the children, with two double beds, one for the girls, one for the boys, with a blanket hanging from the ceiling between the two. There was no bathroom or running water indoors, only a toilet and water tap outside in the back yard.

Our neighbourhood was bounded by Union, Anne, Abbey and Ross-ville Streets. After school and during holidays we could all be found somewhere within these boundaries, either playing on the streets or in a friend's house. The doors of the houses were never locked and all the neighbours looked after one another's children, dispensing first aid or settling disputes as they arose. The only time of the day the streets were fairly quiet was in the evening between 6:30 and 7:30 when the family rosary was said and one could hear the 'Hail Mary, Hail Holy Queen' issuing from every door.

Every house we entered had a familiar feel that made it seem like our own home. On the mantle of every fireplace were two glazed ceramic dogs, one on each end of the mantlepiece, with a clock in the middle and, hanging from one end, the twin symbols of authority: the rosary beads and next to them a thin cane and fine strap used for punishment. The strap was for the boys, the cane for the girls but the threat of their use was greater than their application. On one wall was the Sacred Heart picture and the perpetual light – a miniature oil lamp with a red globe – and at the front door was the Holy Water fount.

When I was two, my mother became ill, exhausted by bearing too many children in too rapid succession and several miscarriages. Her doctor recommended a period of complete rest from child-rearing duties, housekeeping and the sewing she did at home for one of the factories in her spare time.

Eamon and Margaret, my older brother and sister, were cared for during the day by my aunts and I eventually went to live in the house of my father's brother, John. My stay there wasn't planned. As former Officer Commanding, Derry City Battalion of the Irish Republican Army, my father was responsible for ensuring that IRA veterans of the War of Independence and Civil War who had been granted a pension by the Irish Free State government, received the money due them. Because our house was so small my father used a spare room in my Uncle John's flat on William Street as his office and when he went there to work he took me with him. We often stayed until late in the evening and as we were leaving, my Aunt Mary would convince my father that he shouldn't take me out in the rain – or the cold – or because I'd fallen asleep due to the lateness of the hour – so I would spend the night. One night led to another. John and Mary's children were grown so I received the full benefit of my Aunt Mary's attention and a very close bond developed between us, so much so that I looked upon her as my second mother. I was quite happy living there as I saw my father nearly every day, but it was quite some time before I saw my mother. I can still recall looking through the window at the women out on William Street as they passed by John's and Mary's to do their daily shopping, trying to spot my mother among them. I was too young to understand my mother's absence, but to adults, my stay with my aunt and uncle was not an unfamiliar custom. Relatives often assumed responsibility for one another's offspring – it was a continuance of the ancient Irish custom of fostering. Although my mother's condition continued to improve, I stayed at John and Mary's place off and on until I was six.

When I was four I entered Infant School at St Eugene's. From the beginning I enjoyed learning, never had a problem with lessons or homework, and my grades were always excellent, which pleased my father, who took a particular interest in my education. When I graduated into first grade I attended another section of St Eugene's and it was there I first recognised the authoritarian role of the nuns and layteachers who put the fear of God into us.

One nun, Sister Agatha, stands out above the rest as the person who instilled in me a fear of the unknown. This was during the Second World War and every time there was an air raid drill she would make us get under our desks and say an Act of Contrition while she walked up and down between the rows of desks. I remember watching her black robe swishing around her shiny black shoes as she walked past me. One morning Sister Agatha sent me to the Reverend Mother's office for some minor infraction of the rules. The Reverend Mother told me I was possessed by the Devil and threw holy water on me. For years I had a recurring dream in which black, shiny crows would come flying at me calling out 'devil' and I would wake with the fear that perhaps I was possessed.

My main memories of the war are of the blackouts, the air raid drills and being the proud possessor of my own gas mask. One night, I was sitting on my father's lap as he told me a story when we heard several loud explosions in the distance. To allay my fear, my father told me the washtub had fallen from the wall in the shed out back. In reality, it was the noise of bombs exploding during the only bombing of Derry during the Second World War (15 April 1941). Fifteen people were killed in Derry that day but we were fortunate compared to Belfast, where 775 people died.

During the war the Irish Free State, although a member of the British Commonwealth, maintained strict adherence to its policy of neutrality. Northern Ireland was not neutral and this made life difficult for those Republicans who, although they rejected fascism, did not believe in defending the British Empire, which they charged failed to practise democracy in its own backyard. When the United Kingdom entered the war it interned Republican activists. In the Irish Free State Dublin followed suit. Under the guise of preserving Irish neutrality, the Fianna Fail government, under the leadership of Eamon de Valera, passed the Emergency Powers (Amendment) Act in January 1940 which gave the government the right to intern approximately 800 Republican activists during the war years. The living conditions of those interned were appalling but due to war-time censorship this was not public knowledge.

In April 1940, six men went on hunger strike, demanding that the Dublin government grant political status to those interned. The government relented only after two men, Tony D'Arcy and Jack McNella, died. Having won the right to be regarded as political prisoners, the internees were allowed to wear their own clothes – all, that is, except for those transferred to Portlaoise Prison, who were required to wear a prison uniform. These men refused to put on prison clothing which served to identify them as criminals and went naked except for their blankets from 1941 until 1946. For their protest they were kept in solitary confinement from 1941 until 1943. One man, Sean McCaughey, was kept in solitary confinement for five years. On 19 April 1946, seeking release, he went on hunger then thirst strike, but died 17 days later. It was the investigation of his death by Sean MacBride which led to public disclosure of the inhumane treatment meted out to those interned during the war.

Being poor, like the rest of the families in the Bogside, we were used to deprivation, so the food shortages brought about by rationing during the war had less of an effect on us than it did on the Loyalists, who were used to a higher standard of living. But they, like us, supplemented their meagre food allowances by frequent smuggling trips across the border to County Donegal – their patriotism and loyalty to Britain had its limits when the table was empty.

I remember having an almost instinctual understanding that because I lived in the Bogside I was different from people who lived elsewhere in Derry and this knowledge resulted in the only act of cowardice I can ever remember displaying. It was on V-E Day, 8 May 1945, which was also the day my youngest sister, Mary, was born. I was eight and had gone out into the streets to witness the celebration of the end of the war. I got caught up in the excitement, wandered out of our neighbourhood and found myself among a Loyalist crowd. I wanted to share my delight at having a new baby sister and told a woman standing next to me about the new member of my family. She shared my pleasure and asked if perhaps my mother had named my new sister Victoria – an excellent choice if you were a Loyalist. Not wanting to be found out I said, 'Yes', when in fact my mother had named my new sister Mary, after Mary, Queen of Peace, Queen of Ireland and Queen of the Catholic Church. For a brief moment I 'belonged' to the other side as the woman excitedly told others about the baby born on this auspicious day who had been named for Queen Victoria and the victory of democracy over fascism. When I got home I didn't tell anyone about my adventure because I knew I would have been reprimanded for having left the neighbourhood. I also understood that somehow I'd let my family down by lying about Mary's name.

The Bogside community was our extended family. It was there we felt safe and protected from all harm except for the frequent forays by the Royal Ulster Constabulary (RUC), who would disrupt our games and send us scattering for shelter in the nearest house when we got word they were entering the neighbourhood. One day we failed to get the warning soon enough. We were playing one of my favourite games in which we would get an adult to tie a heavy rope high up on a lamp post and on the other end make a large loop. We would then take turns sitting in the loop, and swinging around the lamp post. On this particular day it was my turn and as I was enjoying my swing a group of RUC entered the street unannounced. I scrambled out of the loop, headed for the nearest open door and just as I entered looked back and saw an RUC man with a beet red face grin at me as he reached up with his knife, cut down the rope and took it away with him. Ropes like that were expensive and hard to come by so it was weeks before we could play the game again. This incident did little to further the notion that the police were supposed to be friendly protectors.

The one bright spot of our summer holiday was the yearly trip to Buncrana in County Donegal. If at all possible almost the entire Nationalist population of Derry would head for that oasis 15 miles away in the Irish Free State during the time of the annual Loyalist Derry Apprentice Boy's Parade in mid-August. This parade celebrated the actions of the apprentice boys in 1688 when they slammed shut the doors to the walled city of Derry and held off the invading army of James II until rescued by forces loyal to William of Orange in 1690. It was wiser and safer for Nationalists to absent themselves from Derry when Loyalists commemorated their ancient victory.

To make the trip to Buncrana we took the Lough Swilly Train from the Strand Road Station. In Buncrana we lived in tents, caravans or overcrowded cottages and spent the long summer days on the beach soaking up the sun, swimming in Lough Swilly and savouring the freedom of being in one of the counties of Ulster that wasn't under Loyalist control.[3]

When I was ten, I went to spend the first of many summers at my Great-Uncle Tom McLaughlin's farm outside Buncrana where he lived with his unmarried daughter Rosanne. I went there to help cut the turf which we burned in our fireplace in the winter. Their house was a two-room, thatched cottage and I always felt a sense of peace in the quiet of the place which was lacking in our overcrowded house in the Bogside. It was during my second summer there that I experienced the initial feelings of young love. Mickey was his name.

Mickey's parents lived on a farm which bordered my Uncle Tom's. I had met him the first summer I was there and when I returned the next year we renewed our friendship. A few weeks later he and I were walking up the lane talking and enjoying the late evening sunset. I clearly remember liking the feel of my bare feet on the dirt road that still held the warmth of the sun which had shone all day. All of a sudden Mickey went over to a May bush that still held a few blossoms and picked a sprig which he handed to me saying, in a very formal and grown-up way, 'This is to pledge you to me, we will always be together.' We saw each other a lot in the next four weeks, but when I came back the following summer, Mickey and his family were gone. Unable to make a living on their farm, Mickey's parents did what many other people in the area had done before them – they moved the family to Scotland.

4
Eleven Plus

The Northern Ireland Education Act was passed by the Northern Ireland Parliament in 1948 at the urging of the British government, which had enacted similar legislation a few years earlier.[1] The Act provided free secondary education for those who could pass an examination at the age of eleven, and further provided for university scholarships based on merit. Those who benefited most from this legislation were children from low-income Nationalist families. Denied secondary and university education because their families couldn't afford it, excluded from apprenticeships in Loyalist-controlled industry, faced with either emigration or the dole queue, young people in the Nationalist ghettos for the first time had an alternative to their otherwise bleak future – education.

The first year of the Education Act I was one of the few students at St Eugene's chosen to sit for the examination. I passed with honours and won a scholarship which allowed me to attend Thornhill College (high school) in Derry. I was the first member of my family to go beyond elementary school – my older brother and sister, Eamon and Margaret, had had to leave because my parents couldn't afford their tuition.

Thornhill College, under the administration of the Sisters of Mercy, was a boarding school with an excellent reputation as a finishing school. Young women came from all over Ireland to attend and at the time I entered there were about 200 students, both boarding and day, of which I was one of 20 day students on scholarship. My impression was that those of us who attended on scholarship were tolerated, the Sisters having little choice, but we were never accepted. My lasting memory of Thornhill is that it was cold – physically, socially and educationally.

I was twelve when I enrolled, very tall for my age, long-legged, skinny and awkward, and for the first time I realised I was poor. Most of the students had new uniforms; mine was bought secondhand from Frances Bryson's Thrift Shop. Their books were new, mine were used. My lunch, when I had one, consisted of two slices of bread and butter.

The boarding students went to the convent for a hot meal and the tuition-paying day students had meat sandwiches, flasks of hot soup, and tea and tarts for dessert which they brought from home.

My biggest problem, however, was shoes. It was the policy at Thornhill for pupils to have two pair of shoes, one for outdoors, another for indoors. The nuns recognised the difference between them by a little white button placed on each shoelace of the indoor shoes. My parents couldn't afford to buy me a second pair of shoes so I worked out a solution. I carried little white buttons in my pocket and when we came indoors, as the others were switching into their indoor shoes, I would slip the buttons onto my shoelaces and line up for inspection. I got away with this for quite some time until one day I was caught and sent home. Afraid I wouldn't be allowed to go back, I nagged until my mother gave in and bought another pair of shoes which I had to share with my sister Margaret. I took the shoes with me to wear indoors at school and brought them home at night so Margaret could wear them to work in the evening.

Although my lack of indoor shoes caused me temporary disciplinary problems it was my objection to our history lessons that almost got me expelled. We were taught history by Sister Agnes, English history the first term, Irish history the second. I endured the first term looking forward to the next because I felt sure, from what my father had taught me about Irish history, that I would enjoy it.

Our first Irish history lesson at Thornhill didn't sound familiar at all – in fact, it sounded like a continuation of English history from the first term. During the second lesson I couldn't contain myself and raised my hand. Sister Agnes ignored me and turned to the blackboard. I stood up, 'Sister Agnes, I don't want to learn English history.'

She whirled around, shocked that I would dare speak without permission and glared at me in the silent room. She walked over to me saying, 'This isn't English history it's Irish history. You will learn it and you will sit down and be quiet.'

'No Sister, I won't. This isn't Irish history. It's an English version of Irish history.' With fury in her voice she said, 'Young lady, do you realise you are here on a British scholarship?'

With all the dignity I could muster I replied, 'I'm here because my mother works in a shirt factory and her taxes pay for my education.' I had committed an almost unpardonable sin: I had spoken back to a nun. I was sent to the head office and only after lengthy negotiations was I allowed back into her classroom. From that day forward, Sister Agnes adopted as her personal project methods to break my spirit.

Looking back I realise the nuns and layteachers were little better educated than we were and more interested in keeping order and maintaining discipline than teaching. Until the passage of the Education Act their function had been to provide their students with the proper social graces, combined with piety, as preparation for their future role as wives of their middle-class male counterparts. As teachers they weren't expected to prepare their students for the world of work or professions.

One of my greatest delights during my Thornhill years was provided by my friendship with Pauline Gillespie, whose father managed the cinema at St Columb's Hall. The films changed twice a week, Monday and Thursday, and as Pauline's guest I often attended the matinees after school where we had the privilege of the best seats in the front row of the balcony. Every weekday morning Pauline would stop by my house and we would walk to the bus together. Thornhill was very strict about our appearance. We were required to wear a clean white blouse every day, and because I only had one blouse, I washed it every night and Pauline always had to wait while I ironed it in the morning. As girls who attended Thornhill, we were expected to maintain proper deportment at all times when wearing our uniforms; even getting caught eating an apple on the street was an infraction of their rules. Wearing that uniform set me apart from the other girls in the Bogside who had gone to work in the shirt factories when they left primary school.

One of the major subjects taught at Thornhill was etiquette and for a while I must admit I was something of a snob. I would lecture my brother and sisters at mealtimes, 'Don't grab the food', 'Don't talk with your mouth full', but they soon discouraged me from putting on Thornhill airs by teasing and ridiculing me. There were times when I felt caught between my two worlds – what I was learning at Thornhill and the reality of my life in the Bogside.

We were kept in complete ignorance of our sexuality. The first time I got my menstrual period I went to my mother who, with a look of embarrassment on her face, took me up the stairs to her bedroom. She gave me a clean rag, 'Here, use this. You will get that every month, keep yourself clean.' Except for being told I shouldn't let any boy or man touch me either above or below the waist, I had no sex education. I was given the impression that getting my 'monthly' was something to be ashamed of; it was certainly not to be spoken about. We were taught to deny our feelings. The role model we were expected to emulate was that of the Virgin Mary – to be selfless, devoted mothers, without the pleasures of love-making, was our ultimate goal. Irish girls were, and still are in many respects, raised to be the servants of their fathers, brothers, husbands and sons – to take care of them, keep silent and never ask questions. When I got married at 18, I still didn't know how babies were conceived.

My mother had a hard life. She worked in a shirt factory during the day and brought home sewing to do at night. It seemed she was always pregnant and seldom had time to care for herself. On Saturdays she would clean the house until it was spotless and then begin preparing the Sunday dinner so it would be ready when we came home from Mass the following day.

Saturday nights, my father would usually attend a Gaelic League meeting or a benefit for the Green Cross to raise funds for families of Republican prisoners. Afterwards, he would bring friends home with him who were always made welcome by my mother. Just before he was due to return she would fix her hair, and change into a fresh blouse and clean white apron. After the men had been chatting a while someone would invariably begin to sing and father would call mother in from the kitchen for a song. She would go into the living room, sit in a chair, and with her hands clasped in her lap would sing in her clear, proud voice 'The Bold Fenian Men' or my favourite, 'A Rebel Heart'.

On Sunday morning, mother would hand father his clean white shirt and well-shined shoes. As he left the house for Mass she would brush his coat and send him off. She then got us ready and took us to the next Mass. The Sunday meal was always the best of the week – soup, chicken, vegetables, with either custard and jelly or apple tart for pudding. After the meal my father would take the train to Buncrana to meet his friends at the Atlantic Hotel. In the evening he would return with a big bag of mixed sweets for we children and something special for my mother. From Sunday to Sunday, this pattern hardly ever varied.

With one exception, I never saw my mother and father kiss or hold hands – it was something that wasn't done in those days. The exception was a New Year's Eve when I was only a small child; as the chapel bells rang at midnight, he kissed her and wished her a Happy New Year. But although I never saw outward signs of affection neither did I ever hear them argue and I always had the feeling that they cared very much for each other.

During the years I attended Thornhill I also had to work after school and on weekends. I would get home, change out of my uniform, grab a bite to eat, then rush to Dalton's Pub where I washed glasses and, when older, waited on tables. Derry was a major international military naval port and Dalton's was frequented by men from different countries whose ships pulled into port for short periods of time. They generally treated me and the other girls who worked at Dalton's as through we were their sisters – the main exception being the British who seemed to regard us as fair game for their roving hands and suggestive remarks. Because I was taught this was a sin for which I was somehow responsible, I had to get absolution for these affronts by asking forgiveness from our parish priest in my weekly confession. This caused me to develop a bitter resentment towards both the British military and towards a church that made me assume a responsibility for something I neither welcomed nor encouraged. This led me to question the teachings of the church and finally to the realisation that priests and bishops didn't always practise what they preached to us on Sunday.

They taught us that our endurance of poverty, pain and suffering in this world would be rewarded in the next. Yet I noticed that they always had warm clothes, plenty to eat, and lived in the biggest house in the parish. Slowly it dawned on me that they received the money to live in the style they did from the people in the parish. If your contribution was small or non-existent you were publicly shamed when the names of parishioners and their yearly donations were read from the pulpit. While the church collected money for 'black babies' in Africa or some mission in a far-off land, children in their own parish went hungry or without clothing.

I began to rebel against what was expected of me – kissing the Bishop's ring when I met him on the street and saying three Hail Marys at the grotto outside chapel after Mass. My mother felt I had become possessed and sent for Father McNally to lecture me, an experience I endured in silence. I knew Father McNally was the person I would have to go to if I needed a reference for a job when I got out of Thornhill and if he didn't feel too kindly towards me, my reference was apt to reflect this. It was best to stay in his good graces as far as possible.

Except for the usual harassment from the RUC and periodic displays by Loyalists to reaffirm their sense of superiority, these years were relatively calm. Sinn Fein and the IRA were almost non-existent. The other political party which sought to represent our interests was the Nationalist Party headed by Eddie McAteer, the Derry MP to the NI Parliament at Stormont. However, since 1932, following its failure to gain a hearing for minority concerns at Stormont, the Nationalist

Party had refused to take its seats. In 1945, they decided to re-enter Stormont following the election of a Labour government in Great Britain in the mistaken belief that labour would be more sympathetic to Nationalist concerns.

At the end of December 1945, the Nationalist Party formed the Anti-Partition League (APL), which sought the abolition of the border. In an attempt to enlist support in Derry the APL planned a St Patrick's Day Parade in 1948 which was banned under the Special Powers Act by the Northern Ireland Minister of Home Affairs. The annual Apprentice Boys' Parade was allowed to proceed as usual that year, which further confirmed that we were living in an Orange State run by and for the Orange Order.

In 1951 a second attempt to hold a parade on St Patrick's Day in Derry resulted in the RUC arresting three APL counsellors for marching and carrying the Tricolour (the RI national flag), which was banned under the Special Powers Act. To prevent further Nationalist marches, Stormont passed the Public Order Act in July requiring 48 hours' notice of any parades other than 'traditional' ones – namely those sponsored by Loyalist organisations. Nationalist organisations were generally denied permission to parade when they complied with the law by giving prior notification.

In 1952 the APL was given permission to hold a rally in Derry (but not to parade) on St Patrick's Day. Pauline and I went along. The rally went off peacefully until at the end two Tricolours appeared as if by magic. We joined the hastily formed parade heading for the revered Loyalist site inside the Derry walls. All of a sudden, the RUC and Ulster Special Constabulary (B-Specials) poured out of the Royal Victoria RUC Barracks on the Strand Road and began batoning men, women and children. The B-Specials, a part-time reserve force who carried their own guns, seemed especially vicious that day. I had never witnessed such violence before – there were bleeding and injured bodies all around.

Pauline and I escaped without injury and beat a hasty retreat to my home. We rushed up to my father to tell him about the event. He listened quietly. When we finished he said, 'It was a disgrace. Where was our flag? It was in the gutter', and walked out of the room and went up to bed. He was right: the Tricolour wasn't in its rightful place flying from a flagpole, it had been torn to shreds and trampled in the dirt under the feet of the crowd. (In 1954, Stormont passed the Flags and Emblems Act which forbade the display of the Tricolour or other Nationalist emblems, either in public or private.)

After I had been at Thornhill for two years I began to think of attending Queen's University. My grades would have entitled me to a scholarship and my father encouraged me, but our financial situation at home became so grave that I was forced to leave school when I reached 16 and take a job. I found work at Harkin's Shirt Factory where I discovered the working conditions were deplorable. Harkin was a skinflint and wouldn't turn on the heat. We all sat with our coats on, our fingers stiff with cold, making it difficult to work the sewing machines. The other women kept grumbling, but no one would say or do anything. After a few days I decided on a plan of action. During our lunch break I convinced the others that if we didn't do any work they would have to turn on the heat. All the women said they would back my plan.

About half-an-hour after we started the afternoon shift I gave a prearranged signal. We turned off our machines, picked up our scissors and started banging them on our work tables making a terrible racket. The supervisor approached. 'What's going on?'

I stood up, 'We aren't going to do any more work until you turn on the heat.' He looked around the room, 'And who are "we"?'

At that point all the other women turned on their machines and started back to work. I stood there alone. The supervisor fired me on the spot, grabbed my arm, pushed me out of the room and threw me down the stairs. I had black and blue marks on my arms and legs for days afterward.

My mother talked about suing the supervisor for what he had done to me, but in the end, the matter faded. She did sewing for Harkin's at home and was afraid if she sued they would stop giving her work. This was my first experience of the inability of people to act in their own best interests. Everyone agreed I was right but no one was willing to back me up. I couldn't blame them because jobs were scarce.

A few years later, young women in Derry were enticed with offers of good money and travel if they would go to Asian countries and teach the women there how to make shirts. Several women took up the offer only to see the shirt factories in Derry close as one by one their production costs were undercut by the low wages and reduced manufacturing costs of the overseas factories.

After I was fired from Harkin's I decided to emigrate to England with a friend, Martha Breslin. My sister Margaret was working at Middleton Beach Holiday Camp at Morecambe in Lancaster and I wrote asking if there would be work for Martha and me. Margaret replied that there were jobs available so we took the ferry from Belfast to Heysham where Margaret met us. We began work the following day. We washed dishes for the next six weeks and although the pay was very low we were provided with free room and board. An English man who also worked there suggested that we should consider going to London and getting work in one of the hotels. We were seriously contemplating this when the camp closed at the end of the summer but Margaret put an end to our plans. She had visions of me getting involved with the low-life around Soho and ending up on the streets of London so ordered me to return to Derry. Away from home, Margaret took on the role of my mother and although I put up an argument, in the end I did as I was told. When the summer ended, Martha and I went back to Derry.

Shortly after our return I found work in another shirt factory. I also embarked on what was seen by my parents and the church to be my main vocation – looking for a man to marry and have children with.

5

Emigration, Marriage, Culture Shock

I met the man I was to marry at a dance hall I was forbidden to attend. There were four dance halls in Derry – the Memorial, Capitol, Criterion and Corinthian. Both the Capitol and the Memorial were off-limits to us, the Memorial because it was run by Loyalists and the Capitol because it was frequented by foreigners, mostly members of NATO forces who visited or were stationed in Derry. The Corinthian, patronised by business and professional people, was priced beyond our means. The only dance hall we were allowed to go to was the Criterion run by the Ancient Order of Hibernians (AOH).

Because the Memorial and Capitol had been declared off-limits, Margaret and I decided to see what they were like during one of her trips home from Liverpool where she now lived. At the Memorial we made up stories to hide our Bogside identities. We were barely in the door when a young man named Billy asked me to dance. It was the first time I had talked with a Loyalist my own age in a social setting. He turned out to be very nice and we danced almost every dance but just as the last dance of the evening was ending Margaret came over to us with a made-up story about having to be home early and pulled me out of the room. I was furious that she had forced me to leave and was giving forth to her as we went down the stairs. Just as we got to the front door I heard 'God Save the Queen'. 'There, that's the reason we had to leave', she said. 'You wouldn't have stood up for that song and neither would I. If we hadn't we would have been found out and who knows what would have happened to us!'

A few evenings later – on 12 March 1954 – we got up nerve to go to the Capitol Dance Hall to see the foreigners for ourselves. I was shaking with fear and nervousness when we entered. The place was filled with people wearing French, Dutch, British and US military uniforms and Margaret and I sat in the darkest corner of the room. We managed to avoid requests to dance and were enjoying ourselves simply watching and feeling adventuresome for having come, when, towards the middle of the evening, a tall, fair-haired, good-looking man in a US navy uniform asked me to dance. I hesitated but he seemed harmless so I consented. He introduced himself as Leo Makowski, a Polish-American from Philadelphia.

Leo hadn't planned on coming ashore when his ship, the USS *Johnson*, docked for two weeks in Derry. His dealings with Irish-Americans in Philadelphia had been less than cordial, so instead he had volunteered to stand watches for a number of his shipmates so they could spend extra leave-time ashore. However, the glowing reports he had received of the friendliness and warmth of the Derry people, coupled with the boredom of the ship, led him to the Capitol Dance Hall with Nick Vinci who had a date to meet one of my friends, Bridie Martin. After we had danced several dances, Leo asked if he could walk me home. I replied, 'No, I'm not allowed to go out with a foreigner.'

He laughed, 'I'm not a foreigner, I'm an American.' I still refused his offer but we continued to dance and chat for the rest of the evening. When the evening ended I made for Margaret and we hurried out the door, leaving Leo standing there. As Margaret and I neared our house she looked behind us, 'That fella you were dancing with has followed us.' I ran into the house saying to my father, 'A Yank has followed me. I told him I wasn't allowed to go out with foreigners but he followed me anyway.'

My father went to the door and opened it just as Leo was about to knock. Leo introduced himself: 'Brigid told me you don't allow your daughters to go out with foreigners but I would like to take her out anyway.' Perhaps it was Leo's forthright manner that caused my father to want to take a closer look at this sailor because to my surprise he invited him in for a cup of coffee.

In a flurry of activity I was sent to my Granny's two doors down to borrow her good china. She gave me two cups and saucers, and two silver teaspoons which had little apostle figures on the handles, and admonished me not to drop the china on my way home. At my house my father and Leo were deep in conversation in front of the fire. Leo stayed for about an hour but before he left he had received my father's permission to take me out the following night. Interestingly enough I wasn't consulted in the matter but was delighted to have a date with this good-looking man who had managed to charm my father.

The next evening Leo called for me and we went to see a film at St Columb's Hall. Afterwards, we walked around the downtown area looking in the shop windows and talked. We were both very shy but conversation came easily and when he took me to my door we arranged a date for St Patrick's Day. However, on the night of 16 March he stopped by the house to tell me he couldn't keep our date. US service personnel had been involved in several disturbances on St Patrick's Day in the past, and the new US navy policy was to take the ships out of Derry on 17 March so there would be no danger of a repeat.

Leo and I agreed to go out the following Sunday with Martha Breslin and one of his shipmates. As it turned out his friend had duty that day, so the three of us took a bus to Buncrana and walked along the Crana River to O'Doherty's Castle. Leo took us to dinner at the Lough Swilly Hotel.

The hotel was ornate, with dark wood panelling, deep carpets, crystal chandeliers and lots of windows in the dining room that over-looked the water. Strolling through the hotel in the company of a handsome man who treated me like a lady, I felt I was in a film. At last my Thornhill etiquette course was put to use as I instructed Martha and Leo on the proper use of the silverware in the very formal setting.

After dinner we went to a film at St Mary's Hall, then caught the last bus to Derry. We said goodnight to Martha at the bus station and Leo walked me home. Before he left for his ship we arranged another date. However, two nights later one of his shipmates came to tell me the ship was leaving Derry the following morning, and Leo had watch that night and wanted to see me.

About an hour later I slipped out of the house without telling anyone where I was headed – only 'loose' women went to the dock area and I didn't want to be stopped. Leo spotted me as I reached the ship and a few minutes later managed to slip off. I was scared to death one of the local dock-workers would see me and report me to my parents so when Leo came down the gangplank I grabbed his hand and ran with him around the corner away from the ship. We talked and he kissed me for the first time, then asked if I would consider marrying him when he got out of the navy in a few months. I was flustered and put him off, but suggested we write to one another.

In the months that followed Leo sent me a letter every time the ship pulled into port and I lived for the postman's daily rounds. My family knew I was receiving letters from him but I didn't tell my friends because I didn't really believe this was happening to me – I felt as though I was living in a fairy tale.

When Leo was discharged from the navy, he wrote asking if I would come to Philadelphia to marry him. At 17 I was more in love with love than in love with Leo but I had enjoyed his company, looked forward to his letters and hadn't met anyone else who had taken my fancy, so I responded by saying I would if he could get my father's permission.

When my father received Leo's letter formally asking for my hand in marriage, his initial reaction was positive. Knowing that I was willing to marry, my father wrote back asking Leo to have his parish priest send Father McNally information about his character. The report was favourable and with Father McNally's approval, my father gave his blessing to our marriage. My mother was delighted and confided that although she would miss me, she felt my life would be easier than hers had been if I married Leo and went to the States.

Within a week of receiving my father's consent, Leo sent me a ticket for the SS *Saxonia* which was to sail from Liverpool shortly after the New Year and my eighteenth birthday. To my surprise, I learned that Bridie Martin was marrying Nick Vinci, also from Philadelphia, and that he had sent her a ticket for the same ship.

The day I left Derry there was a big send-off celebration on our street and friends and neighbours all gave me their best wishes and going away presents. Maggie Bradley gave me a suitcase to pack my few possessions. I took very little; Leo had told me not to bother buying a trousseau because he wanted to take me shopping after I arrived. Mrs McDaid gave me a beautiful white missal and rosary beads which I carried the day of my wedding and the Daltons bought me a coat. One woman gave me a nightgown and although I'm sure Leo expected me to wear something slinky on our wedding night, I wore her pink flannel nightdress which covered me quite properly from head to toe!

When the taxi arrived there was a very tearful leave-taking. My father had been quite ill and as he kissed me good-bye said, 'Take a good look at your Daddy because I don't think you will see me again.' At that moment, if either he or my mother had attempted to stop me, I would have remained in Derry. My feelings were very confused as the taxi driver took me to the train station and when the train left Derry I cried my eyes out.

Bridie and I picked up our visas in Belfast and had chest X-rays taken. Tuberculosis was rampant in Ireland at the time and emigrants to the US were required to provide US immigration officials X-ray proof they were TB free. We caught the ferry to Liverpool and after spending the night at my sister Margaret's place we boarded the ocean liner. From Liverpool we sailed to Cobh in the RI to pick up more passengers. I gave some money to one of the crewmembers and asked to have a Mass said for me – in spite of all my questions about the church, I was still a very devout Catholic.

One of the people who got on at Cobh was a young man named Michael from Connemara and he, Bridie and I formed a close friendship during the crossing. Michael's dream was to earn a lot of money so that he could return to Ireland and open a pub or start a business. Bridie and I didn't entertain thoughts of returning to live – we weren't sure if we would ever return for a visit.

Bridie and I travelled tourist class but the cabin we shared seemed luxurious. We enjoyed nightly Irish music sessions on the deck during the four-and-a-half day crossing. This was a period of high emigration from Ireland[1] and one night I sang 'Skibbereen', which told of the sorrow of those forced to leave Ireland during the famine years.

When the ship docked in New York City there was a huge crowd of people waiting for us to disembark and as I scanned the faces I felt myself panic – I couldn't spot Leo. I had forgotten what he looked like. As I walked down the gangplank I kept searching for someone tall in a US Navy uniform. Leo approached me wearing civilian clothes and as he stood in front of me smiling I slowly focused on his face, finally recognising him as the sailor I had had two dates with in Derry. We exchanged awkward hellos and a hasty hug and kiss before picking up my luggage and taking a taxi across town to where we caught the train to Philadelphia. I felt overwhelmed by the noise, crowds, traffic, tall buildings and being with Leo, and kept up a steady stream of chatter to hide my feelings.

From North Philadelphia Station we took a taxi to Leo's mother's house where, he informed me, she was waiting to meet me. As we pulled up in front of the large brownstone house at 2041 East Susquehanna Avenue I was amazed at its size compared to our little house in Derry. Later I was to learn that the house was located in a typical blue-collar, working-class neighbourhood but on first sight it seemed like a mansion and my initial impression was confirmed as we went up the white marble steps before opening the double doors onto a long hallway with a wide staircase. The living room contained a marble fireplace, was well furnished and had a piano and television set – the first one I'd ever seen. We passed the dining room and went into the huge kitchen where his mother was sitting at the table. After Leo introduced us she welcomed me and showed me the bedroom above the kitchen where I was to sleep. I couldn't get over having my own room.

We went back to the kitchen where Mrs Makowski fixed me a cup of tea while she finished making dinner and we sized each other up while Leo sat there beaming and joking. By then I was sure that Leo's family was wealthy: they had a huge upright freezer, a large refrigerator, a telephone and the cabinets above the sink were filled with canned goods.

I met the rest of Leo's family at the dinner table, a festive Polish meal which looked and tasted strange to me although I politely forced myself to eat everything on my plate. Clem was away at college but the others – Gus, Joan, Brona, Tina and Cathy – were all there to meet their oldest brother's Irish wife-to-be. Leo's father had died when he was only eleven and he had taken on the role of 'man-of-the-house' at that early age. Most of the conversation was in Polish until Leo pointed out I didn't speak the language. There was an awkward silence, then Leo's youngest sister Cathy asked me if I spoke Irish; I didn't but I rattled off the Hail Mary in Irish so they would think I did. They were all attempting to be kind but I sensed that they would have preferred Leo to marry a Polish girl and I found myself wondering how Bridie was getting on with her boyfriend's Italian family.

At first I felt estranged from Leo's family. The house was steeped in Polish tradition even though his mother had been born in the States. As the days went by, however, I discovered we all had one unifying belief – our shared Catholic faith. The rites of the universal Catholic Church – the Latin Mass, observation of Lent and Holy Days of Obligation – bridged the gap in our cultural differences in the days leading up to our wedding.

Within two weeks I had a job sewing bathing suits for the Sun Clothing Company in downtown Philadelphia. Like everyone else in Leo's family, I wanted to contribute to my keep by working until Leo and I married, when I would have to stop because Leo didn't want a working wife. One of the highlights of that period was when Leo took me to the St Patrick's Day Parade on North Broad Street. I couldn't get over the difference between this event in Philadelphia and the ones in Derry. There were thousands of people marching, representing every county in Ireland, high school bands playing Irish tunes, everyone wearing a bit of green and the crowds lining the streets all appeared to identify with Ireland that day – the Polish, Germans, Italians, Jews and blacks. I felt very proud to be Irish and pleased with my new country and its people.

Leo and I were married on 16 April 1955 at St Boniface's Church in Philadelphia. I had no family or friends present (Bridie and Nick were also married that day so couldn't attend) but a couple who were friends of my father had somehow learnt of the wedding and just as I was to walk down the aisle they introduced themselves and wished me luck. Having no one to give me away, Leo walked me down the aisle, gave me away, then took me back! After the ceremony we went back to the Makowski house for a typical Polish reception with plenty of homemade food, lots of drink and lively Polish polkas and slow waltzes.

When we were ready to leave on our honeymoon, Leo's uncle and aunt drove us to their house in New Jersey where we spent our wedding night before catching the train to New York City the next morning after Mass. We disembarked at Pennsylvania Station and as we were leaving I heard a voice calling my name. It was Michael from the ship. The day was extremely warm and the sweat was pouring down his face as he stood there with a broom in his hand: 'Well Brigid, I did get a job but it looks like it will be some time before I make the fortune I was talking about!' I was so surprised to see him and so excited about being newly married that I forgot to get his address and to this day I wonder what became of him.

We stayed at the Madison Hotel on Madison Avenue and spent the week sightseeing at Coney Island, Central Park, the Empire State Building and, one night, a blues and jazz club where I saw black performers for the first time. The real treat of the week, however, was when Leo took me to Lord and Taylor's and bought me a black and white houndstooth checked sleeveless dress with a scooped neck and a black jacket. The pièce de résistance was my first pair of high heel shoes. In Derry I was tall for a woman so I could never wear them. Now I could. I wore the shoes the rest of the day, suffering the blisters and pain in glamorous silence feeling like Doris Day in my new outfit!

At the end of the week we returned to Philadelphia and Leo's mother's house, where we lived for about six weeks before moving into our own small flat at 2011 East Susquehanna Avenue, a few doors down from the family home. The flat consisted of a large furnished room with a small kitchen, a bathroom, and a bed which let down out of the wall. Leo had a good job as an apprentice toolmaker and we delighted in setting up house. A friend of his had given us a radio and I frequently heard an ad with a catchy tune which urged people to call 'SAgamore 2-2900 to order a television to be delivered today, no money down, twelve months to pay.' After hearing it several times, I cajoled Leo into letting me make the phone call. This was my first introduction to the American way of buying things on credit, something my family would never dream of doing – we paid cash or went without. From that day on Leo and I joined the ranks of the 'easy terms, no money down' young married couples who were charged exorbitant interest to create the false impression that we were climbing up the ladder of economic success.

I delighted in small pleasures that were entirely new to me – having a refrigerator, weekly shopping trips to the supermarket with its variety of food, doing my wash at a laundromat. But with all the new discoveries, I never dreamt that our common language would cause me embarrassment. Shortly after we moved into our apartment, Leo discovered the alarm clock wasn't working properly and was concerned he wouldn't get up on time in the morning. I told him not to worry, that I would find someone to wake us. I went across the hall and tapped on our neighbour's door. A very nice-looking young man opened it and I gave him my best smile, 'I wonder if you would knock me up in the morning?' He looked startled, 'Would I what?'

'I have to be knocked-up at six tomorrow morning and want to know if you would do that for me.' He grinned at me. 'You're not an American are you?'

'No, but my husband is and he has to get up for work in the morning and our alarm clock isn't working which is why I want you to knock me up.' He broke out laughing, 'Look, you shouldn't use that expression. You better ask your husband to explain what it means.'

I went back to the apartment and said to Leo, 'Gee, these Yanks are funny. The boy across the hall told me to tell you what I said to him and all I asked was for him to knock me up in the morning.'

Leo almost hit the ceiling, 'Damn Brigid, you shouldn't have said that!' And to my mortification he explained that to 'knock-up' meant getting a woman pregnant! We became good friends with the man across the hall and often laughed about the incident but at the time I felt terrible.

Three months after we were married I discovered I was pregnant. While awaiting the birth of our first child I spent my days attempting to make our small flat attractive, meeting Leo every noontime at the factory where he worked and sitting with him while we ate the lunch I had prepared. Several afternoons a week were spent with his mother learning how to prepare the foods Leo liked to eat.

Our first daughter was born at St Mary's Hospital on 12 April, four days before our first wedding anniversary, and the nurses bought us a cake to celebrate the birth of Stanislava (Stella) Marie Makowski and our anniversary. When Stella was a few months old we moved into an unfurnished house at 3251 North Hope Street about twenty minutes by trolley bus from Leo's mother. Our new neighbourhood was mostly

Irish and Irish-American so I felt more at home. I loved taking Stella out walking in her pram and talking with people on the streets. Shortly after we moved I ran into Bridie in a supermarket and we renewed our friendship. She was going through the same problems of adjusting to living in the US as I and we shared our adventures and news from Derry. I taught her to cook Polish dishes and she taught me how to cook Italian.

Because the custom in Philadelphia was to sit outside on the steps on hot summer evenings, I came to know all my neighbours. We would have block parties, closing off the street, creating a miniature carnival with games for the children and different types of ethnic food. On really hot days we would open the fire hydrants so the children could play in the water that gushed out and down the streets. I celebrated my second Christmas in the States by telling Leo I was pregnant once again.

My father died the day before Stella's first birthday although I wasn't informed until two weeks later when I received a letter from my oldest brother Eamon. I was shattered and filled with hurt and anger because my family had not notified me so I could attend his funeral. It helped me not at all to hear that his was the biggest funeral Derry had ever known, nor that words of condolence came from prominent people all over Ireland, nor that the Bishop walked at the head of the burial procession to the city cemetery on the hill overlooking Derry when I hadn't been there to mourn. It was at this point that my homesickness and longing to be back in Derry started to fester inside me – a gnawing ache that never completely left me even though I was content with my marriage, proud of my motherhood and adjusting to life in a new country.

Margaret Simone was born at St Mary's Hospital on 28 October 1957. Leo, rather than seeming disappointed at not having a son, delighted in showing off his three girls as he referred to me and our two daughters. During the next three years we managed to save the minimal down-payment needed for a Veteran's Administration Home Loan and purchased a house in a new suburban development at Collings Lake, New Jersey. Our home at 392 Sherwood Drive was a three-bedroom, ranch-style house with a modern appliance-filled kitchen sited on a quarter acre with pine trees. There were no fences separating any of the back yards so it seemed like we had a huge park at our back door where all the children on the block gathered to play. Our neighbours were all white, working- and lower-middle-class families, who like us were struggling to make ends meet, pay the mortgage and provide a better life for our children.

Because it was a new housing development, Collings Lake lacked the amenities available in Philadelphia, including places of worship. There were no churches or synagogues, and all religious denominations in the area used the same building, the community centre, where Jews had their service on Saturday, Catholics had a Mass on Sunday morning and Protestants their service in the evening. For me this represented a miracle in religious tolerance which could never have occurred in Derry.

It had been five years since I had seen my family and I was determined to go back for a visit. There being no extra money in the kitty, Leo agreed to let me take a part-time job to earn my fare. I got a job waitressing at Halloway's Casino on the Black Horse Pike not far from home. Shortly after I started working I discovered I was pregnant again, and took a temporary leave of absence after working five months.

To our delight our third child was a boy, Leo Patrick, born 31 May 1961. When he was six weeks old I went back to work at Halloway's, taking young Leo with me to sleep in the kitchen in a carrycot while I waited on tables.

One night I was asked to work later than usual because there was a big horse race in Atlantic City and the manager knew we would be busy. After the crowds left, Bill Halloway, who owned the restaurant, introduced me to Noel Coffey. Noel also lived at Collings Lake but we had never met before although I had seen him and his family at Mass. Noel was from Dublin, had served in the British army before moving to the US and I classified him as a typical West Brit.[2] Because Noel came into Halloway's several times a week we became friendly although we clashed in our views about Ireland. However, it was Noel who introduced me to Barney Maguire after my vacation in Ireland and it was Barney who introduced me to Clan-na-Gael.

6
Clan-na-Gael

When I returned to Derry in the autumn of 1961 I was, by every measure applied to emigrants, a success. At the age of 24 I had made a fortunate marriage, was the mother of three healthy children, lived in a modern, well-furnished home, and had become more self-assured and wordly wise than the awkward, shy 18-year-old who had left six years earlier.

In our house the turf fire still burned in the living room but my father's chair stood empty in its corner and my mother had aged. Her beautiful auburn hair was streaked with grey and her stooped shoulders and the lines in her face told of years of sacrifice and hard work. My oldest brother Eamon was single, Margaret was married and living in England, and Teresa, married to Patsy Moore, was living in Derry. Eileen and Mary were working and Sean was still in school. I revelled in the attention I received from my family and delighted in showing photographs of Leo, the children, our house and in general lived up to their expectations of the daughter and sister who had found happiness by leaving Derry.

Derry hadn't changed. The warmth, humour and friendliness of the people I had known enveloped me and their welcome made it seem as though I only had been away on a brief holiday. But although the Bogside looked the same, everything seemed different. The lanes seemed narrower and drearier, the houses smaller and more dilapidated in spite of the sparkling window panes behind white net curtains and the brass door knockers on the front doors, glistering from constant shining. The men remained unemployed, the women continued to work outside the home and children still played on the streets because the area lacked a community centre and parks. Two changes caught my eye. The first was the barbed wire fence and sandbags around the RUC Station in the Bogside, protecting it from the people it was meant to serve. The second was the framed photograph of the newly elected US President, John F. Kennedy and his wife Jackie, which hung in a place of honour next to the Sacred Heart picture in almost every Bogside house. When I told people I had done some canvassing for

Kennedy in the area where I lived in New Jersey, I got the distinct impression they felt I had played a major role in his election!

I spent a lot of time with my cousin Peggy, the daughter of my Aunt Mary and Uncle John, who was married to Tommy Mellon. Tommy had been interned since December 1956 when the IRA had sprung to new life and begun a major campaign directed against British military installations and other key targets aimed at disrupting the operations of the RUC and B-Specials.

'Operation Harvest', or the 'IRA border campaign' as it was popularly named, was masterminded by Sean Cronin, a former officer in the Irish army who had been living in the US. When Cronin returned to Ireland in 1955 he was provided with an introduction to the IRA leadership through Clan-na-Gael, and a few months later he was appointed IRA Director of Operations. When the border campaign began on the night of 11–12 December 1956, a series of operations were carried out through the North, one of which was the destruction of the BBC transmitter in the Rosemont area of Derry. Eight days later Tommy Mellon was interned, under the Special Powers Act, in Crumlin Road Jail, Belfast, as a suspected member of the IRA along with about 100 other men who were picked up in massive swoops in NI in December and January. Except for a vague awareness of the border campaign, I was completely ignorant of what had happened during the years of my absence. My conversations with Peggy provided me with an outline of events which renewed my interest in Republicanism.

One thing I learned vindicated my father's mistrust of De Valera. When, in 1957, the Costello coalition government in the RI fell on a vote of no confidence, partly due to its failure to develop any positive policy calculated to bring about the reunification of Ireland, De Valera again became prime minister when Fianna Fail won the election in March. By July De Valera had reinstituted internment of suspected IRA members as he had done during the Second World War. Although both Costello and De Valera had pledged themselves and their respective governments to end British occupation of NI and achieve reunification, in practice they did nothing. When, in the absence of political initiatives from Dublin, the IRA resorted to a campaign of physical force to achieve these ends, both the De Valera and Costello governments tried to squash the IRA, showing that they were better allies of Britain than of beleaguered Nationalists in NI.

In 1959 De Valera became president of the RI and Sean Lemass replaced him as prime minister. Lemass, who had been Minister of

Defence in the 1923 Republican government of the Second Dail
Eireann, confirmed the rule that there is no more deadly enemy than a
former comrade who has joined the opposition and gained a position
of authority. In 1923 Lemass had supported the anti-partition side in
the Irish Civil War. Now, in 1961, Lemass, acting through his Minister
for Justice, Charles J. Haughey, resurrected the military tribunals
which had functioned in the 1940s under De Valera. By the end of
December 25 men who continued to support the principle of a united
Irish Republic had been tried and convicted by these tribunals.

As my holiday came to an end, Leo sent me a return ticket, a berth
on a luxury ocean liner, the SS *America*, which I was to board in Cobh,
County Cork. The day I left Derry for the second time I felt tremend-
ously torn between wanting to be with Leo and my children and
wanting to remain in Derry. In some respects my leave-taking was
sadder than it had been the first time.

The train trip from Derry to Dublin and the bus ride to Cork
provided my first realisation of how small our island is when compared
to the vastness of the US; Ireland is about the same size as the state of
Maine. My travelling companion was another Derry woman, Mena
McClune, who was returning to her husband and children in
California. After we boarded the ship, I went to the bank to change my
sterling to dollars and while waiting in line engaged in conversation
with the ship's purser. As a result of this brief exchange, a steward
knocked at my cabin door the next day and I was handed an engraved
invitation to dinner at the Captain's table the night before we docked
in New York. I was elated and Mena flabbergasted that I would be
accorded such an honour. Luckily I had packed the perfect dress to
wear on such an occasion – a black crepe cocktail dress which Leo had
given me. I had my hair done in the ship's beauty salon and Mena lent
me a stunning silver necklace and a small beaded purse as accessories;
when I left the cabin to attend the dinner I felt elegant.

That evening represented another fairy tale experience for me and
was the height of my social life to date. The table setting was formal
and candlelit, the food excellent, the service impeccable and for the
first time in my life I drank champagne, served in delicate Waterford
crystal. It was a glorious experience and when it ended I literally
floated back to my cabin and kept Mena up for hours relating everything that had happened.

About a month after I returned from Derry, Noel Coffey introduced
me to Barney Maguire. Barney was from County Donegal but had
been living in Philadelphia for several years. He was a passionate

Republican and we began a heady conversation that went on for hours. This was the first time I had met anyone in the US who espoused the same ideals as my father. Barney suggested I consider joining Clan-na-Gael and invited Leo and me to be his guests at a social they were holding the following week at the Clan-na-Gael's Terence McSwiney Club in Jenkintown outside Philadelphia. At the social Barney introduced me to everyone present, most of whom were in their forties or older, and by the end of the evening it was decided that he would propose me for membership. Another Donegal man, Neil Byrne, agreed to second my nomination. Although Clan-na-Gael was not a secret organisation, since it was legally registered under the US Foreign Agent's Registration Act, it was secretive. To prevent infiltration by those who might not share its aims, new members were normally checked out before being accepted but Barney and Neil felt this wouldn't be necessary in my case – being Paddy Sheil's daughter was recommendation enough.

I met Barney and Neil at the McSwiney Club the night my nomination was proposed to the executive committee and Barney explained the voting procedure. Each committee member was given two small balls, one white, one black, and after discussing the nominee's qualifications each person dropped one ball into a basket. If at the end of the vote three black balls were in the basket, membership was denied.

While waiting for the committee to make its decision, I studied the pictures on the wall of people revered by Republicans ranging from Wolfe Tone, leader of the 1798 rebellion to one of Sean South who, along with Fergal O'Hanlon, had been killed in January 1957 during the first phase of the IRA border campaign; a ballad, 'Sean South of Gerryowen', had been written to commemorate their deaths. When finally summoned to the meeting room the chairperson asked if I was prepared to swear an oath to uphold the Irish Republic of the Second Dail Eireann. When I answered affirmatively, I was sworn into Roisin Dubh, the women's auxiliary of the Major John MacBride Camp of the Philadelphia Clan-na-Gael.[1]

Thus began my 27 year involvement in the campaign to achieve a united Irish republic. My political orientation at that time was pure Republican/Nationalist, based on the naive belief that all Ireland's ills would be solved if Britain gave up its claim to NI. I was prepared to give unquestioning support to any organisation which supported that goal.

The Irish in the US have always provided significant support for Irish resistance to British rule whether that resistance is through

constitutional means or armed rebellion. Although events in Ireland
generally determined the nature and extent of this support, there were
periods when the Irish in the US influenced those at home – one
instance being the appeal by John O'Mahony and Michael Doheny to
their friend John Stephens to establish a revolutionary organisation in
Ireland. Stephens, who had had a long history of involvement in the
cause, heeded their suggestion and formed the IRB in Dublin on St
Patrick's Day, 1858. The Fenian Brotherhood was established in the
US to support the IRB's aim of leading an armed rebellion to establish
an independent democratic Irish republic. During the US Civil War
(1861–5), Irishmen gained valuable military skills which were later put
at the disposal of the IRB. Disagreement over tactics (one of which
was an attempted invasion of Canada as a means of undermining
British colonial interests), led to splits in the Fenian Brotherhood and
those who supported armed rebellion in Ireland formed Clan-na-Gael
in June 1867. For the next 100 years, Clan-na-Gael was to be the major
supplier of money and weapons to the Irish independence movement.

After joining Clan-na-Gael, all my spare time was devoted to its
various activities. I also attended meetings and socials held by various
Irish-American organisations at the Commodore John Barry Irish
Center[2] in Philadelphia where I sold the IRA's monthly newspaper,
United Irishman, and Irish Tricolours (which I made at home on my
sewing machine). I also collected money for dependants of Irish
political prisoners held in Irish and British jails. Although prohibited
from attending the male-only policy-making meetings of Clan-na-Gael,
I was invited to participate in caucus meetings held by the 'Young
Turks', who included Vincent Conlon and Neil Byrne. Vincent had participated in the raid on the RUC Barracks at Brookeborough, County
Fermanagh, which had claimed the lives of South and O'Hanlon. For
several years he was interned at the Curragh Camp in the Republic
(from which he once made a successful but short-lived escape), remaining until internment ended in 1959. I believe one reason I was accepted
into this all-male caucus was because, like them, I was part of the
younger generation of Clan-na-Gael members who felt compelled to
revive and breathe new life into what we saw as a dormant, organisation devoted to celebrating past events.

I saw no reason for women being denied full participation in Clan-
na-Gael and raised the matter at a Roisin Dubh meeting. The other
women agreed and we submitted a resolution to the next Clan-na-Gael
convention which successfully abolished women's auxiliaries and
granted women full membership. In the same vein, I had challenged

the County Derry Society calling itself the Catholic Sons of Derry because, as I pointed out, the name implied that the daughters of Derry were insignificant.

On 26 February 1962 the IRA announced an end to the border campaign. In June at the annual commemoration of Wolfe Tone at Bodenstown Cemetery near Sallins, County Kildare, Sinn Fein president Tomas MacGiolla stated that although the campaign had ended, it had not been a failure and its halt provided an 'opportunity to conserve our resources, consolidate our position, and gird ourselves to move forward with enthusiasm and optimism to the next phase in the struggle for freedom.'[3]

In retrospect, the border campaign floundered because it lacked a political base and therefore the ability to develop the popular support necessary to its success. When, after its initial burst of activity, the campaign failed to make significant gains, it eventually lost the financial backing of Clan-na-Gael which, at the end of December 1961, notified the IRA Army Council that it would be sending no more money. At the time I joined Clan-na-Gael neither it nor the IRA had ever been at a lower ebb.

7

Transitions

In the summer of 1962, Leo and I decided to move back to Philadelphia. His daily journey to and from work was becoming burdensome to him and I wanted to move back so I could participate more fully in Clan-na-Gael activities. We found a red-brick, two-storey house that was ideal for our growing family at 6210 Hasbrook Avenue in the Lawndale section of northeast Philadelphia. We moved into the house shortly before the October confrontation between the US and Russia during President Kennedy's Cuban missile blockade. I was terrified: the world appeared to be on the brink of nuclear war. I was amazed at the general belief that the US would be 'better off dead than red' and felt immense relief when the Russian ships withdrew. I feared Kennedy might 'push the button', to save face following the failed Bay of Pigs invasion of Cuba the previous year.

In September 1962 Cathal Goulding became IRA Chief of Staff and shortly afterward attended a Clan-na-Gael Convention held in Philadelphia. Goulding had come to the US to assess the strengths and weaknesses of Clan-na-Gael support. When Goulding and I were introduced we had a long conversation that marked the beginning of a friendship that later developed into a valued working relationship.

At the beginning of 1963 I discovered I was pregnant and in September our fourth child, Breige, was born. A few weeks before her birth I watched television coverage of the 'March for Jobs and Freedom', led by the Reverend Martin Luther King, Jr, in which over 250,000 people marched on Washington, DC. The various speakers presented a list of grievances from the steps of the Lincoln Memorial outlining the second-class status of black people in the US which, for me, was reminiscent of the position of Nationalists in NI.

Almost from the instant of my arrival in the US I had heard whites saying that black people were dirty, lazy, drank too much, had loose morals and too many children, and if provided with a nice house would shortly wreck it. It all sounded familiar. Loyalists in Derry held that the people who lived in the Bogside were unwilling to work, bred like rabbits and were frivolous. If given a good house they would only tear out the woodwork to burn in the fireplace, and instead of using the bathtub to bathe in they would use it to store coal. The connection in my mind between these racist sentiments led me to the conclusion that the plight of black people in the US and NI Nationalists was similar, but when I attempted to point this out to people I was accused of being a 'nigger lover'. Most people I knew expressed only contempt for the black civil rights movement and its demands for equality – Irish-Americans in particular having chosen to forget the years during which the Irish had been discriminated against in the US.

In November 1963 President Kennedy was assassinated in Dallas by Lee Harvey Oswald who in turn was assassinated by Jack Ruby. The nation halted in its tracks for the next four days as people gathered in front of their television sets and experienced collective mourning at the senseless death of this young and vibrant man whose challenging spirit had ushered in a new era in US politics. Although I had supported Kennedy's candidacy for president, I had become disillusioned shortly after he assumed office because he showed no more concern about Ireland than his predecessors. My feeling of disillusionment deepened after his death when it emerged that the policies of the Kennedy government marked the beginning of the intensification of US military involvement in Vietnam.

In the summer of 1964 my sister Mary obtained work as an *au pair* with a family in Maryland and whenever she had free time came to visit us. I delighted in getting to know my youngest sister, now 19, who was only a young girl when I had left home; having a member of my family close at hand somewhat eased my homesickness.

I made the decision to return to Derry on another holiday in 1965 so, in the Autumn of 1964, I took a job waitressing at John's Restaurant in the Benson Manor in Jenkintown. Although over one million black people lived in the greater Philadelphia area, I came into contact with them for the first time only when we worked together. Dorian, the chef, and most of the kitchen help were black and as time went on I found myself spending more time in the kitchen during my free moments than I did with the other waitresses. As we say in Derry, 'the crack' was better in the kitchen – lots of banter, jokes, songs and serious discussions about US racism and sectarianism in NI – and although our skin colour and accents were different, the similarity of our experiences provided a bond between us.

In 1964, in addition to the work being done by King's Southern Christian Leadership Conference, the Student Nonviolent Coordinating Committee (SNCC) was engaged in voter registration and direct action projects in the Deep South. In June three SNCC volunteers, James Chaney, Andrew Goodman and Michael Schwerner, were murdered and their bodies thrown into a swamp. Earlier, a woman from Detroit, Viola Liuzzo, had also been brutally murdered along a lonely Southern road and I felt as though I had lost a friend when I heard of her death, which could easily have been my own if I had felt free to act on my desire to work as a volunteer for SNCC.

I met the daughter of one of the men who worked in the kitchen at John's Restaurant when Leo and I drove him home one cold, snowy evening. She told me about a programme in North Philadelphia which helped young black students improve their English and math skills. I volunteered to work with the group and spent a few months tutoring and, although I'm not sure how much they learned from my amateur efforts, I gained much satisfaction from the experience.

February and March of 1965 brought a series of events which greatly affected my developing political consciousness and growing disenchantment with the US government. In February, President Lyndon Johnson ordered a bombing campaign of North Vietnam in his undeclared war against the Vietcong. In March, Martin Luther King Jr led a peaceful march in Selma, Alabama and the marchers were beaten, set upon4 by dogs let loose by the police and then hosed off the streets with massive pressurised jets of water spurting from water canons. King then announced he would lead a march from Selma to Montgomery, the state capital of Alabama, to highlight police injustices against civil rights marchers. As the march progressed we witnessed television news reports that exposed the true face of white racist hatred directed towards black demonstrators and their white supporters. All of this took place while I was studying for the examination to obtain US citizenship. I was memorising the US Constitution and Bill of Rights which stated that only Congress, not the President, had the right to declare war (which Johnson ignored), and that every citizen in the US was guaranteed equal treatment under law. I realised how these rights and guarantees were being violated by the very officials obligated to uphold them.

In Northern Ireland, Prime Minister Sean Lemass called on NI Prime Minister Captain Terence O'Neill at Stormont that January – the first meeting between the leadership of the two governments since 1925. The purpose of Lemass's visit, and that of O'Neill's reciprocal trip to Dublin in February, was not to improve the lot of the NI minority community but rather to discuss means of achieving better economic cooperation between the two governments. What was good for business was good enough for Lemass who in 1960 had sought, and achieved, stronger economic ties to Britain by signing the Anglo-Irish Free Trade Agreement. This agreement, which dropped import restrictions, would eventually result in the RI becoming the fifth largest importer of British goods, thus undercutting native Irish industry. Connolly had been farsighted when he warned the Irish people in 1897:

> If you remove the English Army tomorrow and hoist the green flag over Dublin Castle, unless you set about the organization of the Socialist Republic, your efforts would be in vain. England would still rule you. She would rule you through her capitalists, through her landlords, through her financiers, through the whole array of commercial ... institutions she had planted in this country.[1]

In the Summer of 1965 I took Breige and young Leo to Derry leaving Stella and Margaret in the care of their father and his family. I flew to Dublin where I was met by two men sent by Goulding who took us to his mother's house where the children and I spent the night. The next morning Goulding met me for breakfast and I delivered messages to him which could not be entrusted to the regular delivery services. He asked me for my perceptions of the political orientation of Clan-na-Gael members. I responded that although most of them were members of the Democratic Party, in general they were conservative, racist, and supportive of Johnson's policies in Vietnam – the latter due to the Catholic Church's support of the South Vietnamese government and because most Irish-Americans were rabidly anti-Communist.

Goulding told me that a discussion group, the Wolfe Tone Society, had been formed which brought together Sinn Fein members, academics, lawyers and others who were interested in developing a socialist economic programme intended to broaden support for a renewed effort to end partition. The group was particularly concerned about the increasing influence of multinational corporations in the economy of the RI. The Dublin government was inviting multinational firms to locate in the RI, especially the Free Trade Zone adjacent to Shannon International Airport where a new town was being developed to house the people they would employ. Multinationals were being enticed with offers of government funded plant construction, ten years of tax-free profits, the ability to import and export without having to pay duties and, due to the extremely high level of unemployment, an eager and docile workforce. Goulding told me the Wolfe Tone Society was also planning to join forces with the northern based Campaign for Social Justice (CSJ) to organise around the issue of civil rights abuses in NI.

Our conversation gave me hope for the future. Before I left for Derry, Goulding and I exchanged cover mailing addresses so we could correspond after I returned to Philadelphia without fear of our letters being intercepted.

My visit with my family was enjoyable and relaxing, and I delighted in showing off Breige and Leo. My sister Eileen was getting married in November to Jim Collins, a Protestant from County Down and a member of the British Royal Navy. Although my family had no objection to their marriage, our parish priest was putting stumbling blocks in their way so Eileen and Jim were planning to get married in England where there was less difficulty in obtaining the blessing of the Catholic Church. In addition to visiting family and friends in Derry, I also met with members of the Republican movement who were delighted when they learned I had become actively involved in Clan-na-Gael.

I arrived back in Philadelphia in August in time to witness television reports of the eruption of Watts, a black section of Los Angeles, which culminated in a week of rioting during which the Los Angeles police reacted in much the same manner as their counterparts in the southern states. This proved to me that white racism was deep, pervasive and did not stop at the Mason-Dixon line, as northern cities began to explode with the rage felt by black Americans.

The fiftieth anniversary of the 1916 Easter Rising was commemorated on both sides of the Atlantic in April 1966. The Irish of Philadelphia chose to celebrate with a formal, white-tie, invitation-only banquet at the Philadelphia Art Museum with the RI Prime Minister, Sean Lemass, as honoured guest and main speaker. The wealthy elite were celebrating the achievements of Irish men and women whom it was safe to acknowledge because most of them were dead and buried. On the day of the banquet I received a telephone call from Vincent Conlon; he had managed to obtain two tickets and wanted me to go with him to distribute Easter lily emblems to the guests to highlight the anti-Republican policies of the RI government.

The emblem of the Easter lily is the floral symbol worn to commemorate those who died in 1916 and after in the cause of Irish independence. Yet, although the lily is worn at Easter to honour Ireland's war dead, its distribution is made almost impossible. It is illegal to distribute lilies without a permit; failure to have one carries the penalty of a fine, imprisonment or both. But requests for permits are always denied. Republicans, who in any event refuse to acknowledge the authority of a legal system established by a government they regard as illegitimate to begin with, likewise refuse to apply for a permit they know will be denied, and scores of them have served sentences in RI jails for refusing to pay their fines. At the time Lemass came to Philadelphia for the gala Easter Rising celebration, his government had several men and women in jail for the 'crime' of distributing lilies and collecting donations for the families of IRA prisoners jailed in Britain, NI and the RI.

When Vincent arrived that evening I was ready, wearing a formal evening gown I had borrowed from a friend. Leo had no objection to my being Vincent's 'date' because he had come to recognise that my involvement in these activities helped to cure my homesickness.

Security at the entrance to the ballroom was strict but Vincent and I had no trouble entering when we presented our tickets. In the large purse I was carrying were hundreds of lily emblems and leaflets explaining their significance. When we entered the ballroom I approached the band members, holding out a lily and asking if they would wear one to honour Ireland's dead heroes. One man took one and the rest followed his lead, pinning the lily on their outfits. Vincent and I then went to all the tables, putting down a leaflet and asking the people if they would wear a lily. Most of the guests, including Grace Kelly's parents, took one.

Just as we finished Lemass walked in with James Tate, mayor of Philadelphia. I went over to Tate and, explaining its significance, asked if he would wear a lily. He listened politely and took the lily, saying he would be honoured to wear it. I offered to pin the emblem on his dinner jacket while Lemass stood glowering at me. One of Lemass's people motioned to a security guard and Vincent and I were politely but firmly ushered out of the building. We laughed all the way home thinking about Lemass at the head table looking out at all those people wearing Easter lilies!

Leo had become bored with his job, and, having learned that the US government was offering lucrative tax-free wages to people willing to spend 18 months in the Marshall Islands working on the construction of a communications facility, he decided to apply for a position as toolmaker and was accepted. In July 1966, he left for the Marshall Islands where, except for short visits home every six months, he would remain until the end of 1967.

Although I missed Leo a great deal, I managed well on my own and now that I was husband-free, I found myself becoming increasingly involved in Clan-na-Gael activities – one of which was a boycott of British goods as a means of publicising the situation in NI. We also travelled to nearby cities where we held meetings with people interested in establishing Clan-na-Gael camps, and were successful in Baltimore, Maryland; Washington, DC; Scranton, Pennsylvania; and Brunswick, New Jersey.

In June 1966, Seamus Costello, speaking on behalf of IRA/Sinn Fein, gave the historic oration at the Wolfe Tone Commemoration in Bodenstown which marked the new socialist policies of that organisation:

> We believe that the large estates of absentee landlords should be acquired by compulsory acquisition and worked on a co-operative basis with the financial and technical assistance of the State ... our policy is to nationalise the key industries with the eventual aim of co-operative ownership by the workers ... nationalisation of all banks, insurance companies, loan and investment companies.

Not only did workers have the right to use armed force, said Costello; it was also a necessity:

> The lesson of history shows that in the final analysis the Robber Baron must be dis-established by the same methods that he used to enrich himself and retain his ill gotten gains, namely force of arms. To this end we must organise, train and maintain a disciplined armed force which will always be available to strike at the opportune moment.

In August 1966 the Wolfe Tone Society held a conference in Maghera, County Derry, on civil rights violations in NI which was such a success that they planned another for Belfast in November. These conferences formed the core around which was founded the NI Civil Rights Association (NICRA) at the International Hotel, Belfast, on 29 January 1967. NICRA represented a spectrum of Republican/liberal/ left political groups whose first chair was Betty Sinclair, a veteran trade union leader and member of the Irish Communist Party.

The formation of NICRA received a mixed response from Clan-na-Gael members, who equated civil rights with 'black power' in the US with which they wanted no association. In addition, articles in the *United Irishman* were taking an increasingly leftward stance that was at complete variance with the traditional anti-political, pro-military, conservative, pro-Catholic Church ethos of the old guard Clan-na-

Gael members. I, and a few others in the newer generation, were open to anything that might revive the IRA, now, as Goulding had stated publicly, almost dormant. Although I knew that funds and weapons were still finding their way to the IRA Headquarters in Dublin, apathy and inactivity had cut the number of new recruits.

I learned that Rev Ian Paisley was coming to the US in April 1967 for a six-week speaking tour sponsored by the Bob Jones University (BJU) in Greenville, South Carolina. BJU, cited by the Division of Higher Education (US Department of Health, Education and Welfare), as a degree mill whose degrees were worth only the paper they were written upon, had the previous year conferred an honorary Doctorate of Divinity on Paisley for his services to fundamental Protestantism. Of Paisley, Bob Jones Jr said: 'The Reverend Ian Paisley is one of the Godliest men I have ever met. He is definitely being used in the plan of God and he is clearly one of the most effective instruments in the world today.'[2]

The two men have much in common. Paisley is a sworn enemy of the Catholic Church and regards the Pope as the anti-Christ bent on the destruction of the Protestant faith: he sees the unrest in NI as a popish plot. His hatred of Catholicism closely rivals the hatred of blacks expressed by the fundamentalist followers of Rev Bob Jones Jr.

Paisley's speeches in the US were directed against the ecumenical movement, which he regarded as further evidence of a popish plot to destroy Protestantism. When I saw that Paisley had been invited by Rev Carl McIntyre to speak at his church in Collingswood, New Jersey I contacted a few Clan-na-Gael members suggesting we attend to hear first-hand what Paisley was saying.

Six of us – Vincent Conlon, Paddy Groogan, Frank Houlihan, Hugh McDermott, Tom McGuigan and myself – went to the church that night. There is no denying that Paisley is a master orator of the old school and his message of hate directed against the ecumenical movement, the Catholic Church and Nationalists in NI, had his audience of about 300 spellbound. His was a political speech of pure hatred directed at all I held dear and I felt both outrage and fear. Against my better judgement and sense, I felt my anger grow and before I realised what I was doing I was on my feet pointing my finger at Paisley shouting, 'Paisley, there are at least six people here tonight that know you are a liar, no, make that seven.'

Tom McGuigan, sitting next to me, tried to get me to sit down but it was too late. With venom in his voice, Paisley pointed to me: 'There's one of those Fenian's I've been talking about!' Heads turned in our direction and we began to make a hasty exit. There were scuffles as members of the audience tried to stop us leaving.

In January 1968 Leo and I were involved in an automobile accident when our car skidded on a patch of ice and careened into a lamppost. Leo was unscathed but I was knocked unconscious when my head went through the windscreen. I was rushed to hospital, where a priest gave me the last rites. When eventually released from hospital the only visible signs of my ordeal were several scars on my forehead and by the end of March I went back to work at John's Restaurant. However, I did begin to suffer recurring bouts of severe depression which were not helped by events around me – the escalating war in Vietnam and the deaths of Martin Luther King Jr and Robert Kennedy.

President Johnson's increased military involvement in Vietnam was matched by growing resistance to his war policy: marches, teach-ins on university campuses, civil disobedience and symbolic acts of draft card burning as thousands of young men declared themselves willing to go to jail or into exile as an act of resistance to the draft. Senator Eugene McCarthy expressed his opposition by declaring he would challenge Johnson for the Democratic Party presidential nomination. After McCarthy came in a close second to Johnson in the New Hampshire Primary and then won in Wisconsin, Johnson announced he would not seek reelection. Senator Robert Kennedy, who had earlier brushed off suggestions that he run for president, now had a change of heart and threw his hat into the race.

On 5 April, Martin Luther King Jr was assassinated by James Earl Ray as he stood on the balcony of the Lorraine Motel in Memphis where he had gone to lend support to a strike by Memphis municipal garbage collectors. I was at work when the news came of King's death and I experienced an immediate sense of anguish and anger which was not shared by the other waitresses. On one of my trips to the waitress station I overheard them agreeing with one another that 'that black bastard got what he deserved'. Unable to hold back my tears I ran to the kitchen to share my grief with Dorian and the others but my words of condolence sounded trite. In an act of compassion Dorian put his arm around my shoulder, 'You may know we have lost a great leader, Brigid, but I'm afraid that most of white America hasn't a notion of the loss we have *all* suffered.'

In June, when Sirhan Sirhan assassinated Senator Kennedy in Los Angeles after he had won the California presidential primary, I felt I was living in a society gone completely mad. Then, in August, Mayor Richard Daly, who ran the city of Chicago as though it was his fief, turned a blind eye when his police harassed, batoned, and tear-gassed antiwar demonstrators during the Democratic Party National Convention. At the end of that week the police, unrestrained and unable to contain their fury at those they considered to be un-American, ran amuck, stormed the McCarthy headquarters hotel and vented their rage at his campaign staff.

The Democratic Party chose Johnson's vice president, Hubert Humphrey, as their nominee and at the Republican Party Convention held in Miami, Richard M. Nixon was selected as their standard bearer. I had cast my first vote as a US citizen for McCarthy in the Pennsylvania primary but neither Humphrey nor Nixon would get my vote in November.

My depression deepened and, fearing that I might be on the edge of a nervous breakdown, my doctor suggested a change of scenery and complete rest. Leo and I discussed this and agreed that I would go to Derry and stay with my mother as long as necessary to regain my health. The Makowski family agreed to take our youngest child Breige and I arranged for a friend to come in as day-help until Leo came home from work in the evening.

I arrived in Derry on 4 October 1968. The following day was to provide the catalyst for all that has happened in NI since.

8

The Town I Love So Well

Since my last visit my mother had been rehoused in a two-bedroom flat on Columcille Court in a new complex for retired people near the intersection of William and Rossville Streets (later to be known as 'Aggro Corner'). When my sister Eileen came over to welcome me home she was shocked at my appearance – never one to carry excess weight, I was now skin and bones and had a drawn and haggard look. A while later Eileen and my mother went into the kitchen. I could hear them talking softly and wondering what they were saying, went to the door and opened it just as my mother said, 'Don't let Brigid know', which was enough to cause me to start asking questions. I pried out of them the information that a civil rights march was to be held the next day. They both tried to dissuade me from going but at the end of the night I won out and Eileen agreed to call for me the following afternoon.

The civil rights march was the brainchild of the Derry Housing Action Committee (DHAC) under the joint leadership of Eamonn McCann, Johnny White, Finbar O'Doherty and Mickey Montgomery. Throughout the summer of 1968 DHAC had challenged the segregated housing policies of the Loyalist-controlled Derry City Corporation by squatting people in vacant housing units. In order to maintain gerrymandered electoral wards, Nationalists were refused corporation housing units outside of what were considered to be 'their' areas. Instead, a decision was taken to institute urban renewal of the Bogside to rehouse people. The plan included the construction of a complex of high-rise flats on Rossville Street; instead of allowing Bogsiders to move out, the corporation decided to move them up several storeys as a means of containing their growing majority within the election ward assigned them.

Following a successful march in Dungannon, County Tyrone, in August, sponsored by the Campaign for Social Justice and supported by NICRA, in which a surprising 2,500 people marched to support housing reform, DHAC decided to hold a similar march in Derry and asked for NICRA's endorsement. DHAC's civil disobedience tactics had upset the more conservative Nationalist leadership in Derry, who felt the committee was controlled by communists, and they attempted to persuade NICRA that a march in Derry would be unwise. With some reluctance, NICRA agreed to participate and on 31 August an ad hoc planning committee was formed consisting of representatives from NICRA, DHAC, the Derry City Republican Club, James Connolly Society, Derry Labour Party and Derry Labour Party Young Socialists.

The committee announced the march route – from Duke Street in the Waterside, across Craigavon Bridge over the River Foyle, up the hill, through the Derry walls culminating at The Diamond in the centre of the old walled city – and the Loyalists were enraged. This was the first time Nationalists had planned a march into the walled section of Derry since the attempt by Eddie McAteer and the Anti-Partition League in March 1952. The Derry Apprentice Boys announced they would hold their first 'annual' march in Derry that same day, time and route, and then appealed to the NI Home Affairs Minister, William Craig, to ban the civil rights march. Craig complied, citing the Public Order Act; there was no ban placed on the Apprentice Boys' march.

The weather on Saturday 5 October 1968 was grey and overcast with the threat of rain in the air. Eileen and I walked to the Waterside area where the march was assembling. The mood of the crowd was cheerful but apprehensive as no one knew what would happen because of the ban. I saw Mickey Montgomery and Johnny White and they expressed their disappointment at the small turnout. About 400 people had assembled and they felt there would have been more if the march had not been called on a day the Derry City Football Club was having a major match in the city (originally the organisers had thought the Derry team would be playing an away game).[1]

I had a movie camera with me and went around the crowd filming as the march lined up. Because Eileen was three months pregnant, we decided to march towards the back to avoid any possibility of her being jostled if there was trouble. Linking arms and singing 'We Shall Overcome', the march got underway and had started across Craigavon Bridge when it was stopped by the RUC who ordered the crowd to disperse. Policemen began batoning people at the front of the march, injuring Eddie McAteer and his Republican Labour Party colleague, MP Gerry Fitt.

The march halted and Betty Sinclair, speaking through a bullhorn, cautioned us to avoid confrontation. Her words were echoed by McAteer, who was bleeding from his wounds (Fitt had been taken to hospital), and McCann, who added that if we continued the march we should do so in an orderly, non-violent manner. Half-an-hour later, when a decision was taken to move forward, we were attacked front and rear by the RUC who hit everyone they could reach with their batons. The vengeance and hatred on their faces was unbelievable. I dropped my camera but managed to retrieve it while grabbing Eileen's hand, pulling her out of the march, and running with her to a little shop at the entrance of the bridge. There were about 10 or 12 others inside and after we squeezed in the owner shut and locked the door. While we watched through the window we witnessed the RUC bringing water cannons into place, aiming them at the marchers who were trapped on the bridge. As the jets of water thundered out at the crowd, people went flying in all directions. There was complete pandemonium – people screaming and cursing, the uninjured attempting to rescue those who were hurt, as jets of water continued to knock them off their feet. I stood at the window watching in horror, filming the event.[2]

An hour later the march was over. Eileen and I cautiously made our way across the bridge as ambulances carted off the injured. We avoided the Loyalist section by going up Foyle Street and around by the Guild Hall. People out doing their Saturday shopping had learned what had happened and all along William Street knots of angry people gathered in confusion, wondering what to do.

That evening Eileen and I attended a meeting at the City Hotel to watch the day's events on television. This was the first time in the history of NI that television film crews had been sent to cover a Nationalist march, and their film provided the world with stark evidence of RUC brutality towards peaceful protest. We were not asking for a united Ireland but simply seeking to highlight discriminatory housing policies. Observing the RUC on television I was reminded of news reports I had seen of confrontations between civil rights marchers and police in Selma, Alabama and the actions of the Chicago police against the anti-Vietnam War protesters.

That night a group of Bogside youth took matters into their own hands. Unarmed except for rocks and stones they went to The Diamond inside the Derry Walls seeking revenge for the day's outrage and fought with gangs of young Loyalists who sought to defend their turf. The RUC arrived, drove our supporters back into the Bogside, then went on a rampage batoning everyone they encountered.

The next day Eileen and her husband Jim drove me to Fahan outside Buncrana where my mother had rented a small cottage for me. The local gardai, used to seeing the summer cottages dark and empty at that time of year, stopped the first night to investigate. I invited them in for tea and during our conversation they expressed their outrage at the events in Derry. This visit became a nightly ritual of their patrol and often they would drive to the nearest shop to get me milk or cigarettes when I ran out. For the next several weeks I did nothing but sleep, eat, read and take long walks along the shores of Lough Swilly. Slowly I began to regain my old sense of self as the peaceful quiet of County Donegal settled around me.

When I arrived back at my mother's on 14 November, I found the mood in Derry and the rest of NI had changed as a result of the civil rights march – there was to be no turning back from the events of that day. On 9 October McCann had chaired a meeting to establish a community-wide organisation to plan further actions in Derry. At this meeting the Derry Citizens' Action Committee (DCAC) was formed with 16 people chosen to represent several community organisations and the Catholic Church (see Appendix I).

McCann refused an appointment to DCAC when he saw that the young working-class activists and socialists were being supplanted by middle-aged, middle-class, professional and business people, marking the difference between those who wanted to change the system of government in NI and those who sought only to reform it. DCAC's first chair, Ivan Cooper, was a liberal Protestant shirt-factory manager. John Hume, vice chair, was an ex-teacher who had opted out of the priesthood, helped form a credit union in Derry and then made a small fortune from a smoked salmon industry he co-founded and managed. Although Hume had marched on 5 October (as had Cooper), he had refused to participate on the ad hoc organising committee. Now he was to hitch his political star onto the bandwagon of the success of the march. McCann left the DCAC meeting and went to Belfast where People's Democracy (PD) was formed that evening by a group of students from Queen's University which included Bernadette Devlin, Michael Farrell, Kevin Boyle and Cyril Toman.

As a result of the Derry march NICRA had gained increased stature and credibility and was asked to establish new committees throughout NI. They formulated a set of demands which called upon the government to:

- grant universal franchise in local elections and eliminate the company vote
- abolish gerrymandered election district

- end employment discrimination in local government jobs and establish a means to deal with local grievances
- establish a points system to ensure fair housing allocation
- repeal the Special Powers Act and the Public Order Bill
- disband the B-Specials

These demands translated into the slogan of one man—one vote (sic), one family—one house, one man—one job and centred on the key issue of equal voting rights.[3]

The RUC's ugly performance during the 5 October march had had a profound effect upon public opinion in Britain and the RI. The Dublin government sought assurances from the British government that the minority population in NI would be granted the same rights to seek resolution of their grievances as did citizens in Great Britain. Westminster, which had always turned a blind eye to what it regarded as the internal affairs of NI, now wanted answers from Stormont as to how matters had reached such an impasse.

Captain Terence O'Neill, NI prime minister, was not unaware of Nationalist complaints but had adopted a cautious approach lest he rock the Orange Order boat. Faced with growing criticism, O'Neill was forced to appear to take action while he tried to placate both camps. He urged local authorities to begin implementing a fair housing policy while praising the RUC performance in Derry and hinting that if they hadn't taken firm control there would have been deaths instead of merely injuries.

Craig refused requests to hold an inquiry into RUC behaviour, justifying this by stating that Cathal Goulding had been at the march: by implication, therefore, the IRA had been responsible for the violence. But Goulding was in Dublin that day, not on the march, and while there were individual IRA members present, the march was not an IRA activity – in fact, Goulding gave little credence to civil rights marches per se but was willing to support such activity as a tactic to be used in organising support for Sinn Fein/IRA.

DCAC had announced there would be another march in Derry on 16 November to retrace the route of the original one. On 13 November, Craig issued an order banning all marches within the walls of Derry for a month. In defiance of Craig's ban, Eileen and I joined with 15,000 other people to march to The Diamond. Despite a massive presence, the police were overwhelmingly outnumbered. When we reached the police line guarding the Ferryquay Street entrance to the Derry Walls, we halted. The commander in charge, realising he lacked the personnel to enforce Craig's banning order, agreed to Hume's suggestion that a symbolic number be allowed to saunter through the police lines and assemble at The Diamond. March stewards instructed the rest of us to disperse and make our way to The Diamond through various other entrances.

Eileen and I went around the walls and entered through the gate at Shipquay Street on the far side. After we had all reassembled we listened to the speakers; Finbar O'Doherty detailed the injustices directed against Nationalists, and again I was struck with the parallels between the black civil rights movement in the US and our own. 'We are the white negroes', Finbar said, 'of Northern Ireland.' That night the Bogside was elated; we had successfully defied Craig's ban.

A week later, O'Neill announced he was replacing the Derry City Corporation with a Development Commission charged with bringing about economic changes in the city. He said also that he had instructed local housing committees to institute a system of fair housing allocations, appointed an ombudsman to resolve housing and job discrimination complaints and abolished the company vote, and that when the time was 'ripe' he would review the Special Powers Act. On the face of it, it appeared that these were major changes; in actuality, they were little more than promises. The most important demand – electoral reform – had been ignored, and there was no guarantee that O'Neill's small reforms would be implemented by the Unionist Party which controlled Stormont.

I stayed in Derry for five more weeks. During that time I attended educational classes held by the Sinn Fein Republican Club. We read the works of James Connolly, James Fintan Lalor, Wolfe Tone and studied the 1916–22 period to see how and why the original movement for Irish independence had failed. We looked at how successive governments in the RI had broken their promise to work for a united Ireland. Lastly, we analysed the mistakes of the IRA and its policies. Our interests were not simply academic. Sinn Fein was changing. From a Republican Nationalist political stance, it was moving towards a more all-embracing position of Republican Socialism, aimed at uniting the working class regardless of religious, political and geographic differences. The new Sinn Fein socialist programme for Ireland reflected this principle. There was a sense of hope and optimism in the air and although we were not naive enough to believe that the Orange Order would relinquish its control and privilege without a protracted struggle, we did feel we could eventually convince the average working-class Loyalist that we had more in common to unite us than we did to divide us.

These few weeks marked the beginning of my socialist education. I was impressed with the intelligence and knowledge of the young people of Derry; they were articulate, well-educated, and intent on changing their society. They represented the difference between the Derry I had left 13 years earlier and the one I now found – meeting them gave me great hope for the future.

By the time I left I had come to a major personal decision: I wanted to move back to Derry to be a part of the movement for change. I realised that my efforts were being misdirected in the US, that I had a role to play in Ireland. I returned to Philadelphia on 22 December intent on convincing Leo to move with our family to Derry.

9

Battle of the Bogside

Leo and the children met me at the airport in New York City for a glorious reunion. Everyone was happy that I was back and in good form once again. We spent a delightful Christmas together with the holiday week devoted to catching up on family news. Although I had been away only three months the children seemed to have grown years – Stella was now 12, Margaret 11, Leo 7, Breige 5. Within little more than a month's time I would discover I was again pregnant.

The New Year news from family and friends from Derry was dismal. People's Democracy, using Martin Luther King Jr's march from Selma to Montgomery as their model, began a march from Belfast to Derry on New Year's Day designed to expose the true face of the Northern Ireland government. They were not disappointed. Beginning with the original march in Dungannon, every civil rights march since had been thwarted by counter demonstrations by Paisley and his Ulster Protestant Volunteers (UPV) led by Major Ronald Bunting. In each case this was either overlooked or abetted by the RUC and was to prove the case with the PD march as well. Constantly harassed along their 75 mile route by Paisley, Bunting and the UPV, the marchers reached the final leg of their journey on 4 January. Then, according to the march organiser, Michael Farrell:

The march set out from Claudy swelled by several hundred supporters who had come out from Derry ... At Burntollet Bridge several hundred Loyalists hurled rocks and bottles and then charged, armed with clubs and iron bars. It was an ambush ... dozens of marchers were driven off the road and into the river Faughan, some quite badly injured.

There was no doubt that it was a trap. The RUC knew an ambush had been prepared. Heaps of stones had been collected the night before and crowds of cudgel-wielding men had been gathering since early morning while RUC men stood among them laughing and chatting. During the ambush some of the RUC joined in and attacked the marchers too ... It later turned out that nearly a hundred of the ambush party were off-duty B Specials.[1]

If the 5 October civil rights march was the trigger for subsequent events, the ambush at Burntollet Bridge provided the bullet which tore through the fabric shrouding the totalitarian Northern Ireland state.

I telephoned my mother the following week and was told that after the PD march reached Derry the RUC had gone on a drunken rampage in the Bogside and that young people had put up barricades to prevent them from entering the area. The barricades remained in place for five days before Hume and Cooper talked people into dismantling them. However, the sign painted by John Casey would remain as a landmark – 'you are now entering Free Derry' was painted on the end wall of a row of houses at St Columb Street.

To my surprise and delight I found it relatively easy to convince Leo to make a trial move to Derry. He wasn't all that happy with his job and came to regard the move as a potential adventure. In the back of his mind was the notion of starting his own machine shop business to service the toolmaking needs of the multinational companies which had located in the Derry area. We made plans for me to take the children to Ireland in June, make arrangements for the birth of our new child and locate a house for us. Leo would stay in Philadelphia until the end of the summer, join us for a few weeks, then take a job in Greenland for 18 months working on a US government project which, because of the high pay and tax-free salary, would provide him with most of the capital he needed to start a business. To earn extra money for the trip to Derry I went back to work at John's Restaurant at the end of January.

The beginning of the end for the Nationalist Party was signalled by the 24 February election. O'Neill had called for the election in an attempt to shore up his declining support by Unionist Party MPs who were angry about his tentative reforms and the fact that he had sacked Craig for publicly breaking ranks. The election results made it clear that the Nationalists were slipping: Eddie McAteer, the Nationalist Party MP for Derry City since 1949, was defeated by John Hume, who ran on an independent civil rights ticket, and two other NP seats were lost to Ivan Cooper and Paddy O'Hanlon, also independent civil rights candidates.

Excited about my Derry discussion group, I suggested that we do the same at a Clan-na-Gael meeting in Philadelphia and offered the use of my house as a meeting place. Although the number of people who attended varied from week to week, the core group consisted of Frank and Delma Houlihan, Jerry Creegan, Hugh McDermott and myself.

The majority of Clan-na-Gael members, however, were not interested in discussing a socialist programme for Ireland, and were uncertain about NICRA because of its socialist and communist support. When a group of us proposed that Clan-na-Gael carry a civil rights banner in the upcoming Philadelphia St Patrick's Day parade, we were met with some opposition. The motion was finally adopted but with the provision that the banner clearly state that Clan-na-Gael was supporting civil rights in Ireland, not black civil rights in the US.

Brendan Kerr and I dutifully made the banner with its restricted wording 'Clan-na-Gael is supporting civil rights in Ireland' but even so, when word leaked to the parade organising committee, efforts were made to stop us. We informed Michael Cavanaugh, the parade Grand Marshall, that if we were not allowed to participate we would disrupt the parade with acts of civil disobedience. Cavanaugh, realising we meant business, convinced the parade committee to desist. To the sounds of a few boos, more than made up for by cheers and clapping, Hugh McCafferty, John Kelly and I carried the banner the full length of the parade route – the first time there had ever been a show of support for NICRA in the US.

Around this time Jack McKinney (a local journalist), Neil Byrne and Vincent Conlon formed the American Friends of NICRA (AFNICRA) in Philadelphia which I joined. We leafletted, planned rallies and picketed the British Consulate to draw media attention to what was happening in Northern Ireland, but we were not terribly successful. Reporters regarded developments in Birmingham (Alabama), Hanoi, Saigon and Washington as more newsworthy than a 900-year-old political struggle in Ireland which in any event they had been led to believe by British propaganda had been caused solely by religious differences between Protestants and Catholics.

Bernadette Devlin was elected MP to Westminster in a by-election held on 17 April 1969. Two days later a Loyalist mob, aided by the RUC, went on a rampage in Derry, injuring scores of people, including my mother's neighbour Samuel Devenny, who was savagely beaten by the the RUC after they broke into his house and who died a few months later as a result of his injuries. (Devenny lost the 'distinction' of being the first to die in the current troubles when 66-year-old Francis McCloskey died a few days earlier, as a result of a beating he received from the RUC during a demonstration in Dungiven, County Derry.)

On 28 April, Terence O'Neill resigned as Prime Minister. The list of civil rights demands had centred on the adoption of 'one person, one vote', which O'Neill had accepted 'in principle' but in so doing lost the margin of his support in the cabinet. In a manoeuvre which resulted in his election as prime minister, O'Neill's cousin, James Chichester-Clark, resigned from the cabinet in protest over the issue of voting rights. Chichester-Clark became prime minister on 1 May, by one vote over the bid of Brian Faulkner who represented the hard line Unionist Party position of granting no concessions to Nationalists. However, at the end of May, Chichester-Clark announced that universal suffrage would be granted in the next local elections (which did not take place until 30 May 1973 – four years later).

After a final round of good-byes to family and friends, the children and I flew to Ireland at the end of June. I was elated! As we flew over the Atlantic Ocean I recalled the numerous times I had taken the children to Atlantic City just to be by that ocean which touched Ireland's shores as I pondered on the seeming impossibility of ever going back there to live. Now I was on my way home, truly a dream come true.

We settled into mother's small flat while I looked for a place for my family to live. I was in Derry less than a week when my sister Margaret provided a solution. She was buying a three-storey Georgian house with a huge garden on Francis Street across from St Eugene's Cathedral as investment property. She proposed that we move in, and if I was willing to take in boarders to help cover her expenses, she would let us live there rent free. I immediately accepted her offer. The house needed renovations and wouldn't be available for several months, so mother arranged the lease of a caravan to be put on land she owned near Buncrana so I could take the children there for a break when it became too confining for them in her small flat. Having solved our housing problem, I then went to see our family doctor and made arrangements for the birth of my child, due in October.

The children took to Derry as though it were their native place. They had lots of cousins who were the same ages and were soon introduced to all their friends and, as the communal spirit still operated as it had in my childhood, I felt free to let them roam the Bogside, knowing they would be safe. Young Leo even managed to start his own business to earn pocket money: he was already quite an entrepreneur and cute as a fox. He went around to various shops and, announcing himself as Paddy Sheil's grandson, asked if he might haul away their wooden crates for them. Mentioning my father's name gave him entree to half the wooden boxes in the Bogside. He broke them into kindling wood, tied about a dozen each into bundles, then went door to door selling these for five pence a bundle. Before long he had a thriving business going.

Three weeks after we arrived I went to Dublin to meet Goulding, who filled me in on the political activities of Sinn Fein. In the RI they had begun to apply their new political theories of social agitation by organising tenant groups to improve housing conditions in Dublin (which had the worst slums in Europe), as well as in Limerick and Cork. They had also started a campaign to have ground rents abolished – it was still the case that large amounts of land were owned by absentee landlords, mainly English, who leased the land rather than sell it, a prime example being the General Post Office on O'Connell Street, the site of the 1916 Easter Rising, which stood on land which was leased by the Dublin government. In addition, large stretches of Irish rivers ran through estates of English lords and were not available for recreational purposes; Sinn Fein started a series of 'fish-ins' to demand the rivers be open to the public.

In line with their goal of uniting workers north and south as the first step towards ending partition and establishing an Irish socialist republic, Sinn Fein members were also joining trade unions. They tried to show their co-workers how their interests were being undermined in the north by sectarianism and in the south by 'sweetheart' contracts between union leaders and the multinationals. I was heartened by our conversation; Sinn Fein was seriously putting into practice the socialist theories we had discussed the year before in Derry.

Goulding acknowledged the importance of Irish-American financial aid and arms shipments to the IRA and told me about the training camps in counties Donegal, Clare, Tipperary and Wicklow. He also told me the IRA had established arms dumps in various parts of the country and had established a network of safe houses; many people, although members of Fianna Fail or Fine Gael, were willing to support the IRA privately and the list of names included several elected officials. I left the meeting under the distinct impression that the IRA was readying itself militarily to engage the forces of the Crown in NI – without military opposition, Britain would never relinquish a colony.

I joined the James Connolly Republican Club and its political education meetings in Derry, but I began to feel uneasy. We were relying less and less on the writings of Connolly and more and more on those by Russian revolutionaries. While I had no quarrel with the leaders of the Russian Revolution, the USSR was not a model I wished to emulate. I tended to agree with Connolly; a socialist political philosophy for

Ireland had to fit the problems, needs and desires of the Irish people. In a letter to a friend in 1912, he wrote:

> I consider that the problem of the propagation of Socialism in Ireland is a big enough one ... without taking sides in, or getting excited about, what is happening in [the US] ... Political programmes, political phrases and political parties unless they are the expression of the phase of economic development already arrived at in the country where they exist are but fantastic and unreal will-o-the-wisps luring their users to destruction ... Programmes, phrases and parties [in other countries] are no more applicable to Ireland than the programmes, phrases and parties of Ireland are applicable to Timbuctoo. Hence, why get excited about them? [2]

Although he wrote this before the Russian Revolution, I believed Connolly would have remained stalwart in his belief that we could not adopt the Russian model wholesale (nor that of any other country), as a short-cut for what needed to be done in Ireland. However, my initial sense of unease was temporarily overshadowed by events.

Every afternoon, as the RUC day shift was returning to barracks to go off-duty, a ritual known as the 'daily matinee' took place. Around 4 pm, groups of young people would congregate at Aggro Corner to fling stones and insults at the passing RUC patrols before dashing back into the safety of the Bogside. This activity was condemned by priests in Sunday sermons and by the leadership of DCAC who gave them the label of 'hooligans', a term which the Bogside youth quickly adopted as an honoured title reflecting their alienation and disenchantment with their elders. There was a constant stream of these young people in and out of my mother's house because she always made them welcome and delighted in their excited account of the latest escapade. They were not delinquents but, rather, the children of a new generation that was determined not to adopt the complacent attitude of their parents who, while they might rail against their second-class status, did little to change it.

Surprisingly, the annual Orange Order parade on 12 July passed without any major confrontations but as the date of the annual Apprentice Boys' Parade in Derry drew near, there was a definite feeling that trouble was brewing. In anticipation, Sean Keenan, Mickey Montgomery, Johnny White, and Paddy 'Bogside' Doherty set up the Derry Citizens Defence Committee (DCDC) to defend the Bogside and to ensure there would be no repeat of the RUC/Loyalist assaults on our community like those in October 1968, and January and April 1969.

First-aid stations were set up around the community, one in my mother's flat, and young people were put to work gathering materials to barricade entrances into the Bogside. Pint-sized glass milk bottles were collected and money solicited to purchase petrol to make petrol bombs, some of which were stored in coal sheds. As far as humanly possible people prepared to defend their community, knowing they could not depend on the RUC to do so.

There was an eerie sense of anticipation on the morning of 12 August. The huge Lambeg drums boomed steadily inside the Derry Walls as over 15,000 Apprentice Boys and their supporters, which included large numbers of B-Special reservists, assembled for the parade. For me the sound of those drums served as a flash-back to my childhood and I could feel tension and anger mounting within me. Shortly before 4 pm, Eileen and I walked up William Street to watch the parade emerge from the Derry Walls prior to its route along the edge of the Bogside. Our hooligans were at their usual site and we observed the first exchange of rocks between the two groups – the Battle of the Bogside had begun. The RUC and marchers joined forces to charge the group of young rock-throwers who attempted to hold their ground. Eileen and I prudently retreated to mother's flat to prepare to assist those who were certain to appear at our door seeking first-aid.

When we arrived at the flat we found my three daughters with their grandmother. We were told that Leo Patrick had gone with Eileen's and Teresa's boys to play at a friend's house in the Creggan area on the opposite side of the Bogside from the fighting – later we learned they had gone instead to Eileen's apartment in the Rossville Flats, one of the most dangerous sites in the hours ahead. On the roof young people were making and hurling petrol bombs into the street nine floors below, trying to pin down the RUC who were in the vanguard of the assaulting mob.

As word spread through the Bogside and Creggan that a battle was in progress everyone who was physically fit turned out to maintain the barricades. For the first time in living memory Bogsiders collectively and spontaneously rallied to defend their community. At every moment I expected to see armed units of the IRA arrive to defend us but none came nor, as I learned later, were orders ever given for them to be mobilised. The only gun I saw in Republican hands during the next three days was one handgun and the man who owned it lacked the ammunition to arm it. We defended our barricades with paving stones hacked from the sidewalks and streets, and with petrol bombs. Loyalists began hurling petrol bombs back and soon fires were raging around the perimeter of the Bogside facing William and Rossville Streets.

The RUC began indiscriminately firing grenades of CS gas but we quickly learned to protect ourselves from the fumes. We smeared our faces with vasoline and used rags soaked in vinegar to wash out our eyes; buckets filled with vinegar and water were constantly replenished so people could keep their protective rags soaked with the solution.

Our flat was soon filled with people being treated for injuries and several doctors stopped by on their rounds of the first-aid stations to handle the severe cases. The grievously wounded, who couldn't be taken to the local hospital for fear they would be arrested, were driven across the border to the Letterkenny Hospital in County Donegal.

The battle raged through the night. Bernadette Devlin was magnificent. She was our own MP, there to give us heart and encouragement. At one point she helped me steer a wheelbarrow filled with broken paving stones through the rubble as we 'met' without introduction while engaged in common purpose. Infants, young children, and those too feeble to fight were evacuated to Buncrana and early the next morning a decision was taken to evacuate the complex where mother lived. By this time Leo Patrick and his cousins had been retrieved from the Rossville Flats and I took him and my other children to Margaret's house on Francis Street. In the confusion I lost track of mother. Someone I met on the street informed me they had seen her making her way back to her flat to retrieve important documents she had left behind. I caught up with her at the entrance to the flat and tried to dissuade her from going in, but she wouldn't listen to my pleas. There was nothing for me to do but to go in and stay with her while she located the papers.

The flat was in a shambles. The battle raging outside was mirrored by the scene within – waste baskets overflowing with bloody cotton wool used to clean wounds and old bandages which had been replaced by newer ones, cups of half drunk tea and bowls which had contained soup, unheated pots of cold and grey-looking food on the stove. Shoes, socks, torn pants, blouses and shirts taken from wounded bodies were scattered all over the place, which was darkened by the wet blankets covering the windows to keep out the CS gas fumes.

As mother searched for the documents, I heard a commotion in front of the flat; pulling aside one of the blankets I saw a large number of RUC who had broken through the barricades. One of them spotted me and yelled, 'There's one of those Fenian scum in that flat.' Seconds later I heard the sound of breaking glass as CS grenades were fired through the window. I grabbed mother and went into the entrance hall, closing the door to the living room behind us – we were trapped. Lying on the floor clinging to each other, we heard attempts to break open the front door. Mother took her rosary out of her pocket and we both began to pray while tears streamed down our cheeks as we choked and coughed from the CS gas seeping under the living room door. For what seemed an eternity, and certain death at the hands of the RUC if they managed to break in, we lay there and I felt my baby moving restlessly within my womb as if aware of the terror I felt. I vomited and retched while mother continued praying.

Just as it seemed the door was about to burst off its hinges I heard a young voice screaming, 'Hey, those bastards have someone trapped in Mrs Sheil's flat!' followed by a hailstone of rocks and bricks hurling against the walls and sidewalk outside. For the next half-hour we heard sounds of skirmishing outside. I managed to get up and go into the bathroom off the hall to get wet towels to wrap around our faces to ease the effects of the gas. Eventually someone pounded on the door, yelling, 'It's safe to come out, open the door and we'll get you away before they come back!' I unlocked the door to find a group of our young 'hooligans' ready to lead us to safety. Although we needed no urging to flee, a series of shots rang out which increased the speed with which we ran towards the house on Francis Street.

The children were safe but terrified as sounds of fighting drew closer; the RUC were making headway against the Bogside defenders and from our vantage point on the hill we could see two lines of skirmish on William and Great James Street making their way towards us. The Bogside below the hill looked as though the Second World War had come to Derry at last and I was reminded of a film I had seen of the fighting in the Warsaw ghetto. Fires everywhere were issuing clouds of black smoke that mingled with white clouds of CS gas, blotting out the sky. The occasional sounds of gunfire seemed to summon the ambulances with their sirens piercing through the voices of those engaged in the melee of fighting.

I calmed the children and made an instant decision: I would call the US Naval Telecommunications Centre in the Waterside and seek political asylum for my children and myself. The duty officer at the base listened to my plea then put me through to the officer in charge. When I informed him my children and I were US citizens and wanted asylum at the base, he laughed, 'Look lady, I have no authority to do that. You'll just have to take your chances like everyone else and I would suggest that you get out of the city as fast and as best as you can.' No amount of arguing would change his mind so, disillusioned with the US government's claim to be the protector of its citizens overseas, I started back to the house.

On the way I met an IRA member who, when I told him I was planning to take my children across the border, asked me if I would deliver a communication to his contact in Buncrana. Without thinking, I agreed and he gave me a note folded over several times into a compact shape about the size of a 50 pence piece. He told me to instruct his contact to deliver the message to Goulding in Dublin.

When I got back to the house, I told mother and the children we were leaving for Buncrana. We went though the grounds of St Eugene Cathedral and headed for a first-aid station near the Creggan area. As we neared the place I spotted a group of RUC and, fearful of what might happen if we were stopped, I put the note in my mouth, chewed it to a pulp and swallowed it. As a courier I was a failure but my children's safety came first – later I would learn methods of conceal-ment but in those days most of us were novices in the methods of urban guerrilla warfare and I has as much to learn as anyone. This was the first and last time I ever failed to deliver a communication.

We got to the first-aid station and were taken across the border by car. The caravan was overcrowded with my sisters and their children so I dropped my mother off and decided to take my children to a bed and breakfast in Buncrana. The town was jammed with people who, like us, had left the fighting behind and there were no available accommodations; even the Plaza Ballroom, which had been opened to take in people who needed a place to sleep, was jammed to capacity. When it was announced that Irish army bases were being opened to refugees, I decided to take the children to Finner Camp outside Donegal Town.

The camps had been made available by the Irish Prime Minister, Jack Lynch, who had gone on television saying that 'The Irish Govern-ment will not stand by while Nationalists in the North are being besieged.' At the end of the day Lynch's statement prove to be idle words. The RI government did nothing more than make army field hospitals and bases available while dispatching Patrick Hillery, Foreign Minister, to the UN headquarters in New York City to make a half-hearted appeal for UN troops. The Security Council, on a motion from

Britain, supported by the US, adjourned without taking a vote on the request.

The children and I spent the night at Finner Camp but I felt anxious being away from Derry so when I learned a friend was driving back we hitched a lift with him to Buncrana and he dropped me off at the caravan. A few hours later we heard that the British government was sending troops into Derry to take over from the RUC. Leaving the children in the care of friends, I hitched a lift to Derry, arriving about an hour after the troops were in place. As I stood watching them standing by the barricades we had fought so hard to defend, I remarked to a friend standing next to me, 'If they are here to protect us, why are their guns pointed in our direction and not the other way?'

The battle had ended with an agreement between the DCDC and the British Army Commander that the RUC would be kept out of the Bogside. But instead of relief, I had a feeling of despair, an intuitive understanding that our goal to free Ireland from British rule would now be more difficult than ever.

In one respect we were fortunate: although hundreds had been wounded in the previous three days, by some miracle no one had been killed. We were luckier than the people in Belfast, who had taken to the streets in solidarity when they learned of the battle in Derry – there, on the night of 14–15 August, six people had died.

I went to the Grandstand pub with friends to discuss the latest turn of events and was informed by the bartender that Leo had rung and left a message for me to call. I telephoned immediately and he told me he had seen television reports of the fighting, including a shot of me standing by one of the barricades. The situation in Derry appeared serious enough, he said, to warrant my returning to Philadelphia with the children. He was also having second thoughts about our move. I was devastated by his change of mind but realised I had no alternative other than to return to Philadelphia.

In less than two weeks the children and I left Derry. As we departed I had a foreboding of the future. The anxiety I felt when leaving family and friends behind was almost unbearable and I wondered if I would ever see them again. By this time the number of British soldiers in Northern Ireland had been increased from the original 400 to 6,500 – half stationed in Derry, the other half in Belfast.

In the months that followed my return to Philadelphia, the situation in Northern Ireland deteriorated steadily. While political leaders at Stormont, Dublin and London vied unsuccessfully with each other to control matters, it was the action taken by Nationalist and Loyalist

74 Daughter of Derry

people on the streets that determined events. The RUC regarded the political vacuum created by governmental inaction as implied consent to deal with the unrest as they saw fit. I received regular reports from my family about the constant intimidation, harassment, arrests and detentions during almost daily raids by the RUC while, as I had predicted, the British army looked the other way. Neither the RI government nor the IRA came to the aid of the Nationalist community and by the end of 1969 the acronym IRA had come to stand for 'I ran away' and young people chalked that derisive slogan on the walls of housing estates in Derry and Belfast.

Our son Brian was born in October and I was relieved to find that he had suffered no apparent prenatal damage from the effects of the CS gas. About three weeks after I came home from hospital, I and a few other members of Clan-na-Gael were visited by Sean Keenan (Derry) and Joe Cahill (Belfast). Keenan and Cahill told how they had been rebuffed by Goulding and the IRA Council when they had gone to Dublin requesting funds to buy guns and ammunition, and had therefore come to the US seeking Clan-na-Gael support.

Their visit prompted Goulding to travel to the US to discredit them. At a Clan-na-Gael convention in Philadelphia, Golding said that there had been a secret attempt by certain members of Jack Lynch's cabinet to take over and undermine Sinn Fein and the IRA and that Keenan and Cahill were being used by these people, namely, Charles Haughey, Neil Blaney and Kevin Boland. Goulding asserted that in September representatives of the Haughey faction had held secret meetings with the NI IRA leadership who were leery of Sinn Fein's newly adopted socialist programme, and tried to convince them to set up a separate Northern Command. If they did, they were told, support and funds would be made available by the Dublin government. It was Goulding's assessment that social agitation by Sinn Fein in the RI was beginning to erode Fianna Fail's claim to be the true representative of the 'Republican tradition', and was wreaking havoc with the government's attempt to multinationalise the RI economy. I had no reason to disbelieve Goulding and although I knew and respected Keenan, I decided to trust Goulding's judgement on the political situation.[3]

In the months that followed, I began to have serious disagreements with my friends in Clan-na-Gael and AFNICRA about which Republican faction we should support. We were further divided in December when the Sinn Fein National Conference split and the Provisional IRA was founded. The split centred around an IRA Army Council resolution to drop our policy of abstentionism when Sinn Fein members were elected to public office, but there were other dissatisfactions as well. Delegates from NI had been deeply angered by the apparent unwillingness to mobilise Active Service Units (ASU) to defend the Nationalist communities, and increasingly conservatives and socialists disagreed over the new political programme.

I decided to remain loyal to Goulding and the now-entitled Official IRA because, although I realised the need for physical force, I had come to understand that unless armed resistance had a concrete political programme behind it, the Provisional Sinn Fein/IRA was going to fall back into the same old traps of the past. The time had come to build a new political vision for Ireland, and I felt the Official Sinn Fein/IRA would do this. But my decision was costly.

I became more and more alienated from my long-time political allies in Clan-na-Gael and AFNICRA, most of whom supported the Provisional Sinn Fein. My political isolation was made glaringly obvious during the sit-in at the British consulate when most of my former comrades failed to support my stand.

10

Continuing Occupation

The second day of my sit-in at the British Consulate Office began around 7 am when the door was opened by one of the police officers. 'I've brought you a cup of coffee from the vending machine downstairs. Our replacements have arrived so we'll be leaving.'

I took the coffee and thanked him for his kindness. After he left I gave Brian a bottle and called Leo to let him know we were okay. A few minutes after we ended our conversation Delma called and I asked her to hold on while I told Stella and Margaret to go one at a time with Breige and Leo Patrick to the toilet down the hall outside the office and then begin straightening the room so it would look all right when the staff came in for the day.

Delma said that she and several other people would be down shortly and that the morning papers had coverage of the sit-in which Maura would bring when she came. When we finished talking I gave the children a breakfast of cold cereal and milk which Leo had left the night before and talked with them about what might happen in the next few hours.

Delma, Maura and her sister Una arrived shortly before 9 am. Four people were picketing in front of the building and four more would arrive later. Maura handed me a file folder, 'Here are clippings from the papers. The cops outside said only one of us can stay. I think I should go make calls to the reporters who wrote articles and Delma should join the picket line as she is best able to tell people why you are here and what happened yesterday and Una can stay with you.'

While Una and I waited for the staff to arrive I played a tape of rebel music to give us heart. By 11 am neither Barrett nor the staff had come to the office.

Hugh arrived shortly before noon and Una departed. Leo called during his lunch break and I told him we might be staying another night and asked him to bring us sleeping bags and a change of clothes.

Barrett arrived around 1 pm, saying, 'Now that you have gotten all the publicity you came here for, I would suggest you leave so I and my staff can get back to work.'

'I'm quite content to stay, Mr Barrett. As I told you yesterday, so long as the British army and the British government remain on Irish soil, I'm not going to budge out of this office.'

'As you well know, I do not have the ability to meet your demands. I relayed the situation to our Embassy in Washington and they have instructed me to inform you that if you leave this office today, they promise not to take action against you for trespassing.'

'Well, you can just relay this back to Washington, I consider the British government to be trespassers in my country.'

'If you persist you will only make things harder on yourself. If you leave before the end of the day, I will see to it no action is taken against you.'

Having said this he strode into his office. Aside from Brian, who was making baby talk, there was complete silence in the room. A few minutes later, Barrett came out of his office with a briefcase in his hand. 'Just remember, you have until the end of the day. If you stay beyond then you will be arrested and prosecuted.'

After he left, I remarked to Hugh, 'I sense the British government doesn't know how to handle this. It's one thing to drive women and children out of their little houses in Belfast but another to throw me and my children out of their office onto the streets of Philadelphia.'

Shortly after Barrett left, Maura came in to relieve Hugh, who went to get sandwiches. I filled Maura in on the conversation with Barrett and she told me she had arranged for some reporters to come at 2 pm for a follow-up interview. She and I decided I should spend the afternoon telephoning radio talk shows as a means of informing people why I had occupied the consulate.

Several reporters showed up on schedule. One woman irritated me when she tried to infer I wasn't a good mother by implying I was subjecting my children to unnecessary hardship. 'Actually', I replied, 'I feel I'm doing them a favour. The temperature outside is boiling and we don't have air conditioning in our house, at least they're nice and cool here. I wish you would show the same concern for the children of Belfast and Northern Ireland – they are being shot at and some of them have died.'

Sullivan rang after the press had left. 'Brigid, I've been trying to reach you for hours but the telephone has been busy. Frankly, I'm surprised to hear you're still there. What are your chances of being there tomorrow? I'm working on something which I don't want to discuss right now, but if you're still there in the morning I might have some surprise support for you.' I told him I planned on staying as long as possible and promised to call him the next morning.

The guard outside the door changed around 3 pm and still there was no attempt to remove us. Maura figured out how to activate the switchboard so we had access to the visitor's telephone in one corner of the reception room giving us the ability to use one telephone for incoming calls and the other for out-going ones. During the day there were occasional calls from people ringing the consulate on official business. Most of them were taken aback when they heard my Derry accent as I answered the telephone, 'Hello, this is the Irish Republic!'

A little after 5 pm Delma came into the office carrying a huge pot of spaghetti telling me, 'A car pulled up in front a few minutes ago with this nice Italian couple in it and the woman got out asking me to bring this to you. She said she'd been listening to the radio this afternoon and heard you say you were worried about not being able to feed the children except with take-out food. So she made this and said she hoped it would do for tonight's dinner.'

Maura left so Delma could stay and fill me in. She told me there had been a picket line all day, that several passers-by had stopped to join in for a while and that motorists had honked their car horns in support when they drove by. While we were eating Leo telephoned to check on us, saying he would be down shortly with the sleeping bags and clothes. For the next several hours the telephones didn't stop ringing as I took call after call. When Leo arrived I barely had time to talk with him so he sat chatting with the children and then helped the younger ones get ready for bed.

By 9 pm everyone had left. I took the telephones off the hook while I heard the children's prayers and told them a story and we sang a few songs after I tucked them into their sleeping bags. As they were going to sleep I got back on the telephone.

Shortly before midnight, Brian woke up in a fussy mood so I picked him up and tried to comfort him. One of the cops guarding the door came into the room and asked if he could be of any help offering to hold Brian awhile. Brian calmed down in his arms, and we started to chat. His name was George Fencl and surprisingly (to me at least) he was fairly well informed about events in NI. When Brian fell asleep Fencl went back outside. I got into my sleeping bag and tried to relax but it was an hour before I was able to sleep.

The children woke me early Wednesday morning and as I helped them get their breakfast, I went over what I needed to do that morning. I called Leo to give him a report, then telephoned Walter Sullivan as

I'd promised. 'Brigid, I was waiting to hear from you. I have to make one telephone call to get final confirmation on this but how does a press conference with Milton Shapp down there at 11 am sound to you? I got on to his campaign staff yesterday and suggested he might like to give you some support and evidently convinced them the publicity wouldn't do him any harm. They called late last night and said he was willing to hold a press conference with you if they could work it into his schedule. I was told to call this morning to let them know if you were still there and willing to have Shapp do this.'

'Call them right now. Tell them yes, I'm still here and yes, I'd be delighted to have him come down!'

Milton Shapp was the Democratic Party candidate for governor of Pennsylvania. A press conference with him might buy me more time. Sullivan called back in less than five minutes. 'It's on Brigid. Shapp's press officer said to tell you they'll be there around 11 am. They're on the telephone to the press right now setting things up. I'll be down around 11 myself.'

When Maura came in I told her the good news about Shapp. Shortly after 10 am television camera crews came in and started setting up their equipment. A few minutes later a man from Shapp's campaign staff arrived to brief me. As 11 am neared the little reception room was filled with reporters, press photographers and film crews, and when Shapp arrived he could barely make his way into the room. Walter Sullivan came in with him and introduced us. We exchanged a few remarks, then Shapp read a statement to the press in which he saluted me for having the courage of my convictions and described events in NI as tragic. When he finished reading his brief statement, he asked for questions from the press and for the next twenty minutes we both answered their queries. Shapp then announced he was due at a luncheon and shaking my hand, told me I shouldn't hesitate to call his office if I felt he could be of help.

The office was empty by the time Barrett returned. He told me if any of us left the room we would not be allowed back into the office. 'This means if you use the bathroom out in the hall, you will not be allowed to came back into this office.'

I pondered for a moment and replied, 'There are a number of wastepaper baskets in here and I have lots of plastic bags. Those will have to do us.'

Having delivered this ultimatum, Barrett left. I called Shapp's office to report this latest development and asked if there was any way they might appeal to city health officials, 'I'm not going to leave and I'll use the wastebaskets if I have to, but with the children here it seems to me this may constitute a health hazard.' I was clutching at straws but the person I talked with promised to do what they could. It worked. Several hours later one of the guards opened the door and told me we were free to use the toilet.

Around 3 pm there was a knock at the door. It was a delivery person with a colour television with a note from Shapp attached to it: 'Thought you might like to watch the press conference tonight. Also, I hope this helps keep the children contented.' I immediately rang his office and left a message saying how delighted we were to have the TV and to let them know that toilet privileges had been restored.

That evening we watched the news; because of the press conference, our sit-in had been covered by the major networks on their national news programmes. The fact that we were a family protesting together seemed to have caught the interest of the press.

Philadelphia is an ethnic city and the telephone calls of encouragement came from all sorts of people, mostly Polish, German, Italian and Jewish. These calls outnumbered those from Irish-Americans by more than half. Some were crank calls and some were critical of my stand – most of these were from people who were native Irish, the Irish-Irish, I call them; I could tell by their accents, or because they gave the name of their home county in Ireland, that most of them were from the RI. To me this indicated the depth of their slave mentality – my action clearly embarrassed them. But most people rang to give their support, and because of the national coverage, we were getting calls from all over the country.

After the children were settled for the night, I disconnected the telephones and sat down to watch television and relax. Around 10:30 pm Fencl came in to chat and sat with me for a while. He was a nice, jolly man and I learned that the members of the Civil Disobedience Squad who had been assigned to guard the office considered this easy duty. Contrary to their usual behaviour at anti-war demonstrations and civil rights marches, they treated me very politely. Apparently, the fact that I was female, a mother, white, Irish, middle class, had a Polish name and held a minor elected office in the Democratic Party brought me a deference I wouldn't otherwise have received.

When Thursday morning dawned I found it hard to believe we were beginning our fourth day in the consulate. I took a certain amount of satisfaction in knowing that I had disrupted the office and presented the British embassy in Washington with a dilemma it was unable to resolve. We had even got international press coverage, as I discovered when Goulding sent a telegram applauding my stand, saying he had read about the sit-in in the *Irish Independent*.

The day flew by with the routine we had established. The children had been given various tasks to keep them busy. Stella and Margaret kept the younger children amused by playing games with them and they all took turns keeping Brian happy. They were being terrific although I could tell Leo Patrick was becoming restless and anxious to get back home and outside playing with his friends.

The Thursday newspapers had extensive coverage of the Shapp press conference. There was also speculation about how much longer we would stay in the consulate. Barrett and the British embassy continued to make no comment. For me, the situation had turned into a waiting game. I was committed to staying as long as possible. However, I knew it was only a matter of time before the British government would have us removed; the question was when and how they would go about it.

The answer to that question came before noon on Friday when a clerk from the US District Court, accompanied by two US Federal Marshals, came to the office and read out a court order for me to vacate the premises. I replied I wasn't going to leave. They tried unsuccessfully to persuade me to go home. Finally they left.

I got on the telephone to let Leo, friends and the press know that I might not be there much longer, that it was only a matter of time before I was ejected. The hours dragged by as I waited for the police to make a move. I told the children that we would probably be removed sometime that day and instructed them not to walk out on their own but let the police carry them.

Around 9 pm Fencl entered with two Federal Marshals and tried once more to persuade me to leave, 'Time has run out, Brigid, and you are going to have to go. You can make it easy or difficult but you and the children must leave.'

'Well, Fencl, you have your job to do but if you want us out you'll have to carry us.'

'We'll carry you to the elevator.'

'If you do I'll just sit in the hall. I'm not going to walk out of this building.'

Fencl called in several more Federal Marshals and members of the Civil Disobedience Squad and instructed them to carry the children out. I told them to stay calm, that their father was downstairs waiting and that everything would be all right. Leaving Brian with me, the Marshals picked up the other children and took them out of the room.

As she was carried out the door Stella looked at me, raised her right arm, fist clenched and smiled, 'Right on, Mom.'

Five minutes later two Federal Marshals picked me up. Fencl put Brian on my lap and they carried us into the elevator. We were down in the lobby within seconds. They carried us out the front door and as we emerged from the building onto the street a huge cheer went up from the small but loyal group of supporters waiting to greet us. Leo came over as the two men put Brian and me down and put his arm around me as I announced to the press: 'This is typical of the British – they always evict at night, they put the Irish out in the darkness and here it is the same way.'

As cameras went off all around me, I started to cry. The photos in the papers the next day showed my exhaustion and disappointment. The front page of the *Philadelphia Daily News* contained only two photos and a banner headline. One photo was of me being removed and the other showed me crying as Leo hugged me. The banner headline read, 'Charles, Tricia Dance All Night At Grand Old Party on Potomac.' As our 105-hour sit-in ended, Prince Charles was attending a state dinner at the White House.

That evening after we returned home I realised I could no longer remain in the US. My place in Ireland's struggle was in Ireland. I could no longer be a by-stander 3,000 miles removed. Over the next few weeks I convinced Leo to reconsider a move to Ireland. He finally agreed but was firmly against moving to Derry. Instead we compromised on a move to Limerick in the RI at the end of the year. I was overjoyed.

By the end of October the house was up for sale and Leo had located a position with the US government in Greenland for 18 months. He left for Greenland in November after the house was sold and I packed and shipped the things we wanted and sold the rest.

I was given several going-away parties, one by the Philadelphia Democratic Party organisation, the other by an ad hoc committee representing several Irish-American organisations. At the latter I was presented with a plaque which named me Philadelphia's Irish Woman of the Year. To this day this plaque hangs in an honoured place in my kitchen.

Internment

Goulding arranged for us to be met at Shannon Airport and found a cottage for us to move into at Mungret, County Limerick. The cottage was a small country dwelling without indoor plumbing but to me it was as grand as any landlord's mansion and would serve as a base until I could locate a more suitable house in Limerick City. I lit a turf fire, made a cup of tea and settled in.

With Leo in Greenland, the children and I went to Derry for the first Christmas I had spent at home in 16 years. In addition to enjoying the festive time with my family, I also met with local political friends between whom a spirit of friendly cooperation prevailed despite the friction between the top leadership of the Official and Provisional IRA. Although it is the fourth largest city in Ireland, Derry has a small village mentality and individual survival has always depended upon maintaining communal solidarity when faced with adversity. Republicans on both sides sought to preserve communal ties.

In February I located a house on North Circular Road in Limerick and we moved. A young Sinn Fein member, Dolores Roberts, needed a place to live so I engaged her as an au pair in exchange for room and board. In addition to being a great cook, Dolores related very well with my growing family, especially my two teenage daughters. I also rented a room to Barry Doyle, the Official Sinn Fein organiser for Northwest Munster Province.

At the beginning of the year I joined the Limerick Branch of Official Sinn Fein and a few months later was elected by the Northwest Munster Regional Committee to the national executive serving with Michael Murtagh, the other regional representative. I was completely dedicated, and, I confess, quite in awe of the leadership, the most influential of whom were Goulding, Sean Garland, Seamus Costello, Dessie O'Hagan, Mick Ryan and Tomas MacGoilla. At the monthly meetings in Dublin I was generally mute, content to listen and learn.

Aside from a few who voiced the opinion that the leadership should be shot, there was general consensus that the breakaway Provisional IRA would eventually fizzle out. We trusted that people would accept our new political direction and support our renewed military campaign in NI, which we were told by the Official IRA Army Council was in the planning stage. This seemed confirmed by what I presumed to be preliminary actions being carried out by various Active Service Units in NI. Local ASUs had a certain amount of autonomy in conducting selected operations under the direction of their command staff, although major operations had to be sanctioned by the General Headquarters Command (GHQ) in Dublin. One such operation took place not in NI but in the RI, as part of our support for workers' rights, and, in an indirect way, involved me.

On several occasions we had participated in industrial disputes in the RI which had gained us a positive reputation among workers. When strike action at the Mogul Mines in County Tipperary dragged on for months without a sign of resolution, therefore, we were approached to give assistance to the strike effort. Mogul Mines, a Canadian multinational, had acquired the rights to conduct a mining operation at Silvermines, which had the largest deposit of silver ore in Western Europe. After several years of operation, poor working conditions, low wages and an unresponsive management forced the mine workers to take strike action.

One day in June 1971 I was visited by the Officer Commanding (OC) of the local Official IRA ASU and asked if I would be willing to provide accommodation for a man for a few days, which I agreed to do. Martin O'Leary, a 24-year-old Corkman who was tall, soft-spoken and very handsome (he reminded me of Omar Sharif), appeared at my door saying he had been sent by my contact. For the next few days, Martin was in and out of the house and I saw very little of him.

At the weekend some of my relatives came from Derry and we planned a party to be held at my house on Friday night. We were having such a good time we were unaware that Martin had slipped out; we were still up when two men stopped by around 4 am to warn me to remove any traces of Martin's stay. He had been injured and taken to Barrington's Hospital in Limerick. I learned the next day that Martin had left my house and, with a group of volunteers, had gone to Mogul Mines where, in the process of planting explosives, he was injured when they went off prematurely. His comrades put him into the car, drove him to the hospital where they left him on the front steps, and fled. Martin was taken into the hospital still alive and members of his family told us that during his periods of consciousness they were ushered out of the room while he was interrogated by members of the

Special Branch. They also told us they had seen a tape recorder under his bed. Martin refused to give any information.

On Saturday afternoon, Special Branch detectives Jones and Hallisey, accompanied by six armed men, appeared at my door with a search warrant. This would be the first of many searches of my house over the years and, as would continue to be the case, they found nothing incriminating, although the Special Branch must have an entire room set aside to house my personal archive – they have never returned anything.

On Monday representatives from Mogul Mines flew to Ireland to meet with union representatives and settled the strike to the satisfaction of the workers. When we learned of Martin's death three days later, I and a few others went with his parents to the hospital to claim his body. After he was put into a coffin, we placed a Tricolour on top and carried it through Limerick out to the main Cork road where we got into cars and drove Martin home. Outside Cork City we were met by a large contingent which marched with us to the O'Leary house where we held a wake. Martin was buried with full military honours. At Martin's funeral, Goulding paid tribute to him, saying that while he deplored the necessity for armed struggle that resulted in deaths, at the same time:

> It is not within our power to dictate what action the forces of imperialism and exploitation will engage in to repress, coerce and deny ordinary people their God-given rights [making it necessary to speak] the language that would bring these vultures to their senses – the language of the bomb and bullet.

To show their gratitude to Martin the miners held a ceremony to commemorate him and erected a plaque at the entrance to the mine acknowledging the part he played in helping resolve their dispute. A ballad was written to honour his memory.[1]

In March 1971, Brian Faulkner, the son of a Derry shirtmaker, replaced Chichester-Clark as NI prime minister. Faulkner, who had administered internment during the latter stages of the border campaign, was convinced its reintroduction was necessary. He had reason to believe that such a move would not be opposed by the RI government; Lynch had shown that he was thinking along similar lines. In December 1970, Lynch had announced that he had received information that Saor Eire (a small, left-wing fringe group), was planning to kidnap several prominent people. Lynch's admission that he was considering the reintroduction of internment in the RI was a barely concealed hint that if internment was introduced in NI, his government would not oppose the move.

On 22 June, Faulkner issued a directive to General Sir Henry Tuzo, who had replaced General Freeland in February as Commander-in-Chief, NI, that in the future the army had his permission to 'shoot with effect' suspected subversives. Taking him at his word British soldiers killed Seamus Cusack (7 July) and Desmond Beaty (8 July) in Derry during a riot following the death of another man who had been run over by an army truck.

John Hume, realising that he needed to maintain credibility in his home town, met with his newly formed Social Democratic and Labour Party (SDLP) colleagues, Ivan Cooper, Paddy O'Hanlon and Austin Curry, to decide their response to these latest killings. A month earlier, the SDLP had taken Faulkner's bait when he announced he was establishing three new parliamentary committees and that two of the three salaried chair positions would go to members of the majority opposition party in Stormont. Knowing that they would receive these two positions, SDLP MPs had praised Faulkner's decision. Now, with their backs to the Derry wall, the four SDLP MPs announced that unless a public inquiry was called to investigate the circumstances of these latest deaths, they would be forced to withdraw from Stormont. The British government refused to conduct an inquiry and John Taylor, NI Minister for Home Affairs, praised the army. Hume and company were forced to withdraw from Stormont.

At this time a prominent member of the SDLP executive committee approached the Official IRA OC in Derry, offered him all the gelignite he needed and suggested a target – Austin's department store in the walled section of Derry. Because it was felt that the offer was made to encourage the Official IRA to go on the offensive and thus undercut the recruitment gains made by the Provisional IRA, thereby diminishing the Provisionals' growing threat to the SDLP, the offer was declined. The SDLP representative was told that if the SDLP wanted to begin a bombing campaign, they should do so themselves and refrain from criticising those who believed in the armed struggle.[2]

The Provisional IRA had become increasingly active and were beginning to cause real havoc in their campaign of bombing, sniping and full-scale shoot-outs. Unwilling to send in more troops, the British government acceded to Faulkner's request for internment. At 4:30 am on Monday 9 August 1971 'Operation Demetrius' was put into effect. In the pre-dawn light 2,000 British troops pounded on hundreds of doors in Derry, Belfast and other towns and villages and, citing the Special Powers Act as their authority, arrested 342 Nationalists. Those arrested were given no chance to get dressed before being put into trucks and driven off; they couldn't let their families know where they were being taken because they themselves weren't told.

I was in Derry that weekend. Early Monday morning a member of the Provisional IRA came to my mother's flat to tell us of the raid, and in this way the Bogside and Creggan learned the news that almost 100 men had been lifted in Derry. (No women were interned in the early phase, the first was Elizabeth McKee on 1 January 1973. The first two Loyalists were interned in February 1973.)

I dressed hurriedly and went out to talk with people who were gathering at Aggro Corner, trying to assess who was picked up and who escaped and I learnt that Mickey Montgomery was one of those arrested. More and more people gathered, angry, confused, outraged, and spontaneously about 200 of us began to march to the British army observation post on Shipquay Street near The Diamond. With vengeance in our hearts we made our way inside the Derry walls to the post, fortified by barbed wire and sandbags. Oblivious to the pain, I climbed up and over the barbed wire fence with the others and we began to tear the post apart board by board, brick by brick, with our bare hands. I still believe that if reinforcements hadn't come to their assistance we would have demolished the post and stomped the soldiers inside to death. Instead they lived to oppress us another day when we were batoned and tear-gassed back through Shipquay Gate by soldiers and the police. We prevented them from entering our territory by throwing up barricades at every entrance into the Bogside and Creggan, thus establishing the no-go zone known as Free Derry, which became a community run and controlled oasis for the next 12 months. When I finally got back to the flat I was a mass of cuts and bruises, my hose and clothes ripped and torn, and I realised I had lost my shoes.

The following day we began to have a better picture of who had been arrested, although it would be about a week before there was a full assessment; many had managed to escape the net when they were forewarned by their intelligence sources that a move to intern was a likely possibility and had taken refuge across the border. Within 48 hours about 116 men were released because their arrests were deemed a mistake (one of them an elderly blind man). The reason for the many mistaken arrests, the army said, was poor RUC intelligence regarding who should be picked up. But, in the eyes of the RUC who supplied the names, and Faulkner who signed the internment requests, every Nationalist was suspected of being a hard-line Republican therefore it didn't matter if errors were made.

Those who were released gave a harrowing account of what had occurred when they reached the interrogation centers – in the case of those from Derry this was Magilligan, others were taken to either Ballykinlar or Girdwood. They told of receiving severe beatings, being made to run barefooted over broken glass, and forced to stand in a spread-eagle position for hours. Some told of being blindfolded, put into helicopters which unknown to them hovered only a few feet above the ground – they believed they were thousands of feet in the air – and when they refused to answer questions were pushed out the open door. They were the lucky ones – they had been released – 226 remained in custody. Later we learned that 12 men, including Mickey Montgomery and another Derryman, Michael Donnelly, had been taken to Shackelton Barracks at Ballykelly a few miles from Derry and subjected to continuous psychological and physical torture referred to as the 'Five Techniques' for seven days.

Known as the 'Hooded Men', these 12 were forced to wear a heavy black denim hood over their head at all times except while being interrogated, then a bright light was shone into their faces. They were made to listen to constant high-pitched noise; not allowed to sleep; denied food except for occasional pieces of bread and sips of water; and made to stand nearly continuously in a spread-eagle position. They were not allowed to go to the toilet, were exposed to extreme room temperature changes, first hot then cold, and physically tortured. (In October two more men received identical treatment bringing the number of Hooded Men to 14.)

When public outcry forced the British government to appoint a committee chaired by Sir Edmund Compton to investigate the charges of torture by those arrested on 9 August, the committee's terms of reference did not include instructions to investigate the use of the Five Techniques but the committee was forced to include them due to outside pressure.

When I returned to Limerick I plunged into anti-internment activity organised by Official Sinn Fein. We picketed every Saturday outside the British Rail Travel Office on O'Connell Street and talked with people about what was happening in NI. We also held weekly rallies in different locations in the Munster area and when it was discovered that I was a fairly effective speaker, I was increasingly asked to address the crowds that gathered. People in the RI were incensed by the callous and brutal results of the internment round-ups and its aftermath. Many gained first-hand information when another massive exodus of Nationalists crossed the border to settle in the relative safety of RI – large numbers of whom moved to Shannon in County Clare where there was ample housing and available work. At our rallies we also distributed our well-written and researched literature which served to educate people to the value of socialism. The local Provisionals referred to us half-jokingly as the 'Typewriter Brigade', hinting that while Official Sinn Fein spent money on paper and ink, they spent theirs on guns and ammunition but like our counterparts in Derry we co-operated and worked in concert on the anti-internment issue. However, their jibe hit at the core of what had caused the split in 1969 and would continue to haunt the Republican movement as both organisations attempted to maintain credibility with the people in NI whom we had encouraged to take to the streets in 1968.

Although the Provisionals were also holding anti-internment rallies, they were hassled less than we were by the Special Branch because they stuck to the issue of 'Brits-Out' of Northern Ireland and rarely touched on the inept politics of the RI government nor called for, as we did, the establishment of a United Socialist Republic. In an attempt to dissuade people from joining Official Sinn Fein, those who attended our rallies were followed home by Special Branch detectives, visited at their place of work and received more than their fair share of traffic tickets.

In September Loyalists announced the formation of a new paramilitary organisation, the Ulster Defence Association (UDA) which made no secret of the fact they were arming themselves. They also paraded in military-style uniforms without any interference from the RUC or British Army who neglected to arrest them for breaking Faulkner's ban on all marches for a period of one year, announced the same day he introduced internment. It was business as usual in the Loyalist camp.

When the Compton Report was issued on 16 November 1971 it held that while there was evidence of 'ill-treatment' of those picked up in the internment swoops, the committee did not believe this constituted brutality. Brutality, could only be committed by a person who acted 'with indifference to, or [took] pleasure in, the victim's pain', and this, they felt, was not proven to have been the case. But as Mickey Montgomery was to remark later, 'I sure as hell didn't hear the bastards crying when they were beating me!'

Every Nationalist over the age of ten realised the Compton Report was a whitewash of what their son, father, brother, uncle and/or grandfather had experienced after they were lifted. Instances of torture continued to be reported by the ever-increasing numbers who were picked up and taken to Palace Barracks for interrogation. But one must assume that, in line with Lord Compton, the torturers derived no pleasure from their task – they were just stony-faced people who took no pleasure in administering beatings, electric shock, more innovative forms of sensory deprivation and, on occasion, drugs.[3]

Over 60 per cent of the 3,000 arrested in the first six months of internment were released following interrogation. Their release could only be construed as an indication of their innocence – otherwise they would have been interned or charged with an offence. It was this fact which politicised the Nationalist community in Northern Ireland. Internment was intended to intimidate people and cause them to think twice about continuing to seek civil rights reforms. In practice, it had the opposite effect; instead of intimidating people, these arrests resulted in one day's innocent victim becoming the next day's committed activist, totally supported by his/her family for so choosing. New recruits flocked to join both the Official and Provisional IRA.

People in NI were being politicised in a manner which reinforced the Official Sinn Fein theory of how to build a mass movement. One example was a spontaneous rent and rates strike: a few women in Belfast simply announced they would refuse to pay their rent and rates while internment lasted, and within a matter of weeks this had the support of over 40,000 households in NI; in Derry 94 per cent of the Nationalist households refused to pay. Local government virtually ground to a halt. In response, Stormont passed the Payment for Debt (Emergency Powers) Act which allowed local authorities to deduct rents and rates from state benefits. In the end this tactic failed because administering the law became a bureaucratic nightmare.

The Provisionals pulled off a master propaganda coup at one of the large Nationalist flat complexes in Belfast during this period. It was the time of the Grand National Race and the local bookie was flush with the bet money. Knowing the rent collector would be going to the flats to collect on the day of the race, some Provisionals went into the bookie office and took out a 'loan'. They then went around to each flat asking how much each person owed in withheld rent. They gave each tenant this amount plus a month's rent in advance. As the rent collector went door-to-door, the people handed over the money and got their rent books stamped 'paid-in-full' through the following month. The rent collector finished the rounds, left the complex and was promptly relieved of the rent receipts by the Provisionals who then returned the money to the bookie office. There was nothing the housing authority could do; the rent books were already stamped.

Pressure was being put upon the Dublin government to take some form of diplomatic action against the British government's blatantly anti-Nationalist stance in NI and this pressure increased following the release of the Compton Report. Dublin, however, was in the process of negotiating entry into the European Economic Community (EEC), which was linked to that of Britain's, so Lynch had to tread softly. He resolved the dilemma by taking a case against Britain to the European Commission on Human Rights charging that its interrogation procedures were in violation of Article 3 of the Universal Declaration of Human rights. This was a political master stroke: as Lynch undoubtedly knew, the case would take years to be heard; in the meantime, however, he could claim that he had taken decisive action against the British government and the delicate negotiations with Britain over the two countries' EEC application would not be jeopardised.

Leo arrived home from Greenland to spend his first and our second Christmas in Ireland. A week after he returned to Greenland, I answered a knock at the front door. Standing there were two gardai who had come to take me to Limerick Jail to serve a two-week sentence for failing to pay a fine for collecting funds for Republican prisoners' dependants without a permit.

The day I was arrested two Special Branch detectives had asked to see my permit to collect money at our anti-internment table on O'Connell Street. When I told them I didn't have a permit they tried to seize my collection box. Rather than let them take the money, I threw the box in the direction of a group of young people, who scrambled to pick it up. (It was common knowledge that confiscated money was never turned into the gardai station – the detectives spent it in their favourite pub buying drinks for their friends saying, 'This drink is on the IRA,' and I was determined they wouldn't get the opportunity to do this with the money I had collected.)

For failure to have a permit I was given a choice: either pay a fine or serve two weeks in Limerick Jail. I had no intention of paying the fine and had dismissed the whole incident from my mind, but they hadn't. So without giving me prior notice, the gardai had come to take me to serve my two weeks' sentence, leaving me only enough time to scribble a note to Dolores and the children.

Limerick Jail is one of the worst prisons in Ireland and my stay was not pleasant. I refused to do prison work, so I spent most of my day in the cell. During recreational hours I had a chance to get to know the other women, 14 in all, who were in on charges ranging from theft to prostitution. One of them was there for stealing a ham from a supermarket in Dublin and had been given a nine month sentence. Eighteen years of age, she had stolen the ham because her 12 brothers and sisters were hungry, and as the oldest she had felt responsible for getting them something to eat.

The worst features of jail are the boredom and isolation. The two weeks I spent in Limerick Jail aren't worth even commenting on compared to what I knew was happening to my friends in jail elsewhere but forever more I will have some understanding of what it means to be locked away from the rest of the world. Just as a man may experience parenthood but can never know what it feels like to give birth, so a person who had never been in jail can never know what it feels like to be denied the normal things of life. The day before my release I was served with a warrant charging me with IRA membership and incitement stemming from an anti-internment speech I'd given in August 1971.

I was released from the jail on Saturday 29 January 1972. If I hadn't been in Limerick Jail, I would have gone to Derry to participate in the anti-internment march scheduled for the next day. If I hadn't been in jail, I might have convinced Gerry Donaghey, who had been staying at my house, not to go home to Derry, where he became the youngest person to die on the day which became known as 'Sunday, Bloody Sunday'.

12

Even the Skies Wept

The British army's lst Parachute Regiment is the British equivalent of the US Marines' Green Berets. The 'Paras', hand-picked volunteers, are a highly disciplined, efficient, well-trained, elite fighting unit that can be dispatched at a moment's notice to troublespots in the remnants of the British Empire. The regular army takes a dim view of the Paras' involvement in NI, as an article by Simon Hoggart in the *Guardian* on 25 January 1972 reveals that:

> At least two British army units in Belfast made formal requests to brigade headquarters for the Parachute Regiment to be kept out of their areas. Senior officers in these units regard the paratroop's tactics as too rough and on occasions, brutal ... A captain [in a third unit] said: 'They are frankly disliked by many officers here, who regard some of their men as little more than thugs in uniform. I have seen them arrive on the scene, thump up a few people who might be doing nothing more than shouting and jeering ... They seem to think that they can get away with whatever they like.'

In spite of these formally expressed concerns the Paras, under the command of Colonel Derek Wilford, were dispatched to Derry to provide security during a NICRA sponsored anti-internment march on Sunday 30 January 1972 – the first major anti-internment protest since it had been introduced almost six months previously.

Dr Raymond McClean, industrial medical officer for DuPont Chemical Company in Derry, was a former medical officer with the British Royal Air Force. McClean had had occasion to learn of the Paras' tough fighting reputation when he had treated several of them while stationed in the Bahrein Islands in the Persian Gulf in the mid-1960s. McClean had also served as a steward on several previous marches in Derry, and as a result was particularly wary of any signs of potential trouble. When he learned on Friday that the Paras would be in Derry on Sunday, McClean asked why the top fighting unit of the British army was required to undertake a peace-keeping role.

The march was scheduled to start from Bishop's Field in the

Creggan, wind its way through the Bogside, then proceed down Williams Street to culminate in a rally at Guildhall Square adjacent to Shipquay Gate. The march fell under Faulkner's ban. NICRA was told that in no circumstances would the march be allowed anywhere near the Square. Having received assurances from both Official and Provisional IRA that neither organisation would in any way compromise the peaceful nature of the march, NICRA decided to go ahead regardless of the ban.

On the surprisingly sunny but crisp Sunday afternoon, approximately 20,000 people assembled at Bishop's Field and began to march along the designated route. At Aggro Corner, the front line of the march was diverted from its planned destination at Guildhall Square beyond police barricades on Lower William Street, and turned onto Rossville Street heading for the new rally site at Free Derry Corner three blocks away. Some of the crowd, mostly young people, proceeded down Lower William Street to the barricades and began throwing stones. Up to this point there had been no trouble.

McClean was in the middle section of the march and when it was about two blocks from Aggro Corner he noticed several soldiers lying in an empty lot to his left. They were not in normal riot gear and were pointing rifles at the line of march in a menacing manner. When McClean reached Aggro Corner he became aware of a confrontation between the crowd at the police barricades and heard CS gas canisters being fired as well as rubber bullets and saw a water canon spray people with purple-dyed water:

The time was then around 3.40 in the afternoon ... This was the average Derry riot, and was more or less what we had all expected ... Suddenly I heard three or four sharp cracks in rapid succession. These sounds were clearly distinguishable from the sound of rubber bullets or CS gas [canisters] being discharged ... The ominous sharp cracks seemed to have come from the upper William Street area towards the back of the crowd ... [then] I remembered the soldiers I had noticed when coming down William Street.

Within a minute, a man ... came running down William Street calling my name. I asked what was wrong, and he shouted for me to come with him quickly, as two people had been shot at the back of the march. I went with him and someone showed us to the Shield's [*sic*] house, where I found a teenager and a middle-aged man, both of whom had been shot ... The boy's name was Damian Donaghy. I then examined the middle-aged man whose name was John Johnston ... I was treating these two casualties with some first-aiders for approximately fifteen minutes, when I heard the sound of several gun shots in the vicinity, coming in rapid succession.[1]

A background statement issued by the British government information service contended that the first three shots fired that day were fired at troops stationed *behind the barricades*, the fourth was fired by them after 'a member of the machine-gun platoon saw a man about to light a nail bomb. As the man prepared to throw, an order was made to shoot him. He fell and was dragged away.'

An eyewitness at the scene of the shooting was Fulvio Grimaldi, an Italian journalist who was interviewed on RTE Radio, Dublin, on 31 January. He reported:

I have travelled in many countries. I have seen many civil wars and revolutions and wars. I have never seen such a cold-blooded murder, organised disciplined murder, planned murder ... There hadn't been one shot fired at them [the Paras]. There hadn't been one nail bomb thrown at them. They just jumped out, and with unbelievable murderous fury, shot into the fleeing crowd ... I saw a young fellow who had been wounded, crouching against the wall. He was shouting, 'don't shoot, don't shoot'. A paratrooper approached and shot him from about one yard. I saw a young boy of 15 protecting his girl-friend against the wall and then proceeding to try and rescue her by going out with a handkerchief and with the other hand on his hat. A paratrooper approached, shot him from about one yard into the stomach, and shot the girl into the arm. I saw a priest approaching a fallen boy in the middle of the square, trying to help him, give him the last rites perhaps – I saw a paratrooper kneel down and take aim at him and shoot at him, and the priest just got away by lying flat on his belly. I saw a French colleague of mine, shouting 'press, press' and raising high his arms, who went into the middle to give help to a fallen person. I saw the paratroopers kneeling down and aiming at him, and it's only by a fantastic acrobatic jump he did that he got away ... It was panic, it was despair, it was frustration. I saw people crying, old men crying, young boys, who had lost their friends ... Crying and not understanding. There was astonishment. There was bewilderment, there was rage and frustration. It was unbelievable.[2]

Thirteen civilians were dead – Gerry Donaghey, at 17, was the youngest – and 18 were wounded. When John Johnston later died from his wounds, his death brought the total to 45 people who had died in Derry since July 1969, when Samuel Devenny became our first victim in the current 'troubles'. Forty-five members of our Derry family – 4 sisters and 41 brothers – were dead as a direct result of our desire to be treated as first-class citizens. No member of the security forces was killed that day. Only one soldier was wounded – when he accidently shot himself through the foot. The afternoon that started out filled with sun was now deluged with rain.

A few weeks later I went to Derry and, as I often do when I'm in need of comfort, slept with my mother in her bed. In the still darkness she told me how she had responded to having Damian Donaghy and John Johnston brought wounded to her flat and of the horror of the deaths that followed – all of whom were people she knew.

That night she had been unable to sleep and feeling a need to grieve, she left her flat around 2 am to walk to the place where the 13 had been shot earlier that day. The streets were eerily empty, the wind at gale force and rain lashing down. 'All of a sudden', she said, 'there was silence as the wind stopped for a minute. When the wind started blowing again it sounded like the voices of the dead crying for vengeance for all those who had died, going back to the days of the famine. I felt surrounded by all their spirits.'

She reached the area at the Rossville flats where the people had fallen and saw a large, blood-stained, civil rights banner fluttering about the sidewalk, kept from blowing away by the stick it was attached to. She gathered up four heavy rocks lying on the ground, caught hold of the banner and fastened down one corner with one of the rocks. Then she spread the banner out flat on the ground and used the remaining rocks to secure it. When she finished she knelt down and cried while she prayed. As she was telling me her story I put my arms around her, shedding my first tears over our latest losses. When she ended her story we hugged each other, and rocking back and forth, cried together.

Television and newspaper reports of the events of that Sunday resulted in a storm of protest directed at Westminster. In response, the government appointed Lord Widgery, Lord Chief Justice of England, to conduct an inquiry. In the RI ordinary citizens, who in general had become immune to the troubles in NI, were collectively outraged when they learned about the massacre. There were calls for a general strike. To defuse the situation and diminish public pressure for his government to take formal sanction against the British government, Lynch declared Tuesday 1 February, the day of the funerals in Derry, a day of national mourning and announced the closure of factories, schools and public buildings. Meanwhile in major cities throughout the RI people had taken to the streets on Sunday evening and Monday. The day of the funerals over 30,000 people marched to the British Embassy on Merrian Row in Dublin and there a group, led by Seamus Costello, set fire to the building with petrol bombs, burning it to the ground.

When the Widgery Committee staff established an office in Derry to take statements and select witnesses to give testimony before the committee, Dr McClean submitted a formal statement and made himself available as a witness. In addition to having treated the first two people wounded on Bloody Sunday, McClean had examined four of those who died and had been present at the formal post mortem conducted by the Derry city coroner at the Altnagelvin Hospital on 31 January. His offer to testify before the committee was turned down. Instead the committee selected Dr Kevin Swords, who had examined only one of the victims, my young friend Gerry Donaghey. Swords was called solely to give testimony as to whether or not Gerry had had anything in his pockets.

When the Widgery Report was made public on 19 April McClean was amazed to learn that: 'Nowhere in the report was there any consideration of the concrete forensic evidence produced by the post mortem examination, and of whether this concrete evidence was consistent or otherwise with eyewitness accounts of the incidents.'[3]

In his testimony, Swords stated emphatically that Gerry's pockets were empty when he examined him. The committee, however, chose to believe the testimony of a soldier who claimed to have found four nail bombs in Gerry's pockets after the doctor finished his examination. The Widgery Committee posthumously convicted Gerry, and the others who died that day, of having committed 'terrorist offences', then stated that 'none of the marchers should have been there in the first place'. This was the same justification that had been given to absolve the Ohio State National Guard when they killed four unarmed students during an anti-Vietnam War protest at Kent State University on 4 May 1970.

The Widgery Report was such a blatant tailoring of evidence to suit government needs that a new phrase was coined in Derry to question someone's veracity – 'Are you pulling a Widgery on me?'[4]

Ireland's leading poet, Thomas Kinsella, composed *Butcher's Dozen*, in which the ghost of Gerry Donaghey says:

A bomber I, I travelled light
– Four pounds of nails and gelignite
About my person, hid so well
They seemed to vanish where I fell.
When the bullet stopped my breath
A doctor sought the cause of death.
He upped my shirt, undid my fly,
Twice he moved my limbs awry,
And noticed nothing. By and by
A soldier, with his sharper eye,
Beheld the four elusive rockets
Stuffed in my coat and trouser pockets,
Yes, they must be strict with us,
Even in death, so treacherous!

Eventually all those murdered that day were absolved of the terrorist charges levelled against them, but in such a manner as to go unnoticed in the world press. In December 1974 the British government awarded the families of the dead a total of £41,500 in compensation – an average of £2,964.29 per victim.

The paratroopers who shot them were awarded medals for their performance and their commander, Colonel Derek Wilford, was included on the 1973 Queen's Honours List and awarded an Order of the British Empire.

13

Green, Orange and Whitelaw

The day after the funerals I was cleaning the bedroom where Gerry had slept. As I picked up a shirt he had left behind, I was overwhelmed by anguish and rage. I have never taken the life of another person nor do I ever anticipate doing so, but if I had had a gun at that moment I would have had no hesitation in shooting British soldiers until my ammunition ran out.

After Bloody Sunday the Official IRA GHQ sanctioned retaliatory action against the Paras; the target was Para headquarters at Aldershot in England. The deployment of explosives in the officers' mess hall was brilliantly executed but the results were disastrous. On 22 February the bombs went off prematurely, killing five cleaning women, a chaplain and a gardener and the operation backfired in a welter of recriminations. The Official IRA was castigated as having murdered 'innocent' civilians and depicted as mindless terrorists. But these accusations begged an answer to my question of whether or not civilians who work for, or citizens who collaborate with, an army can be truly be regarded as innocent when that army is used by the government to deny its citizens the right to peaceful protest. Since 15 August 1969, the British army had patrolled our streets, aiding the RUC, Ulster Defence Regiment (the disbanded B-Specials in new guise), and the Stormont government in their continuing efforts to deny us our civil rights. The British army was an army of occupation, we were its target, and in light of this I agreed with Connolly that:

> There is no such thing as a humane or civilised war. War may be forced upon a subject race or subject class to put an end to subjection of race, class or sex. When so waged it must be waged thoroughly and relentlessly, but with no delusion as to its elevating nature, or civilizing methods ... agitation to attain a political or economic end must rest upon an implied willingness and ability to use force. Without that it is mere wind and attitudinising.[1]

Derry has always served as my touchstone of reality and Bloody

Sunday was to serve as a demarcation point in my political understanding. Something was amiss with the political programme of Official
Sinn Fein. When I voiced my concerns to other members in Derry I
discovered that many shared my perception that our party had
adopted a theory and method which was out of step with the Nationalist population and hindering our ability to respond to events in a
positive and politically constructive manner. In keeping with our two-
pronged approach to the different political realities which prevailed on
each side of the border, we concentrated in the RI on exposing the
economic inequities resulting from partition. In NI we sought through
the civil rights movement to bring about the democratisation of
Stormont which, we felt, once achieved, would enable us to begin to
unite the working class, north and south, into a cohesive national
liberation movement. There was no delusion that in this final stage
there would undoubtedly be the need for armed struggle but in the
interim, it had been decided to downplay the military role of the
Official IRA and to carry out only defensive operations.

While I don't see myself as an intellectual I do regard myself as
having a good instinctual intelligence. Some of my Derry political
colleagues became involved in a theoretical debate over which model
of revolution we should follow in breaking our connection with Britain.
I came to the conclusion that the real problem was that people do not
always respond to events in lock-step perfection according to some
preconceived theoretical ideal.

An urban architect can develop the most efficient sidewalk system to
enable pedestrians to get from one point to another only to find that
people often forge their own, more efficient, short-cuts. We were in
the same position as the architect. By the beginning of 1972, Nationalists in NI, having decided upon their own political short-cut, were
calling for the abolition of Stormont while we, in line with our stages
theory, were locked into the position of calling for its democratisation.
Lacking the political wisdom to adapt our theory to the practical
wisdom of the people, we found ourselves increasingly isolated. What
was worse, we had worked to get the people to take to the streets in
peaceful protest, but had failed to defend them when they were
batoned off the streets, dragged from their homes, and murdered in
cold blood. As a result, we were losing popular support to the Provisional IRA and its campaign of armed resistance. In March 1972 the
Provisionals' military success forced a temporary cease-fire and led to a
meeting in Dublin with Harold Wilson, leader of the British Labour
Party opposition. Then in July, during a second cease-fire, the

Provisionals' leadership flew to London for talks with William Whitelaw, Leader of the House of Commons. Although these talks led nowhere, they were perceived as the outcome of the Provisional IRA's military operations rather than of any political strategy.

Whether to seek Stormont's democratisation or its abolition became a moot issue when British Prime Minister, Edward Heath, informed Faulkner that in the future Westminster would administer security matters in NI and, when Faulkner objected, threatening to resign, announced the suspension of Stormont. William Whitelaw was appointed NI Secretary of State and on 30 March the British Parliament passed the Northern Ireland (Temporary Provisions) Bill which ended home rule. Henceforth, NI was to be administered directly by Westminster.

Goulding issued a statement saying that Official Sinn Fein regarded the suspension of Stormont and the imposition of direct rule as a 'retrograde step ... what we want is a democratisation of the system in Northern Ireland.' For the the first time I found myself in total disagreement with Goulding and Official Sinn Fein policy. I was delighted to see Stormont go. Britain could no longer be seen as a remote puppet master; it was clear, finally, who pulled the strings and who the real enemy was. Members of the Official IRA felt the same way. On 10 April, the Derry Official IRA ASU killed two British soldiers in direct violation of the GHQ directive that ASUs should not carry out offensive operations. The armchair generals in Dublin were faced with a potential revolt by their volunteers on the ground.

The RI's case against me for IRA membership and incitement had been heard in the lower courts and was now scheduled to go to trial in Dublin on 5 May. Like other Republicans, I refused to recognise the legitimacy of the courts and had ignored the original warrant served on me when I was released from Limerick Jail and failed to respond to summons to appear at the earlier hearings. After a lengthy and heated exchange with a friend visiting from the US who was a supporter of the Republican cause, I was persuaded to appear at my trial in the Dublin Central Court. The trial was unusual on two counts: I was the first woman in the history of Ireland to be charged with IRA membership and I was the last person to be tried by jury for a political offence in the RI.

The charge of IRA membership was dropped for lack of sufficient evidence and the jury found me not guilty on the incitement charge because the state failed to prove its case. To the dismay of my solicitor, who was afraid I would be cited for contempt of court, I couldn't resist making a statement to the judge that while I applauded the verdict of the jury, I couldn't help but notice that there was not one woman on it and that this should be rectified in the future. When I emerged from the courthouse, the garda who had testified against me on the incitement charge came up and shook my hand saying he was delighted I had got off – such were the contradictions I continued to encounter!

On 31 May, Desmond O'Malley, Minister for Justice, succeeded in obtaining legislative approval for an amendment to the 1939 Offences Against the State Act abolishing jury trials for political offences. In the future, these trials would be conducted by a panel of three state-appointed judges. In December, the law was further amended to allow a person to be convicted of IRA membership solely on the testimony of a Garda District Superintendent; the burden of proof lay with the accused.

On 29 May 1972 the Official IRA called an unconditional cease-fire which eventually became permanent. This decision resulted in intense and bitter arguments within the organisation. The cease-fire was not called from a position of strength and its only achievement was an early release date for our interned members, but it was justified as a legitimate response to the public outcry after the Derry ASU killed a Derryman from the Creggan, Ranger William Best, on 20 May while he was home on leave from the British army.

Best was killed in retaliation for the death the day before of 15-year-old Manus Deery, who had been murdered by the British army. The protesters stated that Best shouldn't have been killed because he was one of 'ours' and had never served in NI, but again, I had to ask myself the question, why was the death of Best any different from that of a British soldier from Lancaster or Liverpool? It seemed to me one couldn't have it both ways – British soldiers are British soldiers no matter where they were born or raised. The fact that the British had never stationed any of their three Irish regiments in NI only meant that their deployment elsewhere freed three other regiments for service in NI.

In my opinion, what was worse was that after the cease-fire Goulding, MacGoilla and others in the Official Sinn Fein leadership began spouting a holier-than-thou line. They denounced the Provisional IRA as fascists, while those who disagreed with them politically, including members of their own organisation, were accused of being Trotskyites and ultra-leftists.

Leo, having completed his contract in Greenland, arrived home in June and immediately found work. His former boss at General Electric in Philadelphia, who had been selected to manage EI, a GE subsidiary located in the industrial estate at Shannon, gave Leo a job within a week of his arrival. Finding a house to purchase in Shannon Town was not so simple.

We went to see Michael McNamara, who was in charge of housing allocation for Shannon Free Airport Development Company (SFADCo). He told us that there were no vacancies, although SFADCo had ads in several papers urging people to come to Shannon and move into their newly constructed housing units. I suspected the 'lack of vacancies' was due to the fact that SFADCo management didn't want a known Republican moving into the area so I went to see Rory Cohan, the Branch Secretary of the Irish Transport and General Workers Union (ITGWU) in Shannon, whom I had met previously. Cohan contacted Michael Mullins, General Secretary of ITGWU, who in turn told McNamara that if we were denied housing he would call a general strike of all ITGWU members at the Shannon Industrial Estate. The next day we received a letter from McNamara informing us that we had been allocated a house.

I wasn't the only 'dangerous' new resident in Shannon. When Stella turned 16 she had joined Official Sinn Fein and our other two daughters, Margaret and Breige, were members of the Republican youth group, Fianna Eireann. Now that he had joined us, I told Leo, I would confine my political activity to local matters. I did have my fingers crossed behind my back when I made this promise but I think Leo knew this anyway. Besides, to my way of thinking, the situation in Derry was a 'local' matter.

When the British army entered Derry in August in 1969 the Bogside became, as agreed by the DCDC and the British army commander, a no-go area for the RUC. After the introduction of internment, the Bogside and Creggan became no-go areas for the army as well. It only entered the 800 acres known as Free Derry when heavily armed 'snatch squads' invaded in Saracen armoured cars (referred to as 'pigs'), and then each incursion was announced by women banging dustbin lids on the pavement to sound the alarm all along their route. At night we were alerted to soldiers entering on foot by dogs barking. Frequently a family pet was found dead the next morning – either shot or poisoned by these British patrols in order to silence them.

The residents of Free Derry had opted out of the NI state. Community services were provided by the skilled, but unemployed, men and women in the area. Radio Free Derry and the *Barricade Bulletin*, the local newspaper, kept the community up to date; the Free Derry Police handled minor crime and disputes. During the night the Official and Provisional IRA patrolled the streets and maintained automobile check points at the limited entrances into the area. There was actually very little crime; the main offences were undermining security or collaborating with the enemy, for which the penalties ranged from warnings to tarring and feathering (later kneecapping). In extreme instances death sentences were carried out after it was established beyond reasonable doubt that a person had committed a traitorous act – such as informing or repeatedly collaborating with the security forces.

For the authorities such close-knit communities were an obvious source of frustration. British soldiers and the RUC were easily spotted, and British intelligence on the Republican forces dwindled. In late 1971, in an effort to penetrate Nationalist areas, the British government introduced the Special Air Service (SAS), also known as Mobile Field Reconnaissance (MRF), into NI. SAS was, and is, a counter-insurgency and covert operations force. Established after the Second World War and officially assigned to NATO, its function is to carry out acts of sabotage and reconnaissance behind enemy lines – in our case, behind IRA and Republican lines. The British government did not formally acknowledge the SAS presence in NI until 1976, but we saw signs of them all around.

Generally, SAS operated in teams of four, which were trained to hide in stake-outs for days on end; MRF were mobile units of three or less who travelled in unmarked cars. Both SAS and MRF personnel wore civilian clothes and were provided with special surveillance devices, weapons and equipment. Their weapons were usually the same as those used by local insurgents, so that their use would be blamed on local rebels, and they used bogus businesses as fronts for their operations. At the Four Square Laundry, for example, which SAS opened in a Nationalist area of Belfast in the summer of 1972, SAS examined clothing brought in for potentially incriminating evidence against their owners. SAS/MRF also carried out assassinations. MRF later admitted responsibility for the deaths of two Nationalists in 1972 – Paddy McVeigh on 12 May and Daniel Rooney on 27 September – and the wounding of four others on 22 June. In all these instances, the MRF unit wore civilian clothes and fired from unmarked cars.

Free Derry was especially difficult for the SAS because strangers were immediately detected and reported. With the army and RUC denied access and SAS surveillance hindered, a decision was made to remove forcibly the 40 or so barricades around Free Derry in an exercise named 'Operation Motorman'. Whitelaw obtained permission from NATO headquarters (and an okay from President Richard Nixon) to release an additional 4,000 British troops from their NATO commitment and on 27 July these troops were sent to NI. This major influx of troops and their equipment, especially the Chieftain tanks which were put on ships and ferried up Lough Foyle to Derry, provided ample warning that a major operation was in progress and all Official and Provisional IRA members were ordered to go across the border to safety.

As fate would have it, having been in Derry when the barricades were originally installed, my children and I were there when they were forcibly removed. This time, however, Leo was with us. The factory where he worked had closed for two weeks' holiday and we had come to Derry. Around 4 am on 31 July 1972, we were woken by a tremendous noise of near-deafening proportions and a bright light from the searchlights trained into the area from the Derry walls. Free Derry was being invaded by 5,000 British troops with tanks, bulldozers and earth-removing equipment which smashed through, flattened and removed the barricades surrounding the area. Three hours later our streets were once again patrolled by the British army. The ratio of soldiers to civilians was 1:4; any attempt to defend the area would have resulted in a blood-bath making the Battle of the Bogside seem a picnic by comparison.

Two unarmed youths, Daniel Hegarty and Seamus Bradley, were killed during the invasion. I attended a meeting to protest over their deaths and a statement was drafted calling upon the people to resist the presence of the troops on our streets. Printed in the *Derry Journal* the next day, it warned the British government:

That every hour of every day every British soldier is ... in the eyes of the people of the area ... a leper .... Here we had a community which organised and ran itself without any 'help' from all those institutions which are supposed to be necessary, and we managed well enough ... The only thing we demand of them or want from them is that they get the hell out of our area and out of our lives so that we can build our own future in a free, socialist Ireland.

Having taken over Free Derry, the army put everyone under house arrest, then proceeded with a house-to-house search. Doors were

smashed in, floor boards torn up, bathtubs torn out; people were
threatened and intimidated in an attempt to extract information. When
they came to my mother's flat, we were ordered to stand spread-eagled
against the wall. My mother refused, saying to the lieutenant in charge,
'I'm not one bit afraid of you. The only person I'm afraid of is the man
above.' The Lieutenant pulled out his notebook and pen, 'What's his
name?'

'Who?'

'Give me the name of the man who lives in the upstairs flat.'

'I'll not give you anything, just get out of my house.'

Whereupon, the Lieutenant went with his troops to search the flat
upstairs and we could hear them dismantling the place. After the
search party left Tommy Doherty, the upstairs neighbour, came down
and said to mother, 'Mrs Sheils, they told me you said you were afraid
of me. What did I ever do to you?'

'I didn't tell them I was afraid of you, I told them I was afraid of the
man above.'

Tommy slapped his forehead with the palm of his hand and started
laughing. 'Mrs Sheils, would you please in the future not refer to God
as "the man above"! These stupid squaddies haven't got any sense, they
thought you meant me and wrecked my place!'

Leo had never before witnessed a 'security operation' and he was
absolutely appalled. He had been steeped in the Second World War
patriotic belief that the British were allies and comrades-in-arms and
had had friendly encounters with British soldiers when he was in the
US Navy. But now, he realised, simply because he was in the Bogside,
he was regarded by British soldiers as an enemy. It was a difference
between night and day – one moment a friend, the next an enemy. He
was also outraged at the lack of regard for personal privacy; the
individual rights guaranteed in the US Bill of Rights that US citizens
take so much for granted, he realised, didn't apply in NI. He began to
understand why people in Derry would take up arms. As he said to me,
'If this had happened in Philadelphia, if foreign troops came into our
neighbourhood like they have here, I'd have been the first to pick up a
gun to defend my home. I now know how the people in Poland must
have felt during the Nazi occupation and how they must feel today
under the communists.'

I knew I would never convince Leo that socialism was better than
the so-called free enterprise system in the US, but at least he now
understood why I was involved in the political struggle in Ireland.

14

Bullets and Ballot Boxes

In the autumn of 1972 dissension over what was perceived by some to be an outmoded political strategy, combined with massive disagreement over the cease-fire, deepened and intensified within Official Sinn Fein/IRA. The cease-fire had been called at a time of escalating activity by the British amy and Loyalist paramilitary groups – the two most prominent being the Ulster Volunteer Force (UVF) which had ties to Ian Paisley's Ulster Constitutional Defence Committee, and the Ulster Freedom Fighters (UFF), the military wing of the UDA which was aligned with William Craig and his newly formed Vanguard organisation (February 1972). In its February 1972 bulletin the UDA agreed with a letter attributed to a woman supporter which stated:

I have reached the stage where I no longer have any compassion for any nationalist, man, woman, or child. After years of destruction, murder, intimidation, I have been driven against my better feelings to the decision – it's them or us ... Why have they (loyalist paramilitaries) not started to hit back in the only way these nationalist bastards understand? That is, ruthless, indiscriminate killing ... If I had a flamethrower I would roast the slimy excreta that pass for human beings.[1]

The Nationalist and Loyalist working class were further apart than ever. When Stormont was suspended the backlash of Loyalist anger and rage at the loss of 'their' parliament marked the beginning of a spate of brutal and grisly sectarian assassinations. These were carried out by a variety of Loyalist paramilitary organisations who began killing Catholics because they were Catholic, regardless of their political sympathies or involvement. From April through December 1972, 82 Catholics were murdered by Loyalist paramilitaries.

Some of these Loyalist murder squads were unmistakably sadistic:

- 12 July: one of the few Catholic members of the UDR was branded with a red-hot iron, stabbed several times then shot dead in East Belfast.

- 13 August: a man was stabbed 150 times before being strangled in the Oldpark area of Belfast.
- 24 October: two farmers were hacked to death with pitchforks on their farm in County Fermanagh.
- 2 December: a 23 year-old man was branded and his hands and feet almost burnt off with a blow-torch in East Belfast.

These Loyalist sectarian murder squads did not confine their activities to NI. The last two killings of 1972 and the first two of 1973 occurred across the border in the RI. On 28 December two people were murdered in County Cavan and on New Year's Eve, a young couple was murdered near Buncrana and their bodies then dumped at the end of a lane near Burnfoot a few miles from the border. The man had been castrated and his penis stuffed into the woman's mouth. Learning of these deaths I couldn't help but be reminded of the mutilations and killings of blacks by the Ku Klux Klan in the southern US.

The Official IRA reserved the right to terminate the cease-fire if it was determined there was a need to defend Nationalists against aggressive attacks by either the British army or sectarian forces. With the clear indication that there was an upsurge of Loyalist assassination squad activity, many in the Official IRA felt that the cease-fire must come to an end. A second issue was the Official Sinn Fein view that the suspension of Stormont was a defeat rather than a victory. The aim, said the dissenters, should be forming an alliance between north and south, and ultimately reunification; trying to improve the political centre of one or the other, as our call for a democratised Stormont implied, was an implicit acceptance of the division of Ireland into Protestant and Catholic nations.

In an attempt to open up debate on political and military strategies, Seamus Costello, Official IRA Director of Operations, and Sean Garland, Official Sinn Fein National Organiser, jointly formulated a policy document for discussion at the 1972 Official Sinn Fein National Conference. The document, 'A Brief Examination of the Republican Position: An Attempt to Formulate the Correct Demands and Methods of Struggle', was sharply critical. It held that our attempt to develop class consciousness among the Nationalist and Loyalist working class to gain support for our revolutionary objectives had led to confusion rather than clarification; that the organisation was seen to be seeking reforms not revolution; and, finally, that our demand for a democratised six county state had led us into the dangerous position of expecting the British army to play a progressive role in Northern Ireland and had given:

A lot of people in the country and many of our members ... the idea that we are not in favour of the 'National Struggle' or the ending of this Struggle. This is one of the reasons why the Provisional IRA are still a force today and why they will not fade away for a long time yet.

The Costello-Garland document made a strong case for not separating the call for a democratic reform in NI from the national struggle as a whole. The document also stated that the demand for civil rights guarantees should be extended to the RI, which itself was becoming increasingly repressive. The document concluded:

In this country more and more the events of the past few years demonstrate that the struggle for democracy is also the national struggle since it is the British power and influence that maintains the undemocratic structures and it is the Nationalist population that suffers under this system.

Garland and Costello met with the various regional committees to gain support for their position prior to the annual national conference in December. Their supporters on the National Committee were Mickey Montgomery, Billy McMillen, Jack Lynch and Jim Kerr. Their opposition consisted of Goulding, MacGoilla, Sean Kenny, Mick Ryan, Dessie O'Hagan and Eamonn Smullens.

Smullens, Director of Economic Affairs, had already ruffled the feathers of the North Munster Regional Committee when he had come to one of our meetings and instructed us to appoint a certain person as industrial organiser for our area. When we disagreed with his suggestion, Smullens came to the next meeting with the OC of the Munster Official IRA who ordered us to accept Smullen's directive. Again we refused on the grounds that the appointment was a local political decision and we were not going to be dictated to by either the national office or the army. Also, despite the cease-fire, certain ASUs in North Munster had continued to provide training for volunteers from NI as well as weapons to ASUs in NI, particularly Derry. When the Official IRA GHQ realised they were losing control of the training and education of new volunteers to those they regarded as political deviants they established a new training camp under their direction in County Cork. The training, however, was not done with an eye to suspending the cease-fire in NI, but rather in preparation for some distant day when the time would be ripe for a general armed insurrection. Volunteers began to drift away from the Official IRA and to join the Provisional IRA.

There has always been a constant stream of people in and out of my house from around the country. Now my kitchen table in our new house in Shannon became a mini forum for a continuing debate leading up to the national conference as people attempted to define where they stood on the clearly developing split over policy. One person who felt caught in the middle, and who was typical of many others, including myself, was Malachy McGurran. Since 1971 Malachy, based in Derry, had been Official Sinn Fein Organiser for Counties Derry and Donegal in Northwest Ulster. Malachy was a year older than I; as a young man he had fought in the 1956–62 border campaign and as a result of his involvement had spent time in prison. Like myself he had come to realise that there was a need to move away from a purely military conception of struggle towards a solid political programme complemented by military action. However, unlike me, he had a strong distaste for the Provisional Sinn Fein/IRA; in his opinion its military action was unprincipled because it lacked political justification. While I agreed that the Provisionals had failed to develop a clear-cut political policy and remained trapped by the IRA apolitical past, I felt it unfair to denigrate the bravery of the Provisional IRA volunteers. In fact, I felt the Official IRA GHQ was being less than honest because, despite our cease-fire, our ASUs continued to carry out some GHQ sanctioned operations but were instructed not to claim responsibility for them. On the political side, anyone who disagreed with the leadership was castigated. This attitude of 'if you aren't with us, you're against us' resulted in a particularly obnoxious article in the November 1972 issue of the *United Irishman* in which Bernadette Devlin McAliskey, Michael Farrell and Eamonn McCann were referred to as 'parasitic sub-life'. It was a cheap shot against three people whose commitment and dedication to ending British rule in Ireland was beyond question. The article was so vicious that many members refused to distribute the paper, some of whom were suspended as a result.

At the national conference, the Costello-Garland policy document was discussed during a heated debate. Those in opposition argued that any resumption of the armed struggle in NI would only hurt attempts to win elections in the RI. Furthermore, the conditions in NI were not yet ripe for building the base of political support necessary for a working-class alliance. To resume military activity would only alienate further the Loyalist working class and work against our long-term goal of achieving a socialist republic.

Those in favour of the document said that our policy put too much emphasis on appeasing Loyalists rather than protecting Nationalists; that the cease-fire had served to strengthen Nationalist support for SDLP and Provisional Sinn Fein/IRA; that we had lost sight of the fact that the real enemy was British imperialism which was propping up the Loyalist state; and that our first priority was to abolish partition – unless and until that happened we would be faced with the myriad economic, social and political problems posed by that border.

The Costello-Garland proposal was adopted as policy and I felt that once tempers cooled down and calm reason prevailed we would regain our solidarity and move forward in a constructive manner and get on with what I considered to be the main argument in favour – ending partition.

We needed this solidarity. The year 1972 had been the worst of the decade. Four hundred and sixty-eight people had died in NI (322 civilians, 146 security forces) and 4,876 had been injured (3,813 civilians, 1,063 security forces). We had had Bloody Sunday, the imposition of direct rule by Britain, the removal of the barricades in Free Derry, and the continued suspension of habeas corpus. While some internees had been released, several were rearrested and detained to wait for trials which often never took place. Those convicted were designated 'criminals' rather than political prisoners. A hunger strike by Billy McKee (of the Short Strand fame) won them 'Special Category' status on 20 June 1972, however; by September there were 184 'special category' prisoners in NI prisons.

In the RI Official and Provisional IRA remand prisoners had been held for months in Mountjoy Jail awaiting trial. On 18 May they rioted, an act which resulted in 178 prisoners (40 of them on remand), being removed to the Curragh detention barracks before being sent to various other prisons where they were held under military guard. Three days after the riot, an 'emergency' prison bill was passed by the Dublin Parliament authorising the Minister for Justice, Desmond O'Malley, to transfer prisoners who were not considered to be 'ordinary' prisoners (i.e. those convicted for political offences), to military custody under the designation of 'extraordinary' prisoner.

Censorship was also imposed in the RI under Section 31 of the Broadcasting Act when the Minister for Posts and Telegraphs, Gerry Collins, acting on the instructions of Prime Minister Lynch, issued a directive to the state-owned Radio Telefis Eireann (RTE) prohibiting radio and television broadcasts of any material which 'could be calculated to promote ... the IRA or the attaining of any particular objective by violent means'. Kevin O'Kelly broke this ban on 19 November 1972 by airing an 'anonymous' interview with Sean MacStiofain, Provisional IRA Chief of Staff. When O'Kelly was backed by the RTE Board of Directors after he refused to reveal the source of the interview, the Board was replaced by the government and O'Kelly was sentenced to six months for contempt. Since that time the censorship ban has remained and although Loyalist 'men of violence' can be, and are, interviewed on RTE, Republicans are banned – including those who hold elective office.

I had kept my promise to Leo. After our move to Shannon, I confined my political activity to our new community. I became the Official Sinn Fein representative to the Shannon Town Alliance which also had representatives from Fianna Fail, Fine Gael, the Labour Party and Provisional Sinn Fein. I also took occasional jobs to earn extra money to help out with the increased expenses of furnishing our new home and the needs of our growing children.

The only trips I took were occasional visits to my mother, although I did make a special trip to Derry in May 1973 to work in the election campaign of Mickey Montgomery, who was running as Official Sinn Fein candidate for the first local elections held in NI in six years – Provisional Sinn Fein boycotted the election. As the election was to be run on the proportional voting system for the first time since 1920, thousands of newly enfranchised Nationalists would be voting for the first time and there was excitement in the Derry air as the election drew near – Nationalists realised that they had an opportunity to gain a majority on the Derry Corporation. In her attempt at fairness to the 'boys', as she termed the members of both Official and Provisional IRA, my mother had two signs in her window – one urging people to boycott the election and the other urging them to vote for Mickey Montgomery.

Mary was home on holiday from the US and on election day she and I undertook to supply sandwiches for our election agents stationed at polling places to ensure there were no attempts at fraud or denial of voting rights. At one of the polling places Mary and I noticed that two RUC members stationed there to keep an eye on things had removed their bullet-proof vests which were lying on a table next to where they were sitting. I conferred with Mary as we distributed our sandwiches and we devised a plan of action. As we were about to leave we went over to the RUC men and began chatting with them. When Mary learned that one of them had been in Washington, DC on holiday, she embarked on a conversation about the various merits of that city. Meanwhile, I bent down to read a newspaper lying on the table, opening it to cover the vests. When Mary had the two men sufficiently diverted, I swept the two vests into the box, now empty of sandwiches, and asked one of the men if I could take the paper with me. He said I could, so I put it in the box to cover the vest and, telling Mary she didn't have to leave on my account, made a hasty exit. As we had agreed, Mary came out almost immediately and we ran off down the street to the house of an Official IRA member I knew and handed over the vests.

When the election results were tabulated we were elated to learn that Mickey had won and that Nationalists held a majority of the 27 seats on the Derry Corporation. At their first meeting, the councillors chose Dr Raymond McClean (SDLP) as mayor and Jackie Allen (Unionist Party) as deputy mayor, whereupon the SDLP pompously announced that this indicated that power-sharing could indeed work. However, the rest of NI, with the exception of Newry, Mourne and Fermanagh District Councils, remained firmly in the hands of Loyalists.

15

Treacherous Comrades

I resigned from Official Sinn Fein after Seamus Costello was court-martialled and dismissed from the Official IRA in July 1974.

After the 1972 national conference, the executive committee refused to implement the policy adopted by the delegates. The Goulding-MacGoilla faction, attempting to reverse the decision, began to pursue their vendetta against those who had voted for the policy. Unable to withstand the pressure, Garland turned his back on Costello and their joint resolution and sought to have the decision reversed by the 1973 conference.

In the meantime, the Goulding-MacGoilla-Garland group became increasingly Stalinist. They began to discredit and purge the opposition and to isolate and undermine Costello. They submitted a resolution to change the policy through the Army Council, knowing that army discipline required delegates to the national conference who were IRA volunteers to vote in favour of any army resolution or face automatic expulsion for failure to follow orders. Finally, throwing the democratic process out the window altogether, local branches were set up on paper and people who supported the anti-Costello faction were accredited to vote at the national conference. To sweeten this bitter pill, and with the realisation that volunteer discontent stemmed from their disagreement with the ceasefire, ASUs were told that the GHQ was planning a major operation against the British army which would involve all northern units in the near future.

After travelling around the country to assess his support, Costello decided to fight back. In so doing, however, he was himself thwarting army discipline. By prior agreement with those who supported his position, it was decided that an amendment to the Army Council resolution reaffirming the 1972 mandate would be proposed from the floor of the conference by the Derry-Donegal Regional Committee. The 'Costello Amendment', proposed by Johnny White and seconded by Terry Robson, resulted in pandemonium. Tempers flared and long-time friendships were strained to the breaking point. When the vote was taken Official IRA delegates who favoured the amendment found themselves trapped by army discipline requiring them to vote against their political conscience, and the amendment was defeated.

Afterwards, in an attempt to remove him from the party, Costello was charged with having committed 'irregularities' at the conference but the committee which heard the evidence voted against his expulsion. Having failed to oust him from the party, the executive committee then voted to suspend Costello for six months and denied him permission to seek re-election as an Official Sinn Fein candidate to his seat on the Wicklow County Council and the Bray Urban District Council in 1974.[1] Costello chose to run as an Independent Official Sinn Fein candidate and received the highest vote in both races, outpolling Fianna Fail, Fine Gale and Labour candidates. Having failed to undercut Costello politically, the anti-Costello faction then decided to remove him from the army and instigated court-martial proceedings against him.

At that time I had a part-time job at Bunratty Castle washing dishes after the nightly banquet. The night before the Costello court-martial, I was visited at work by two men who ordered me to be ready at 6 am, when I would be driven to Mornington in County Meath where I was to appear as a witness on Costello's behalf. When the men picked me up they were reluctant to talk, so I curled up in the back seat and slept until we reached our destination. As we entered the enclosure which shielded the two adjacent houses from the country road, I noticed armed volunteers on foot patrol supplied with walkie-talkies and we were frisked for weapons by other volunteers. I went into the nearest house and greeted those present – Goulding, Garland, MacGoilla, Michael Ryan, Des O'Hagan, Sean Kenny, Derry Dineen, Tony Hafferman, Malachy McGurran, all members of the GHQ, and the other people in the room – Barry Doyle, Dolores Roberts, John Donovan and Sigrid Mienel. Goulding, in a rather distant manner, informed me I was in the wrong house, that I should go next door where I would find Costello. Feeling dismissed, I left.

In the second house were Costello, Ronnie Bunting, Sean Flynn and Jim Kerr (who were also on the GHQ), along with Jack Lynch.[2] Costello calmly told me he wanted me to testify to what I had told him after the recent national conference, namely that I had observed Sean Kenny handing out voting cards to people whom I knew were not members – one of whom was Sigrid Mienel – and instructing them to vote against the Costello Amendment.

Finally we were summoned to the other house and the court convened. McGurran read the charges against Costello: he had engaged in conduct which undermined the Official IRA and had misappropriated army funds. Ronnie Bunting and I were denied the right to present our testimony but considering that one of the three judges hearing the evidence was Sean Kenny, I wasn't surprised they didn't want me to speak. At the end of the day it really didn't matter: Jesus could have testified on Costello's behalf and it wouldn't have changed the verdict. The kangaroo court found Costello guilty of all charges and dismissed him from the Official IRA with ignominy.

After the verdict, Costello and the rest of us left immediately. I caught a lift to Shannon with one of his supporters from Limerick. I was stunned, sickened and angered by the spectacle I had just witnessed and by the time I got home, I realised I could no longer remain a member of the organisation. Within a few days, I had sent my letter of resignation. It was not an easy decision, but I was convinced that no person of principle could continue to support such un-democratic, totalitarian behaviour. This was no longer the organisation my father had helped found. In one respect the Provisional Sinn Fein was correct: our adoption of politics as the primary goal had had a negative effect. But then, in my judgement, the Provisionals' lack of political development, which left them as a purely military movement, was also in error.

I had once heard Costello express the view that a political party is only a vehicle to revolution; when it fails to work consistently towards that goal, it becomes time to change vehicles. Having come to the conclusion that Official Sinn Fein was no longer the proper vehicle, I was quite open when Costello approached me about the possibility of forming a new party.

When the Official Sinn Fein leadership learned of Costello's decision to form a new party, they tried to block him. The GHQ contacted the Official IRA OC and the regional organiser in North Munster and ordered them to inform the Garda Special Branch in Limerick of an operation Costello was planning. The two men complied with the directive but Costello got wind of this and the operation was called off. When a member of the GHQ was confronted with the fact that they had informed Special Branch, he freely admitted, with no sign of regret, that they had done so.[3]

Costello called a meeting of former Official Sinn Fein members from around the country to discuss the pros and cons of forming a new Republican socialist party. The response was overwhelmingly favourable. The group also discussed setting up a separate but complementary military organisation to be headed by Costello but it was decided to delay its formation until after the new party was firmly established. This would provide the necessary time to create an army command structure, select volunteers, and gather the necessary finances to train and arm the ASUs.

In spite of this positive response, Costello held back hoping that the split with the Officials could be avoided. He made one last effort to heal the breach at the 1974 national convention, to which he and Tommy McCourt, who was from Derry but living in the Dublin area, were elected delegates. To test the waters, McCourt preceded Costello into the conference and presented his delegate credentials at which point he was told he had been expelled from the party. Having anticipated this response, McCourt pulled his written resignation from his pocket, handed it over and left. He went to Costello who was waiting outside and told him it would be an exercise in futility to attempt to gain entrance. That evening, on a motion from the chair, the conference voted to dismiss Costello from the party on grounds of 'general unsuitability'. Costello supporters had been so thoroughly purged from both the party and the army that there were only 15 votes against the motion. The way was now open for Costello and those of us who shared his viewpoint to proceed as we saw fit.

The first meeting of our new party was held on 8 December 1974 at the Spa Hotel, Lucan, County Dublin. There were nearly 80 delegates present representing Belfast, Derry City, Dublin, and Counties Armagh, Derry, Donegal, Wicklow, Cork, Tipperary, Limerick and Clare. A great deal of time was devoted to deciding on a name. With the clear understanding that we would take our socialist direction from James Connolly, the debate was over whether the name should be that of the party he had started in 1896, the Irish Socialist Republican Party, or something new. In the end we chose the name favoured by Costello, the Irish Republican Socialist Party (IRSP).

Party structure was democratic centralist; differences of opinion were to be expressed through an internal bulletin and debated in open forum. Policy was another matter; this would take time to develop. But on one principle we were unanimous: the quest for national liberation and the need to bring about social and economic change would be intertwined. Our central objective was to 'end Imperialist Rule in Ireland and establish a 32 County Democratic Socialist Republic with the working class in control of the means of production, distribution and exchange' – the same goal as Connolly although in one respect his task in 1896 has been easier than our own: he didn't have a border to contend with. Finally, we committed ourselves to working in a broad front with other organisations which shared our political viewpoint.[4] Because we lacked the time to give them adequate consideration, it was decided to refer all proposed policy documents back to local and regional committees and to reconvene the national conference in April 1975.

Along with other people from North Munster, Stella and I left the meeting excited and anxious to begin to establish an IRSP base in our area. Shortly thereafter we joined with others in Ennis and Shannon to form the James Connolly IRSP Branch. Within a month of the December meeting the national membership had grown by leaps and bounds. In some areas, entire Official Sinn Fein branches resigned and joined IRSP. The Divis Flats complex on the Falls Road in Belfast, which housed over 7,000 people, had so many IRSP members it became known, tongue in cheek, as 'the planet of the Irps'. In Derry, almost 180 people joined in the first few months of 1975, completely eclipsing Official Sinn Fein.

The public launching of the IRSP, co-chaired by Costello and Bernadette Devlin McAliskey, was held in February at Father Matthew Hall in Dublin. The 400 or so people who attended represented a broad spectrum of left political viewpoints – traditional Republicans, revolutionary Republican socialists, Communists (both Marxist-Leninists and Stalinists), Trotskyists, Young Socialists, Anarchists, Cultural Nationalists and liberals – with a complex variety of personal, political, social, and historical motives for wanting to be part of a new political movement. All these differences created an excitement of their own and in the year ahead the wheat would be sorted from the chaff as IRSP slowly began to develop.

The new party immediately felt the full brunt of Official Sinn Fein/ IRA anger. Having laid down its guns against the British army, the Official IRA picked them up again and turned them against our members. On 20 February 1975, Hugh Ferguson, a Belfast IRSP member, was killed. A local Belfast group calling itself the People's Liberation Army (PLA) was hastily formed to defend IRSP members against these attacks. MacGoilla called for a truce after Sean Garland was shot and wounded outside his flat in Dublin on 1 March, and an uneasy truce was arranged in mid-March, with Senator Michael Mullins as the mutually accepted go-between. But the killings continued. During negotiations Danny Loughran (IRSP) and Billy McMillen (Official IRA Belfast Brigade Commander) were killed on 4 and 28 April, while over 30 IRSP members and sympathisers were wounded. On 7 May an assassination attempt was made on Costello as he drove away from a meeting in Waterford. In mid-May the Officials agreed to end their armed attack against us, although the GHQ directive to assassinate Costello was never rescinded.

The British administration in NI and the Fine Gael/Labour coalition government (1973–7) in the RI took repressive measures in an attempt to destroy our fledgling party. When approximately 40 Sinn Fein members in Long Kesh Prison in NI resigned and joined the IRSP they were immediately stripped of their status as Special Category prisoners and reclassified as criminal offenders. Recognising this move as the thin edge of the wedge in abolishing Republicans' right to be treated as political prisoners, 20 IRSP prisoners went on hunger strike. The prison authorities were forced to back down, and IRSP members were reclassified as Special Category prisoners.

IRSP members in NI were singled out for more than their fair share of RUC repression. In the RI, too, the Special Branch stepped up its surveillance and harassment. Those of us who were old hands at this sort of intimidation took it more or less in our stride but new members found their commitment tested in ways we could never have devised. The most common form of harassment was a week of constant surveillance combined with police 'visits' at a member's home, workplace, school or university. Arrests were frequent.

Stella and I began to lose track of the number of times our homes were searched or we were picked up for questioning. My tactic when I was held for the standard 48 hours was to give nothing more than the required information – name, address, age – then pick out a spot on the wall, stare at it and quietly hum a song to myself while they attempted to question me. My refusal to engage in conversation or answer questions often resulted in threats directed against Leo – 'he could lose his job because of you', or 'we could see to it he loses his resident status and is deported' – or against my children – 'we'll see to it your kids never get a job'. I would just keep humming away. One time I chose 'Take it Down From the Mast'; after about an hour one of the men questioning me hit me in the head, kicked my shins and yelled at me to shut up, 'Don't you know any other damn song?'[5] This was my own way of mentally torturing them, but for me, the humming served as a mantra and had a soothing effect.

The UDA also took advantage of the feud by carrying out a bombing operation in June 1975 designed to incriminate the IRSP. Had it been successful, the bombing would have resulted in the deaths of large numbers of Official Sinn Fein members, including the leadership.

The UDA had a history of operations in the RI and were suspected of having strong links to SAS undercover operations there, to which the coalition government turned a blind eye.[6] One UDA bombing on 17 May 1974 resulted in 33 deaths – to date the highest death toll in either Ireland or England in any one day since 1968. Discussions between the RI and British governments had resulted in the Sunningdale Agreement, under which a power sharing executive was to be created at Stormont that would involve both Loyalist and Nationalist members in administering the day-to-day affairs in NI. Sunningdale came and went in the first six months of 1974, brought down after a four-day general strike by Loyalists and the UDA's retaliatory action. It planted three car bombs on a major roadway in Dublin and one at a downtown bus stop in Monaghan on 17 May, all four timed to go off during rush hour. No prior warnings were given. After the incident and the 33 deaths the UDA press officer commented, 'I am very happy about the bombings in Dublin. There is war with the Free State and now we are laughing at them.'[7]

The UDA's June 1975 operation was equally murderous, although this time it was mass killings with a twist – the IRSP was to be blamed. The idea was to blow up a train carrying Official Sinn Fein members to the annual Wolfe Tone commemoration at Bodenstown, but the bomb failed to go off until the train had passed. The UDA unit planting the bomb, however, had been spotted by a local man, Christopher Phelan, who was savagely stabbed to death. Gardai investigating the bombing found Phelan's body and the murder weapon, which had a clear set of fingerprints on it.

During the following week the gardai arrested Costello, McCourt, Nicky Kelly and three other IRSP members under section 30 of the Offences Against the State Act. None of their fingerprints matched those on the murder weapon and the curious line of questioning directed at them sought to ascertain their knowledge of Loyalist paramilitary organisations in the Dublin area.

MacGoilla stated that in light of the recent truce, it was unlikely that the IRSP was responsible for the bombing; in his opinion, the Special Branch would do well to look to Loyalist involvement. None the less the IRSP's public image was severely damaged. The press and police alike portrayed it as culpable.

Several months later, a UDA member was killed by his own bomb in County Derry and it emerged that his fingerprints matched those on the weapon which killed Phelan. When this information was revealed there was no attempt by the media to retract any of its earlier damaging anti-IRSP articles. What was headline news in June became back page material in October.

16

The Heavy Gang

There is no denying the fact that robbery is a major source of funds for Republican groups – bank, post office, payroll. Having no government treasury at their disposal, Republicans regard robberies, particularly bank robberies, as a form of 'preemptive nationalisation'. One such operation, which in an unprecedented admission was claimed four years after the fact by the Provisional IRA, was the Cork to Dublin mail train robbery at Kearneystown, near Sallins, County Kildare, on the morning of 31 March 1976. Known as the Sallins Train Robbery, four of the five people who carried out the operation wore hoods which made identification nearly impossible; neither the 12 mailbags which contained the money, nor the money itself was ever recovered. The gardai had no concrete leads other than their suspicion that a Republican group might have carried out the robbery. But which group? IRSP won the draw. Later that day three IRSP members, Osgur Breatnach, Sean Gallagher and Gerry Roche were picked up, questioned, then released.

On 4 April, Chief Superintendent John Joy held a staff meeting to discuss the case and appointed Inspector Ned 'Buffalo' Ryan to head the investigation. John Courtney of the Technical Bureau was to assist him. Courtney directed a newly created unit that would come to be known as the 'Heavy Gang', whose sole function was interrogation. At the meeting a list was compiled containing the names of 19 people to be brought in for questioning – all but one (Brian McNally had recently resigned), were members of IRSP. Fifteen of these people were arrested under Section 30 of the Offences Against the State Act over the next four days: Breatnach, Roche, Gallagher (their second arrest), Seamus Costello, John Fitzpatrick, Nicky Kelly, Brian McNally, Ronnie Bunting, Bob Lee, Jim Doherty (5 April); Mick Plunkett, Noel Doyle, Ite Ni Chionnaith (6 April); Caoilte Breatnach (7 April); Mick Barrett (8 April). An additional 25 people were picked up, all but 6 of whom were IRSP members. Mairead Casey, Secretary of the IRSP Dublin Regional Committee, and her sister Maura, were arrested when they went to the IRSP National Office on the evening of 5 April and found Special Branch detectives inside who had gained entrance using a key they had found among Costello's possessions. Over the next two days detectives ransacked the office, searching, removing and even burning files.

Nine of those arrested were selected for 'in-depth' interrogation by members of the Heavy Gang – Roche, Gallagher, Fitzpatrick, Kelly, McNally, Plunkett, Doyle, Barrett and Osgur Breatnach. They were repeatedly beaten with batons or rubber truncheons on the head, arms, legs, stomach and back. Their feet were trodden upon. Some of them were handcuffed, forced to lie on their stomachs with their feet forced between their arms, then beaten and kicked. Others were made to stand spread-eagled against the wall and beaten in this position. Their feet were kicked from under them and when they fell to the ground they were beaten again, kicked, and hit with chairs. Some were stripped naked during the beating process, others partially stripped. Their hair was pulled from their head. They were repeatedly beaten on the ears; some were lifted by their ears off the ground. All were denied sleep and some denied food and water for as long as 24 hours. All were held beyond the legal limit of 48 hours by the expedient of release then rearrest – for Roche, Breatnach and Gallagher their third arrest, for others their second. As a result of the torture techniques, four of the men – Kelly, Breatnach, Fitzpatrick and McNally – signed 'confessions'.

The nine were moved from place to place during interrogation, making it difficult for family and friends to locate them. When Osgur Breatnach's parents managed to determine where he was being held, they asked the High Court to issue a writ of habeas corpus. In court the doctor who had examined Breatnach testified he was suffering from headache, loss of memory, pain in the back of his head and neck, and evidenced signs of concussion. Dr Noel Smith stated that Breatnach had a large swelling on the top rear part of his head, bruises on his arms, buttocks and both legs. He told the court Breatnach should be sent to hospital for X-rays. The court ordered his immediate release and directed him to be sent to hospital.

When it became likely that others might take similar court action, Costello, Roche and Gallagher were released on the evening of 7 April. They immediately held a press conference and in an editorial on 9 April, the *Irish Times* tied Costello's allegations of gardai mistreatment to a recent directive from Patrick Cooney, Minister for Justice:

In recent weeks disquiet has been caused by Mr Cooney's decision to

change prison regulations in order to allow defendants in custody to
consult only with a solicitor approved by the Minister for Justice. The
leader of the Irish Republican Socialist Party, Mr Seamus Costello,
has alleged at a Dublin Press Conference that he was arrested on
Monday morning, questioned until Wednesday when he was released, then re-arrested, brought to Rathmines and there questioned in the Garda station until his release on Wednesday. At the
same conference a number of members of the IRSP – a registered
political party –showed bruises to reporters and made allegations
of brutality against the Gardai.

While the press conference was being held, Kelly, Plunkett, Fitzpatrick and McNally were being charged with the train robbery before
Justice D. J. O'hUadhaigh at a specially convened sitting of the Dublin
District Court. The court sat in secret behind locked doors; neither the
public nor press was informed. None of the four had been allowed to
see an attorney and they were not legally represented at the hearing.
After being charged the four were remanded back into gardai custody
in the Bridewell Gardai Station, although prisoners remanded in custody
were normally sent to Mountjoy Prison unless they were involved in
extradition proceedings. Back in the Bridewell, McNally and Fitzpatrick were placed in one cell, Kelly and Plunkett in another. This
violated the Garda Code of Prison Rules which required that persons
charged with the same offence be kept separate and stipulated that
Section 30 prisoners were *always* to be segregated. The reason for
violating these rules became obvious during the trial, when the four
were accused of beating each other up in an attempt to incriminate
their interrogators.

On 8 April, although under a writ of habeas corpus, Osgur
Breatnach was rearrested for the fourth time as he left hospital and
charged with being an accomplice in the robbery. He was then
released by the court but immediately rearrested and charged again.
Barrett was also charged.

Bail for the six was set at £10,000 each but attempts to provide it
were denied on one excuse or another for almost a month. This delay
gave sufficient time for all injuries sustained during interrogation to
heal. Conditions of their release required that they surrender their
passports and report twice a week, Thursday and Sunday, to the gardai.

On 20 April, IRSP announced that we were asking Amnesty International (AI) to conduct an investigation into the conduct of the Heavy
Gang and that 12 IRSP members were instigating a civil suit against

the government which would be handled by the Association for Legal Justice and financed by by the Susan Langley Trust, a US-Canadian organisation. The announcement that IRSP intended to wage a legal battle against the state set a precedent for the Republican movement. Heretofore, it had been Republican practice not to recognise the courts for the same reason that they had adopted abstentionism: the NI and RI courts, like their legislative bodies, were illegitimate extensions of illegal governments. IRSP believed that non-recognition of the courts allowed the state to use its laws to its benefit against Republicans who were often falsely accused and convicted, and it was our intention to challenge state repression both politically and legally.

Under RI law, before a case can be brought to court, a book of evidence, in which the state sets out the evidence it will use in prosecuting the case, must be produced and provided to the accused no more than 30 days after he or she is charged. No such protection applied in the case of the IRSP Six. In June the court granted a first exemption in the 30 day requirement in answer to Detective Inspector Ryan's claim that more time was needed for the gardai to take statements from 700 'witnesses', i.e., every person who had, in one way or another, handled the money that had been stolen. In September and again in October further extensions were granted, with the final date for providing the book of evidence set for 9 December. When the day arrived and the gardai had again failed to produce the evidence, the judge dropped the charges.

The IRSP Six were released. Freed from the legal constraints against pre-trial statements, they held a press conference to expose the torture techniques of the Heavy Gang. The IRSP announced that despite the release of our members, we would continue our civil action against the state. This placed the government in an awkward position: if it had continued with the robbery case, the charges of torture and brutality would have emerged during the trial; even without the trial, however, police abuses would still be exposed through the civil suit. The Director of Public Prosecutions (DPP) and gardai decided to have another go at a frame-up.

On 17 December 1976, Nicky Kelly, Mick Plunkett, Brian McNally and Osgur Breatnach were arrested and recharged with the robbery. This time they were charged in the no-jury Special Criminal Court where their case would be heard by three judges rather than a jury. The major evidence against them was their signed confessions, although neither Fitzpatrick, who had also signed a 'confession', nor Barrett, was recharged. At the time of the robbery both Fitzpatrick and Barrett had stayed overnight in Limerick at the house of Tom and Betty Hayes, who were willing to so testify. Scheduled to start in May 1977, various legal appeals delayed the trial of the now 'IRSP Four' until January 1978.

The IRSP Four case was an obvious example of the similarities between repression in NI and the RI. Our local IRSP committee pointed out that the gardai Heavy Gang was little different from the RUC's Regional Crime Squads; both were an elite group of Special Branch inspectors and detectives whose sole responsibility was interrogation. Likewise, the methods of physical and mental abuse were similar, although in NI these practices were more acceptable and were carried out on a regular basis at Castlereagh Detention Centre near Belfast or Gough Barracks, Armagh City. In the RI the actions of the Heavy Gang directed at IRSP members was more of a trial run – could they get away with it?

Almost every protest against the prosecution of the IRSP Four was illegal under section 4 of the 1972 Offences Against the State (Amendment) Act which provides that:

Any public statement or any meeting, procession or demonstration intended or of such character as to be likely, directly or indirectly, to influence court, person or authority, including a party or witness, concerned with the institution, conduct or defence of any civil or criminal proceedings constitutes an interference with the course of justice, is unlawful, and, an offence with a liability on summary conviction to a fine not exceeding £200 or to imprisonment for a term not exceeding twelve months, or both, or on conviction or indictment to a fine not exceeding £1,000 or to imprisonment for a term not exceeding five years or both.

Every time we spoke out, held a meeting, ran a benefit, marched in a demonstration or picketed the court to protest the frame-up of our friends and colleagues, we were in contempt of court.

On 21 July 1976 the British ambassador, Christopher Ewart-Biggs, was assassinated by the Provisional IRA. The Dublin government decided to call a State of Emergency, only to find that the one instituted during the Second World War was still in effect. With egg on their faces they cancelled the old and brought in the new. The government also passed the 1976 Emergency Powers Act (EPA). This act extended the length of time the police could hold a person in custody without charging them from two seven days, increased the sentence for membership in a proscribed organisation from two to five years, and provided the Irish defence forces with powers of search and arrest. After the EPA was enacted, President Cearbhall O'Dalaigh, a former Attorney General and Chief Justice, referred the EPA to the Supreme Court to test its constitutionality; the Court held that it met the constitutional test. A few weeks later the Minister for Defence, Patrick Donnegan, castigated President O'Dalaigh for having referred the legislation to the Supreme Court and called him a 'thundering disgrace'. 'The army must stand behind the state', he proclaimed. O'Dalaigh decided that Donnegan's statement was a slur on the office of the President; as a result, he felt, the only honourable recourse open to him was to resign, which he did on 22 October.[1]

In the fall of 1976 our household was reduced by two when Stella, now 20, and Margaret, 19, moved into their own flat. Although they lived only a few blocks away and we saw them nearly every day, the house felt lonesome without their sparkling energy. Stella was as active as I in IRSP although her seat on the national committee meant that she went to meetings in Dublin at least once a month while I concentrated mostly on local activities. I am more inclined to work on an individual basis, finding it difficult to participate on committees except for short periods of time and then only for a specific purpose. It was important, I believed, to establish a strong local base for IRSP which Costello also favoured.

I wrote and produced a number of leaflets reflecting IRSP policy on various local, regional and national issues. With leaflets in hand I would go to the main entrance of the Shannon Industrial Estate at plant closing time at least once a week and as cars halted for the traffic light, I would give the leaflets to the workers on their way home. After a while they began to look forward to my presence always anxious to see what I had to give them. Later, when I saw some of them in the town centre, we would chat – sometimes they would agree with the viewpoint expressed in the leaflet, other times not, but at least we had a conversation about the matter.

I also announced I would be opening a citizen's advice centre in my house. I offered to help people resolve their housing complaints with Shannon Development Company and to provide assistance in obtaining their benefit entitlements from the social welfare department. No issue or problem was too difficult to tackle. I thoroughly enjoyed doing battle with the various bureaucrats, although to my surprise I found that some welcomed my intervention when it allowed them to resolve a matter which they felt they couldn't do on their own initiative.

I continued to be active on the Shannon Town Alliance, this time as IRSP's representative. One issue that concerned the alliance was that of establishing a Shannon Town Commission. As the creation of SFADCo, Shannon Town was little more than a multinational 'company town' and had no legal standing or town council.

Shannon was a miniature international village which, as we ourselves were an international family, made it a good place for us to live. Leo and the children didn't feel as alienated as they might have if we had remained in Limerick or had moved to Derry. All the families in the town were 'first' families and their children first-generation Shannon-ites; everyone was from somewhere else – Europe, North America, South America, Asia or another town in Ireland. Several Chilean families, refugees from Pinochet's regime, lived near us.

After the CIA backed coup, the Irish government had agreed to accept approximately 25 Chileans and their families as political refugees and several families settled in Shannon.[2] I and other IRSP members felt great solidarity with our new neighbours, supporters of Salvador Allende, President of Chile's first elected socialist govern-ment, who had been assassinated during the coup. We did what we could to help them adjust to their new environment and worked with their Chile Solidarity Committee. One particular friend was Benjamin 'Benji' Duarte. Benji was most approving of my one-person leafleting campaign and although his English was poor and my Spanish non-existent, we had great conversations about the plight of workers in both our countries and the difficulties of achieving a socialist govern-ment. Benji had been active in the Chilean labour movement and after Leo helped him and his friends to join the union in their workplace, he quickly figured out how weak the Irish labour movement was. But he wasn't too discouraged; he started his own one-person campaign to educate his co-workers about the need to strengthen the union.

Because we lived so near the Shannon International Airport, we were constantly visited by people who arrived on flights from other countries. Most of these people were politically active in their own countries and either knew us, as was the case of US visitors, or knew of us from friends who gave them our address. Arriving at our house as their first stop in Ireland often provided many of them a welcome they didn't anticipate when they frequently found themselves being fol-lowed, or stopped and questioned, by the Special Branch or the newly formed Task Force (the political police). When Leo arrived home for his daily lunch break he never knew who he might find at our kitchen table. He established two house rules: he wouldn't give up our bed to anyone and even though he smoked a pipe, insisted that no one smoke at the kitchen table while he ate his meals. Otherwise he took the ebb and flow of people through our house in his stride.

17

Seamus is Dead

Seamus Costello was assassinated shortly after noon on 5 October 1977. He was sitting alone reading a newspaper in his car on Northbrook Avenue off North Circular Road in the dock area of Dublin, where he had gone to keep an appointment.

I was preparing Leo's lunch when Seamus's death was announced on the one o'clock news. He had been shot; the Richmond Hospital pronounced him dead on arrival. I froze, not wanting to believe what I had heard. Within 15 minutes Stella, crying and almost hysterical, arrived at the house. She said she was leaving for Dublin immediately to help with the funeral arrangements. I decided to remain in Shannon until the wake the next day in Bray; people had to be told the news and arrangements had to be made for wreaths and telegrams to be sent from the Munster area. As we had a cup of coffee Stella and I went through the myriad possible assassins. Special Branch? SAS? UDA? Official IRA? Task Force? Belfast dissidents?

Seamus was born in 1939 in Bray, County Wicklow, RI, the eldest of nine children. He first became interested in Republican politics in 1953 when he read accounts of the arrest and sentencing of Goulding, Manus Canning and Sean Stephenson (MacStiofain) for their part in an arms raid on the British Army Officers Training Corps School at Felstead in Essex. The raid had been successful but the three were caught when police spotted their overloaded van in the middle of the night.

At the age of 16 Seamus applied to join the IRA and by the following year he was commanding an ASU in South Derry as part of the 1956–62 border campaign. The campaign opened on the night of 12 December 1956 with a series of coordinated IRA attacks in the border area; Seamus's ASU burned down the Quarter Sessions Courthouse at Magherafelt, County Derry. A few weeks later in a safe house Seamus lost part of a finger when a Thompson machine gun went off accidentally. He was sent back to Dublin for medical treatment and shortly thereafter was arrested and sentenced to six months in Mount-joy Jail. After his release he was rearrested and interned, spending almost two years in the Curragh internment camp.

He always referred to his time in the Curragh as his 'university years' because it was there that he began his study of socialism and analysed the failures of the border campaign. Along with others, Seamus concluded that the campaign, although widely supported, lacked popular involvement – a result, in turn, of Sinn Fein/IRA's poorly articulated political programme.

After his release from the Curragh, Seamus helped to restructure Sinn Fein/IRA. Meanwhile, he worked as a car salesman and very soon became the firm's top salesman. When the firm learned of his membership in Sinn Fein it tried to fire him but backed down when he threatened to mount a daily picket. In 1964 he married and he and his wife Maeliosa settled in Bray.

Seamus was one of the major forces pushing for abolition of Sinn Fein's abstentionist policy. He helped convince the organisation to contest local elections in selected areas, and in 1967, Seamus himself won a seat on the Wicklow County Council and the Bray Urban District Council as a Sinn Fein candidate. His major base of support was the Bray Trades Council and the Bray Tenants Association, which he had helped found. He was also involved with credit unions and small farmers' organisations.

It was during this period that Seamus developed his belief that a strong local base was necessary for a successful socialist movement. People had to be educated and encouraged to act in their own best interests. When a particular issue was being discussed – housing, road repairs, water and sewage, access to local beaches, land speculation, etc. – Seamus always managed to turn out large deputations of local citizens to support the Sinn Fein position. A good socialist, he argued, acted with rather than for the people, and he warned against the danger of becoming merely a 'social worker' – in other words, of maintaining instead of changing the political system. It was his conviction that almost every Irish county had within its borders all the problems common to the nation: small farmers trying to eke out a living on unproductive farms, inadequate housing, high unemployment, industrial workers with depressed standards of living.

I first met Seamus when I was elected to the Sinn Fein national committee in 1971, although we didn't form a close working relationship until after 1972 when we found we were on the same side during the developing schism in Official Sinn Fein which led to the formation of IRSP in 1974. During that time Seamus seemed to be everywhere at once and I never knew when he would show up at my door to discuss a matter or to get my opinion on something before taking off for his next consultation. Seamus trusted my gut reaction to situations and people. In one instance he accepted my positive assessment of a person who had come to us with an offer of help. Others wanted to have nothing to do with the man, they didn't trust him, I did. Seamus acted on my judgement and the man delivered as promised.

No one who met Seamus could remain unaffected by his personality. Some people revered him, others disliked him, and some vacillated between the two poles, but no one underestimated or lacked respect for his principled political commitment.

When people disagreed with him on a political point, he didn't trivialise the disagreement or take it personally. He took time to discuss the particular issue, forcefully presenting his point of view while remaining open to arguments that might cause him to rethink his position. This attitude is what caused him to pursue the political disagreement with Goulding, Garland and MacGoilla through to its eventual impasse – but when it became apparent there was a need to part company, Seamus didn't do so with enmity. He was strongly opposed to feuding among Republicans and after the split refused to sanction or condone those who wanted to raid Official IRA arms dumps. When the feud broke out he did everything in his power to resolve it. And although we were the most damaged by the feud, he was still willing to hold out his hand to those who had been his former allies. When he spoke at a commemoration ceremony in April 1975 to honour three IRA volunteers who died at Crossbarry on 19 March 1921 during the War of Independence, he addressed his remarks to the leadership of Official Sinn Fein who had chosen not to participate in the commemoration. Seamus called upon them to forget past differences and join with IRSP to support a broad front effort to achieve national liberation and socialism because:

Such unity is essential and the IRSP thought that a beginning could have been made here today. We want to build a society where our children can live in peace and prosperity, a society where they will control the wealth of this country. Petty differences and recriminations must be forgotten and the necessary leadership given to the Irish people. No republican or socialist can afford to allow themself to be manipulated in creating disunity in the anti-imperialist forces.

Seamus was not a saint. At times he could be exasperating, domineering, manipulative, ruthless and calculating, but this was balanced by his bravery, sincerity, warmth, humour, idealism and total dedication. He had all the qualities of a charismatic leader.

Even those who had had political disagreements with Seamus mourned his death; one such was Bernadette Devlin McAliskey. Seamus had persuaded her to help form IRSP, but she left after about a year because of differences over policy. In her graveside tribute Bernadette said of him:

> Seamus Costello was cut down in the prime of his life before he could make a bigger contribution to emancipation. As a speaker he was without equal, his main appeal was to reason and not to emotions. He was one of the greatest revolutionaries in 800 years of Irish history. He will not be easy to replace.

In the Irish tradition of walking a loved one to their final resting place, Seamus was carried in his coffin from the Church of the Holy Redeemer, Bray, to St Peter's Cemetery, Little Bray, on the shoulders of his personal and political family. A colour party of nine, six of them dressed in combat jackets and black berets, flanked the coffin while a lone piper played laments and 26 women carried wreaths. Over 6,000 mourners marched in the cortege of local and national elected officials and politicians, representatives of the trade union movement, tenant and farming organisations, republican and socialist friends and neighbours. The graveside ceremony was presided over by Nora Connolly O'Brien, the daughter of James Connolly, who said in her remarks:

> My father told his court martial [in 1916] that the British had no right to be in Ireland. Seamus Costello felt the same way. He was the greatest follower of my father's teaching in this generation and I hope that his example shall be followed and that his vision for Ireland will be realised in this generation.

Seamus's coffin, draped with the Starry Plough (the flag of James Connolly's Irish Citizen Army), and the Tricolour, on which rested a black beret, was lowered into the grave. The last post played to the accompaniment of a roll of drums, after which reveille was sounded by two buglers. The colour party stood at attention and saluted; then, on orders issued from two people in the crowd, six Irish National

Liberation Army (INLA) volunteers fired a volley of shots into the air in final tribute.

Seamus's fate had been strangely foretold by Dr Noel Browne, former RI Minister of Health (1948–51) in an article on the Amherst Conference on Northern Ireland held at the University of Massachusetts from 28 August through 3 September 1975. Sponsored by the Committee for an Irish Forum, Seamus was invited to attend, along with Johnny White (IRSP National Organiser), to present the IRSP viewpoint. Most political parties in Ireland sent representatives as did the UDA and Orange Order. (Provisional Sinn Fein representatives were denied visas.) Each group was allowed two hours to present their position but there was such interest in Seamus's presentation that his lasted three, and, by popular demand, he was asked to speak again in the evening. Writing about Seamus's presentation, Browne, no friend of the Republican movement, wrote:

> Seamus Costello spoke for the IRSP and gave a scintillating display of good humour, history, politics and hard facts. No one who listened to his three hours in the afternoon, and by unanimous demand two hours ... in the evening, now doubts but that they will have to shoot him or jail him, or get out of his way but they certainly won't stop him. Costello, the Revolutionary Marxist Socialist, whose ambition is a secular, pluralist united socialist republic, won't go away until he gets it. I've never heard his brand of republicanism before .... Is it not a triumph [because of censorship by] the venomous Dublin political denigration machine, that none of us has even read, heard of or seen this man's remarkable dialectical skill and political ability? [1]

In a country as small as Ireland where everyone knows their neighbour's daily business before nightfall, there was no possibility that Seamus's assassin would remain anonymous for long. Maeliosa Costello spent four years attempting to get the state to hold an inquest, taking her request on appeal from court to court until finally the Supreme Court held in her favour. The inquest into the cause of Seamus's death was held on 19 November 1982. An eyewitness reported having heard a gunshot at the scene and then 'saw a man who seemed to be reloading a black sawn-off shotgun. The man then fired two more shots into [Seamus's] car.' The witness described the man as 'about 25 to 30 years old, about 5 ft 6 in tall, and with dark short hair cut straight.' The gardai reported they had no leads on his assassin. The jury returned a verdict of death due to lacerations caused by shotgun discharged by a person or persons unknown.

It is my firmly held belief that the delay in holding the inquest resulted from the fact that the gardai knew more than they wanted revealed. Since the formation of IRSP, the Special Branch had placed Seamus under 24-hour surveillance. He never went anywhere without his followers. Yet on the day Seamus was assassinated his watchers were strangely absent. Why?

The INLA undertook their own investigation and eventually established beyond reasonable doubt that Jim Flynn, Official IRA, had done the deed and he was executed. Although Flynn pulled the trigger that killed Seamus, those that gave the order are still at liberty.

18

Justice Denied

Miriam Daly, a social history lecturer at Queen's University, Belfast, assumed the chair of a party shattered and numbed by the death of Seamus Costello. The beginning of her term as national chair was marred by the death of Colm McNutt, an 18-year-old IRSP member from Derry, who was killed by an SAS team on 12 December 1977. Two SAS undercover agents, sitting in a car parked in a lot on William Street, opened fire on Colm as he walked past. His death was to mark the beginning of what was eventually exposed as an SAS operation to execute known Republicans which resulted in ten deaths in NI between December 1977 and November 1978.[1]

One major issue that concerned us was the upcoming trial of Nicky Kelly, Osgur Breatnach, Mick Plunkett and Brian McNally for the Sallins train robbery. As the result of our request to the Irish branch of Amnesty International (AI) that they conduct an inquiry into the brutal interrogation methods of the Heavy Gang, AI had sent Angela Wright of their International Secretariat and Douwe Korff, a Dutch lawyer, to undertake an investigation. In addition to taking statements from the IRSP Four, Wright and Korff took statements from 24 non-IRSP people whose allegations of similar treatment while in gardai custody had been gathered by AI-Ireland.

In June 1977, shortly after the AI delegation completed its investigation, a general election brought a change in government – Fianna Fail was back in power, Jack Lynch was again prime minister and Gerry Collins was Minister for Justice. AI submitted its report to the Lynch government on 27 August; the government did not release the report until 17 October.

In its report, AI expressed five concerns:

- Maltreatment of persons in police stations appears to have occurred in a number of cases examined by the delegates.
- Maltreatment appears to have been systematically carried out by detectives who appear to specialise in the use of oppressive

methods in extracting statements from persons suspected of involvement in serious politically motivated crimes.

- In a number of cases reported to the Amnesty International delegation impediments in access to legal counsel seem to have aggravated the risk of violation of detained person's rights.

- Insufficient safeguards exist in law regarding the rights of suspects while they are in police custody. The Judges Rules for the guidance of police when questioning suspects are not legally binding, and rights guaranteed under the Constitution such as the right to Habeas Corpus, do not eliminate the risk of maltreatment, as is shown in the cases examined by the Amnesty International mission.

- The Special Criminal Court has seemingly failed or refused to scrutinise allegations of maltreatment according to principles of law which govern the burden of proof with regard to the admissibility of statements.

Patrick Cooney, Minister for Justice at the time of the AI investigation, had refused to meet with the AI team. The AI report, however, quoted a statement he had made in Dail Eireann on 18 February 1977 regarding the legal position in relation to voluntary statements:

It is the law [under the Judges Rules] that no statement made by an accused person may be admitted in evidence if it was not a voluntary statement. This means that the statement must not have been obtained as a result of physical pressure or a threat or an inducement. If any question is raised as to whether a statement was voluntary, the onus of proof is on the prosecution and in any case of doubt the statement is inadmissible.

The AI report went on to state that despite Cooney's assurances:

The Special Criminal Court has rarely dismissed a case on the grounds that the prosecution failed to establish beyond doubt that statements were voluntary, but has thus far appeared consistently to accept police testimony as against the accused. From an examination of seven cases appearing before the Special Court in the past, it appears to Amnesty International that, despite the standards proclaimed by the former Minister for Justice [Patrick Cooney], the onus of proof has in effect been on the defence to establish beyond all reasonable doubt that maltreatment did occur, rather than on the prosecution to prove it did not. In a recent case examined by the mission [IRSP Four] it was alleged in court that three persons had been maltreated soon after their arrival at the police station and had signed incriminating statements within the first 12 hours of detention. They had not been brought before a court for five days. The Special Criminal Court ruled that this was not in violation of the requirement in Irish law to bring accused persons before the court at the first opportunity.

When the government published the AI report, all mention of the Special Criminal Court, which had been brought into being by the previous Lynch government, was removed.

AI formally requested the government to conduct a public inquiry of the charges of maltreatment which, as a signatory of the United Nations Declaration Against Torture, the government was obligated to do.[2] Instead the new Minister for Justice, Gerry Collins, appointed Justice Barra O'Briain to head a three-member committee of inquiry to consider means to safeguard persons in garda custody '... *for the protection of members of the Garda Siochana against unjustified allegations of such ill-treatment*' (my emphasis).[3] The O'Briain Committee was specifically prohibited from investigating charges of past gardai illtreatment which therefore excluded those of the IRSP members arrested in April 1976.

On 18 January 1978, the European Court of Human Rights delivered its verdict in the case brought before it by the RI government which had charged the British government with inflicting torture on the Hooded Men. The Court held that 'the use of the five techniques constituted a practice of inhuman and degrading treatment which practice was in breach of Article 3 of the European Convention on Human Rights'.[4]

The RI, which had instituted the court action in 1971 to avoid taking diplomatic action against the British government, was now being hoisted with its own petard: the AI report showed that the Heavy Gang used torture techniques similar to those used in NI. Against this background the IRSP Four trial began in the Special Criminal Courts in Dublin on 19 January 1978.

The trial was held in the same courtroom in which I had been absolved of IRA membership and acquitted of the charge of incitement in 1972. Now the room was used exclusively for sittings of the Special Criminal Court. Two jury boxes on either side of the room were empty, and the place of the jury had been taken by three judges, who, in this trial, were James McMahon, presiding, John Garavan and John William O'Connor.

The day I went with some other IRSP members to observe the trial proceedings we found our way to the court house barred by locked gates and were questioned at length by one of the twelve gardai at the entrance who wanted to know why we wanted to enter. After we repeatedly insisted that it was our constitutional right to be allowed to observe the trail, he finally opened the gate. Once inside we were asked our name, age, address, occupation, place of employment and reason for attending the trial. This procedure wasn't exclusive to IRSP members but was carried out on every citizen who wanted to observe the trial and was obviously done to discourage attendance.

When we gave our reasons for wanting to observe we were less than honest; if we had said that we wanted to confirm for ourselves the reports that Judge O'Connor was constantly falling asleep, it is doubtful we would have been allowed inside. The first public account of the 'sleeping judge' appeared in an article written by Niall Kiely in the *Hibernia* weekly review on 3 February. Although fearful that the publication might be held in contempt under section 4 of the Offences Against the State Act for its critical assessment of the court proceedings, Kiely wrote:

> Justice John O'Connor seemed to fall asleep last Wednesday: the courtroom is high-ceilinged but the well of the court is packed and very stuffy by mid-afternoon. At 2.42 p.m. his head was only inches above the bench but three minutes later he sat up and began to write; at 3.10 his head seemed to be actually resting on the bench but two minutes later he again sat up.

Everyone in the courtroom knew the judge was falling asleep with regularity, yet, like the Emperor with no clothes, everyone – the defence, the prosecution, the other two judges – pretended it wasn't happening. It was a legal embarrassment that no one wanted to tackle: the defence because it might prejudice their relationship with the other judges, the prosecution because it might result in a mistrial, Justices McMahon and Garavan because they didn't want to humiliate a colleague.

Finally, on 26 April, the defence attorneys approached the bench and pointed out the problem, hoping this might resolve the matter. When it didn't, they made a statement in open court asking the court to discharge itself and order a new trial. When this request was refused the defence made an application for a mistrial to the High Court which was also refused. They then appealed to the Supreme Court.

On 3 May the Supreme Court turned down the request on the

grounds that the delay in bringing the application disentitled the accused from being granted a new trial and furthermore, because the Special Criminal Court, in its refusal to stop the trial, stated that Justice O'Connor was following the evidence, this 'amounted to a rejection of the factual basis for the complaint now being made and therefore is not subject to appeal.'[5]

The next afternoon Judge O'Connor fell asleep again and the defence called for a break. After the break, Mick Plunkett stood up saying, 'My defence council may be bound by the Supreme Court ruling but I want it put on the record that Judge O'Connor appeared to be asleep before the break.' He was told by Justice McMahon to sit down and let his council defend him. On 11 May, Kiely wrote another article about the 'sleeping judge', yet the trial continued.

On 6 June Judge O'Connor failed to appear for the start of that day's court session – shortly before leaving his house that morning he suffered a heart attack and died. The longest trial in the history of the state came to an end and a new trial was ordered to start on 10 October.

In the interim between trials IRSP received a request to send representatives to meet with two members of the US Congress, Joshua Eilberg and Hamilton Fish, Jr, who were conducting a fact-finding trip as members of the US House of Representatives Judiciary Committee. Eilberg and Fish were charged with investigating systematic refusals to grant US travel visas to Republicans and in so doing found that 'it was necessary to seek up-to-date evaluations on social, political, and economic conditions, especially in Northern Ireland, which had a direct impact on visa decisions.'[6] The IRSP national executive delegated Mick Plunkett, James Daly (Miriam's husband) and me to meet with the congressional delegation, which we did on 1 September at the Shelbourne Hotel in Dublin. One of their main concerns was the judicial system in Ireland and they were very surprised to learn of the allegations against the RI of human rights violations made by IRSP and others. We presented them with detailed information including a copy of the AI report and they promised to investigate the matter further, but in their final report to the US Congress they chose to confine their concern with human rights violations to NI only.

The new presiding judge in the second IRSP Four trial was Liam Hamilton, the same one who had heard the application for habeas corpus on behalf of Breatnach and had ordered him to hospital on 7 April 1976. The other two judges were Gerard Clarke and Cathal

O'Floinn. On 11 October Mick Plunkett was discharged as a defendant; he had not signed a self-incriminating statement and there was no other evidence linking him with the robbery. The only evidence against the other three was their signed statements; the period from 11 October through 1 December was taken up with whether or not those statements were given voluntarily or forced from them as a result of torture. It came down to whether the judges believed the defendants or the gardai.

On 1 December the court ruled in favour of accepting the signed statements as evidence:

> The court accepts that inherent in its findings with regard to each of the accused, it has drawn the inference that the injuries that they suffered at the time of their respective medical examinations were self-inflicted or inflicted by collaboration with persons other than members of the Garda Siochana.

On 9 December, after giving his testimony, Nicky Kelly decided he would never be given justice by the court and jumped bail. Two days later the Special Criminal Court found the IRSP Three guilty of the Sallins train robbery. Breatnach was sentenced to twelve years, McNally nine. They said they would appeal the decision. On 15 December Nicky Kelly, despite his absence from the courtroom, was given a sentence of 12 years.

In sentencing Breatnach, McNally and Kelly the Republic of Ireland had conveniently absolved itself of carrying out torture for its own political ends. When the O'Briain Committee made its report to the government in September 1978, one of its recommendations had been that the government should set up a tribunal to investigate complaints against the Garda Siochana. The government's reply was that 'this will need careful consideration'. Today, ten years on, they are still giving the recommendation careful consideration.

About a week before Christmas Eve, there was a knock on our front door late at night. When I opened it I found Nicky Kelly standing outside and I hurriedly brought him into the house. There was a nationwide search out for him and already I'd been visited twice by the Special Branch in their attempts to locate him. Nicky looked wrecked and the strain of the past few months had aged him beyond his 27 years. Over a cup of tea he told me he was contemplating going to the US and wanted me to contact certain people in IRSP to see if this could be arranged. I told him I would but in the meantime he would have to stay somewhere else as it wasn't safe for him at our place. I made arrangements for him to stay at the house of a friend in Shannon which would never be suspected of harbouring a fugitive. The next morning I made the necessary telephone calls and later that day two people came from Dublin to discuss the details of getting Nicky to the US. While the arrangements were being made, we decided Nicky would be safer out of Shannon and I told them I knew just the place to take him – a farm house in the middle of County Clare and that I would make the arrangements in the next several days. I also agreed to contact some of my friends in the US and ask them to help Nicky when he arrived. The two people left and I invited Nicky to come to my house for our family Christmas Eve celebration and dinner the next day; over the next two days there would be less surveillance as the gardai and Special Branch would be down to a token duty roster.

We had a delightful Christmas Eve dinner and Nicky enjoyed our traditional Polish meal. We also drank lots of good cheer and the next morning all the adults slept late, being more interested in recovering from the night before than making the Christmas dinner – all, that is, except Nicky who cheerfully went about preparing a complete and delicious meal, rejecting all offers of half-hearted assistance.

The next morning a friend drove me to the house I had in mind for Nicky. I explained to the couple that I had a young friend who felt himself to be on the verge of a nervous breakdown because of a traumatic break-up with his girlfriend and was so upset that he had contemplated suicide. I told them that I felt a complete rest would do him a world of good and asked if they would put him up for a few weeks in exchange for his helping out on the farm. They readily agreed to play the good Samaritans and we arranged for me to bring Nicky out the next evening.

Nicky stayed with the couple about three weeks, by which time the arrangements had been made for him to leave the country. The day we picked him up he seemed relieved to leave the farm – as we were driving back to Shannon he told me if he had stayed much longer he really would have cracked up. The couple were pacifists and he told us a tale about the night they were all sitting around the open fire in the kitchen relaxing after a hard day's work. 'All of a sudden', Nicky said, 'a mouse made an appearance and the cat made a leap for it. The couple were shocked at the cat's behaviour and chucked it out the door with a lecture on not killing other creatures. I realised they were deadly serious in their attempt to prevent the cat from doing what was part of its natural instinct and I had all I could do to not burst out laughing my head off at their strange behaviour. It was then I realised one could carry pacifism a bit too far!' To this day the couple on the farm have no idea who they had staying with them those few weeks.

Nicky and our friends stayed the night at the safe house in Shannon and the following morning left for Dublin. The next time I heard of him he was safe in the US living on a farm in the Appalachian Mountains.

Although the Lynch government decided not to renew the State of Emergency when it came up for review in 1978, it did establish the Gardai Task Force, a 40-member anti-terrorist squad, in January 1979. The Task Force, like the 600-member Special Branch, was armed, principally with Uzi machine guns. During the year there was a sharp increase in the number of Section 30 arrests with detention for the legally allowed limit of 48 hours. In 1978, 912 people were arrested under Section 30; in 1979 the number increased to 1,431.[7] It literally got to the point that every time I left Shannon I could count on being stopped, if not pulled in for a few hours of questioning. When I was a passenger in a car going to Limerick or Ennis, I was assigned the task of watching out for Special Branch or Task Force cars, which were all identical Ford Cortinas with Dublin licence plates. Before long I felt I had made the acquaintance of every member of the Task Force and half the Special Branch. They even sought to get at me through my family.

Shortly after the announcement that Pope John Paul II would be making a historical first papal visit to Ireland, the Makowski family received an invitation to meet him – an invitation extended to all people of Polish descent who resided in Ireland. The reception was scheduled for Sunday 30 September at the Papal Nuncio's residence adjacent to Phoenix Park in Dublin just prior to the Pope's public appearance to conduct mass.

Leo was over the moon with excitement, hardly able to contain his joy and certainly unable to talk of anything else. We attended two meetings in Dublin with the other people who had been invited, about 400 in all, where we were taught several prayers in phonetic Polish and learned two Polish hymns. We were told that it would be appreciated, for those who cared to do so, to wear Polish native dress and to prepare Polish dishes to be eaten.

I made Breige, who had just turned sixteen, a Polish peasant dress to wear and baked kruchiekes, a Polish biscuit. On the Saturday before the visit, Leo, Breige, Brian, Leo Patrick and I drove to Dublin where we had arranged to spend the night at Maeliosa Costello's house. Margaret was now living in London where she had gone to work and Stella had absolutely no interest in the outing.

Sunday morning we were up at daybreak. I ironed Breige's outfit and helped her dress – tall, blond and big boned, she looked the epitome of a Polish peasant fairy princess and Leo was near to bursting with pride at her appearance. We arrived early at the Jesuit College where we were to check in, receive our official passes, and be given last-minute instructions before going to the Papal Nuncio's house. The woman in charge of handing out the passes read the names of people arranged in alphabetical order. She came to and passed over Makowski and Leo and I looked at each other in puzzlement. When she finished, Leo went over to the woman and told her we had been omitted. She checked her original list against the pass list: our name was on the first but not the second. She assured Leo there had been a mistake and told him we should go to the residence with her and she would straighten the matter out once we arrived.

When we got to the Nuncio's residence, she went inside and we waited at the entrance. A few minutes later she came out accompanied by a red-haired Special Branch detective who, with a smirk on his face, said to Leo, 'You and the rest of your family may go inside but your wife is considered a security risk and we can't take the chance of letting her in.' Without a moment's hesitation, Leo replied, 'If my wife isn't allowed in, then I and the rest of my family don't consider ourselves welcome either.' Taking my arm, he turned me around, told the children to follow us and we all walked to the special section in Phoenix Park reserved for the Polish contingent and waited, like every other person in the park that day, for the Pope to appear on the platform.

Hunger For Justice

The last time I saw Patsy O'Hara alive he burst into my kitchen brimming over with infectious good-humour, beaming from ear to ear as he gave me a hug, 'God it's good to be in a Derry woman's house! I'm starving with the hunger, can you make me a fry?'[1] That was in January 1979. A year later Patsy was sentenced to serve eight years in an H-Block cell in Long Kesh Prison. A member of the INLA, he was classified as a criminal offender. The next time I saw him was 22 May 1981 at his parents' home in Derry where he was lying in a coffin dead at the age of 24 after a 61-day hunger strike. He gave his life in an attempt to win political status for himself and others.

Engaging in a hunger strike to redress a grievance is a time-honoured and respected tradition in Ireland. Under ancient Brehon Law, if a person felt themselves to be unjustly accused by another, the accused would go to the door of the accuser and begin a fast; the accuser was expected to begin a counter-fast, and whoever lasted the longest was considered by the community to be in the right.

At the time of Patsy's death there were approximately 1,450 political prisoners in Northern jails, 70 of whom were women. Of this number, about 400 convicted prior to March 1976, were classified as Special Category, i.e. political prisoners. The other 1,050 − 750 Republicans, 300 Loyalists − convicted after that date were designated as criminal offenders although they were sentenced for having committed the same type of offences as the 400. It is safe to say that 99 per cent of these prisoners, given normal times, would never have seen the inside of a police station, let alone a prison.

The British are past masters at using word substitution to protect their image. Thus, as the colonial war intensified in NI, internment became detention; interrogation centres were renamed holding centres; Long Kesh Internment Compound was redesignated Her Majesty's Prison, the Maze; guerrilla fighters were called terrorists; the Ulster Special Constabulary (B-Specials) was reoutfitted as the Ulster Defence Regiment (UDR); and the war itself designated as an outbreak of terrorist activity. In keeping with these euphemistic changes, in 1972, after Billy McKee's hunger strike, the government granted political status to prisoners-of-war under the designation of Special Category prisoner, only to take it away in 1976 when they adopted their policy of 'Ulsterisation, Criminalisation and Normalisation' at which point prisoners-of-war *cum* political prisoners became criminals.

When the introduction of internment in 1971 began to result in adverse publicity for the British government other means were sought to accomplish the same ends. In 1972, the British Parliament appointed Lord Diplock to chair a commission to consider:

What arrangements for the administration of justice in Northern Ireland could be made in order to deal more effectively with terrorist [sic] organisations by bringing to book, otherwise than by internment by the Executive, individuals involved in terrorist activities, particularly those who plan and direct, but do not necessarily take part in, terrorist acts.[2]

The major recommendation of the commission, after taking a look at the precedent established in the RI for juryless, three-judge Special Criminal Courts to try 'subversive crimes' was to establish what became known as the Diplock Courts – juryless courts presided over by one judge. One benefit cited by the Diplock Report of one judge as opposed to three, was 'to shorten trials so as to enable more cases to be dealt with by the same number of judges and to reduce the current delay between committal and trial'.

Another Diplock recommendation was to suspend the 'current technical rules, practice and judicial discretions as to the admissibility of confessions ... for the duration of the emergency' and allow signed confessions to be admitted in evidence with the burden of proof that these confessions were not obtained by torture or inhumane treatment being placed on the accused rather than the accuser. The report also recommended that bail be granted only in unusual circumstances. The recommendations for the Diplock Report were incorporated into the Northern Ireland (Emergency Provisions) Act in July 1973. Executive internment was to be replaced by executive extra-judicial detentions via farcical trials which violated every principle of English common law.

The new legislation allowed a person to be charged with possession of a proscribed article (explosive, firearm ammunition, etc.) if it was found in a place (or automobile, vessel or aircraft) normally occupied by the person – even if the person was not present or in physical possession of the proscribed article at the time of a search.[3] The Act also extended the time a person could be held for questioning from 48 to 72 hours. A year later the police were to be given the authority to detain a suspect for an additional five days after passage of the 1974 Prevention of Terrorism Act (PTA). The PTA also gave the British Home Secretary power to exclude a citizen of one part of the UK from another. Thus, for instance, if a native of Derry was living and working in London and went home to Derry for a holiday, that person could be prevented from returning to London when his or her holiday ended.

To answer critics who charged that the Diplock courts were a violation of civil liberties and human rights, the government appointed Lord Gardiner to head a commission charged with the responsibility for studying the matter. The Gardiner Commission Report (January 1975) held that the Diplock Courts were not a violation of civil liberties or human rights and recommended their continuance. The report praised one major side benefit of abolishing juries: it resulted in a major saving of time – 'as much as two hours a day' by eliminating the time-consuming aspects of a jury trial – choosing, swearing in, instructing and summing up. Unfortunately, the report bemoaned, this time-saving factor had been overlooked due to: 'The greatly increased success of the Royal Ulster Constabulary in bringing prosecutions against alleged terrorists, which has markedly added to the workload of the court'.[4]

The Gardiner Commission also recommended the phasing out of detention (internment) and urged the government to: 'Find suitable sites on which to begin construction immediately of both the temporary cellular prison for 700 and the permanent prison for 400–500, for which plans have already been announced'.[5]

The site chosen for the new permanent prison was adjacent to the Long Kesh Internment Compound and would be renamed Her Majesty's Prison, the Maze. The new prison would be called H-Block by the inmates because each self-contained unit was in the shape of the letter H; the cross bar in the centre was the administrative section, the four wings on either side containing 25 cells that were 10 by 8 feet and intended to house one prisoner although, as convictions increased, often they housed two.

On a positive note the Gardiner Commission did recommend retaining that section of the 1973 Northern Ireland (Temporary Provisions) Act which abolished capital punishment for murder, but only because to reintroduce it would 'lead sections of the public to regard those executed as martyrs'.

In keeping with the newly announced policy of Ulsterisation, the

British army's 'law and order' role was to be phased out to the RUC and the part-time UDR with back-up provided by the British troops when needed (normalisation). In December 1975 Roy Mason, Secretary of State for Northern Ireland, announced that Special Category status would be ended on 1 March 1976 – anyone convicted of 'terrorist' crimes committed after that date would be treated as an ordinary criminal offender (criminalisation). To sweeten the directive ending Special Category status, Mason announced there would be a 50 per cent remission of all sentences, regardless of category, for those who were of good behaviour. At the time it was ended there were approximately 1,119 Special Category prisoners.

With the Diplock courts given a clean bill of health, new legislation allowing increased powers of arrest and time for interrogation, and new prison facilities being built, all was in place for what would become a conveyer belt system of internment by trial. The key to start the conveyor moving men and women through the process that led to Long Kesh (the Maze) and Armagh Women's Prison was provided by the new Castlereigh Detention Centre, a centralised facility for carrying out the most modern methods of interrogation, which was opened in mid-1976 by Kenneth Newman, RUC Chief Constable. On 26 July 1976, Newman issued a directive placing himself in command and control of those responsible for interrogation and issued new guidelines, the importance of which:

> Lay in the distinction ... made between an 'interview' – the result of which criminal charges were to be preferred – and an 'interrogation' conducted for the purpose of obtaining intelligence. The directive stipulated that the Judges Rules, the suspect's main safeguard from abuse during his [sic] detention in police custody, applied to an 'interview': it clearly implied, however, that Judges Rules did not apply to an 'interrogation'.[6]

The chorus of a ballad written by Frances Brolly, a school teacher who had been interned in Long Kesh (1973–5), sums up the response of those denied Special Category status:

> I'll wear no convict's uniform
> Nor meekly serve my time
> That Britain might brand Ireland's fight
> Eight hundred years of crime.

The first person sentenced under the new criminalisation policy was Kieran Nugent. He was convicted for hijacking a van and when taken to Long Kesh Prison on 15 September 1976, refused to put on a prison uniform, choosing to wrap himself in a blanket instead. For the next 42 months, until he was released, this is all he wore. Nugent's refusal to be branded a criminal and wear a prison uniform marked the beginning of what became known as the blanket protest and would eventually involve hundreds of other Republicans at Long Kesh. Women at Armagh had been allowed to wear their own clothing since 1972 and this did not change with the ending of Special Category status, although some 30 women began a limited no-work protest to support the blanketmen.

In order to break the blanket protest the men were locked in their cells 23 hours a day and for three days a month were confined for 24 hours in a completely bare cell. They were denied exercise, given no reading material, no radio, no compassionate leave and lost their remission. Toilet facilities consisted of a chamber pot in their cell which was emptied once a day by the trustees. The only rights the protesting prisoners were granted was one letter and one half-hour visit per month, although most of them refused to take the visit because to do so would require them to put on a prison uniform. Those that took the visit were subjected to degrading body searches which involved forcing them to squat naked over a mirror and be subjected to searches by guards who used their fingers to probe the anus and then the prisoner's mouth.

By mid-1977, Castlereagh was in full-scale operation. It was here that the majority of suspects were taken for the three to seven days of interrogation – during which time they were unable to contact either an attorney or a relative. The interrogation methods used by the Regional Crime Squad's 'heavy brigade' resulted in the signed confessions that provided the only evidence in over 60 per cent of the convictions handed out by the Diplock courts. From July 1976 through October 1979, 5,067 people were brought in for questioning at Castlereagh, of this number only 1,964 (39 per cent) were charged with an offence. (Gough Barracks, which opened in November 1977, had questioned 897 people by the end of October 1979; of that number only 197 (22 per cent) were charged with an offence.) The low ratio of those charged relative to the numbers interrogated is indicative of two features of the war against 'terrorism': (1) large numbers of people were brought in and subjected to 'interviews' in order to intimidate them as well as to gather intelligence; and (2) refusal to talk or sign a 'confession' while undergoing the brutal interrogation methods was regarded by those being questioned as a further act of resistance to British rule.

When a person was to be charged after interrogation at Castlereagh, they were taken to Townhall Street Police Station near Castlereagh city centre and signed over on a prisoner arrest form. Prisoners were given a medical examination at Townhall Station only when they requested one, a practice which changed when it became apparent to the police at Townhall that an increasing number of prisoners from Castlereagh showed evidence of injuries. As a result:

> Senior police officers at Townhall Street became concerned that they might be blamed for the injuries and were anxious to put themselves and their men in the clear. They discussed the problem with Dr [Robert] Irwin and their own superiors and, as a result, it was decided to offer a medical examination to every prisoner who arrived at Townhall Street from Castlereagh.[7]

Dr Irwin was one of several senior medical officers assigned by the Department of Health and Social Security to examine prisoners at various police facilities. He was also secretary of the Forensic Medical Officers Association (FMOA), and in early 1977 he began to observe from the condition of prisoners at Townhall and Crumlin Road Jail, Belfast, that there was an increase in the number of reported and confirmed assaults on prisoners during interrogation. Other police surgeons reported a similar trend.

On 22 April 1977 FMOA filed a complaint with the Police Authority based on their observations of injured remand prisoners. On 22 June Newman responded that these injuries were self-inflicted by the prisoners in an attempt to embarrass the RUC. (This prompted a slogan which began to appear on Derry housing estate walls, 'Help the police, beat yourself up.')

In July the police surgeons requested a formal meeting with Newman to discuss the situation; the request was denied. The doctors threatened to go public with their complaints, and Newman was forced to meet with them. As a result of this meeting Newman appointed RUC Deputy Chief Jack Hermon to head a liaison committee between the RUC and police surgeons to provide a conduit for police surgeon complaints. When Amnesty International conducted an investigation of alleged assaults during interrogation in NI (November–December

1977) the investigative team was denied access to the Hermon committee files.

When AI submitted their report to the government in May 1978, it stated that 'Amnesty International believes that maltreatment of suspected terrorists by the RUC has taken place with sufficient frequency to warrant the establishment of a public inquiry to investigate it.' The government asked AI to give the Department of Public Prosecution (DPP) the names of the 39 people AI said corroborated its charges so the DPP could look into the matter (30 of these cases had already been reported to the DPP for possible legal action). AI refused to turn over the names and insisted that the government hold a public inquiry into their charges. The government prevaricated, then set up the Bennett Committee to examine police procedures and practice during interrogation. It did not, however, call for an investigation of the cases cited by AI. Although theirs was not a public inquiry, the Bennett Committee investigation did confirm AI charges that maltreatment had taken place during interrogation.

Beginning in March 1978, the trustees in the H-Block started overturning chamber pots in the prisoners' cells. Prisoners were frequently beaten en route to their weekly shower. Their response was to refuse to take their showers and to empty their chamber pots out of the windows of their cells. The windows were boarded up, and the prisoners then resorted to smearing their faeces on the walls of their cells. Thus began 'the dirty protest' in H-Blocks 3, 4 and 5.

In May 1979 an election in the UK resulted in the Labour Party defeat by the Conservatives. Margaret Thatcher became the new prime minister. Five weeks earlier the INLA had assassinated the man who was slated to become the new Secretary of State in NI in the event of a Conservative Party victory. Airey Neave, Margaret Thatcher's political adviser and intimate friend, had stated that he favoured the return of capital punishment in NI combined with a new get-tough policy to defeat the INLA/IRA.

The H-Block/Armagh Committee was established in October 1979 to support the protesting prisoners' demand that they be granted the same privileges accorded to those who had Special Category status:

- The right to wear their own clothes.
- The right to refrain from penal work.
- The right to free association with other political prisoners.
- The right to organise their own educational and recreational facilities, and to receive one letter, visit and parcel a week.

● The restoration of the right to earn remission of sentence.

The H-Block/Armagh Committee was composed of a broad spectrum of left political groups, including the IRSP, Provisional Sinn Fein, Relatives Action Committee, People's Democracy, and trade unions. Its first chair was Father Piaras O'Dull; other prominent members were Miriam Daly, Bernadette Devlin McAliskey, Gerry Adams and Osgur Breatnach.

In February 1980, 30 women at Armagh Prison joined the 425 protesting prisoners in Long Kesh by engaging in their own 'no-wash, dirty protest' after several of them were beaten up during a cell search. The government and the prisoners were at loggerheads.

Between June 1980 and January 1981 there were several assassination attempts made on prominent Republicans. Five of the victims were current or former members of IRSP: Miriam Daly, Ronnie and Suzanne Bunting, Noel Little and Bernadette Devlin McAliskey. They were all shot by assailants who had broken into their homes. Suzanne survived, as did Bernadette and her husband Michael, who was also shot. The three others – Miriam, Ronnie and Noel – died as a result of their wounds.[8] This was a time of constant funerals. I began to feel as though I had no tears left to shed.

On 11 October 1980, the *Irish Times* printed the following communiqué issued by the INLA/IRA blanketmen:

We demand, as of right, political recognition and that we be accorded the status of political prisoners. We claim this right as captured combatants in the continuing struggle for national liberation and self-determination. We refute most strongly the term 'criminal' with which the British have attempted to label us and our struggle.

When the British government turned a deaf ear, the prisoners announced that a hunger strike would commence, to continue until their five demands were granted. On the morning of 27 October 1980, seven men refused their breakfast, one of whom was INLA volunteer Kevin Lynch. On 1 December, three women at Armagh Women's Prison also embarked on hunger strike. On the 53rd day of the protest, when Sean McKenna lapsed into a coma, the British government issued a statement that they were prepared to negotiate and grant certain concessions if the prisoners began taking food. Fearful that McKenna might die before negotiations were completed, the men went off hunger strike on 18 December and the women ended theirs the following morning.

That night Bernadette rang me, and with elation in her voice said, 'The prisoners have won!' To which I replied, 'We'll see Bernadette, we'll see.' To my sorrow, I was proven right. The Thatcher government reneged on its promise to negotiate so, on 1 March 1981, Bobby Sands began a second hunger strike. He was joined by Francis Hughes on 15 March, and Patsy O'Hara and Raymond McCreesh on 22 March.

Bobby Sands died on 5 May. Francis Hughes died on 12 May and Patsy O'Hara and Raymond McCreesh both died on 21 May. They were replaced by four others – Joe McDonnell, Brendan McLaughlin, Kieran Doherty and Kevin Lynch. Having already been on hunger-strike for 53 days during the previous protest, Kevin was under no delusion about what he faced in the days ahead: his body, denied food, would begin to feed upon itself.

A committee of the Irish Commission for Justice and Peace (ICJP) and Father Denis Faul, prison chaplain at Long Kesh, decided to intervene on behalf of the prisoners – an intervention which wasn't welcomed. The prisoners wanted no outside element to conduct negotiations for them; they wanted to deal with the British government though their own elected representatives who, like themselves, were protesting prisoners.

One member of the ICJP committee was Hugh Logue whom I hadn't seen since he briefly joined my sit-in at the British Consulate in Philadelphia. He was now a high ranking member of SDLP. The ICJP represented the Catholic hierarchy. Neither ICJP nor SDLP was considered sympathetic to prisoners as both the church and the SDLP had denounced the armed struggle and neither agreed with the social-ist viewpoint of the IRSP.

Both ICJP and Father Faul realised the weak link in the hunger strike lay in the prisoners' relatives. At a meeting, after eight young men had died, Father Faul told the relatives that the situation was 'hopeless' and described the hunger strikers' determination as 'lemming-mentality'. 'They [the hunger-strikers] must be helped', he said 'to help themselves by getting them off the hunger strike.' Shortly after this meeting, Mrs Eilis McDonnell, whose son Joe was one of the hunger strikers who had died, read a statement issued by the relatives which put the blame for these deaths squarely where it belonged – with the British government:

It is unknown in Irish history for eight young men to die on hunger strike for the principle of human dignity. We, the prisoners' wives, fathers, mothers, brothers and sisters ... find the British government guilty of the most callous cruelty and lack of responsibility, care and compassion in the present hunger strike crisis. We, the relatives, stand in full support of the protesting prisoners.

In the words of Mickey Devine, INLA volunteer from Derry, who was the last of the ten to die (20 August), going on hunger strike was the last resort of those who felt that every other attempt to call attention to their plight had failed. Just before embarking on his hunger strike Mickey wrote:

There is nothing that any human being values more than life. Every person clings to it with every ounce of strength of their being. To willingly surrender it is to acknowledge the greatest sacrifice anyone can make. Not only to die, but to choose a death which is slow and agonising, further serves to illustrate the depths of courage and sincerity among the men in the H-Blocks of Long Kesh. What it takes to willingly undergo this ordeal, willingly undergo suffering, none of us can possibly imagine ... [but] all we have to give is our lives.[9]

The Dublin government remained silent. Charles Haughey, the new leader of Fianna Fail and prime minister until 11 June, when his government was replaced by a Fine Gael/Labour Coalition, made promises to the sisters of Bobby Sands and Patsy O'Hara which he failed to keep. Garret FitzGerald, Haughey's successor, also turned his back on the problem. My sister, Teresa Moore, was a member of a delegation who met with FitzGerald in Dublin on 6 August. Teresa got down on her knees in front of him to beg him to exert pressure on the Thatcher government to negotiate a settlement. Muttering vague, empty phrases FitzGerald left the meeting and had the delegation forcibly ejected from his office when they began a sit-in.

Both Haughey and FitzGerald reflect what Frantz Fanon has described as the 'black skin, white mask' syndrome: the formerly colonised who attempt to prove their worth by adopting a harsher attitude towards dissent than the former colonial administrators.[10] When Bobby Sands was elected as MP to the British Parliament during his hunger strike, the British government let him die rather than seek a settlement with the prisoners. In the 11 June election in the RI, ten prisoners ran on a H-Block/Armagh ticket; two of them, hunger-strikers Kieran Doherty and Paddy Agnew, were elected TDs to Dail

Eireann. FitzGerald and Haughey stood by and let the two die thus proving they were twice as adamant as Thatcher. Haughey and Fitz-Gerald may have white faces but they wear Union Jack masks.

There are no words to describe the depth of despair I felt as each young man died. Each death was like that of one of my own children, especially those of Patsy O'Hara and Mickey Devine, whom I knew. Nor are there words of praise high enough for the determination of these young men, whose average age was 25. Although ten died, a total of 23 embarked on hunger strike before it ended on 3 October. The only one who went off voluntarily was Brendan McLaughlin because his ulcer made it impossible to continue. The other 22, including those who died, went without food for an average of 51 days; the longest was Kieran Doherty, who died after 73 days, the shortest was Jim Devine (no relation to Mickey), who was on hunger strike only 13 days before it ended. These young men captured the hearts of the vast majority of the nation and won the active support of a growing majority of previously silent people, north and south – people who were willing to risk gardai, RUC, UDR and British army harassment when they marched, leafletted, wore black arm-bands, flew black flags at the death of each hunger striker and attended the funerals in their tens of thousands.

The hunger strike was hardest on the families of those young men. Against their most deeply held instincts, they were willing to help their sons, brothers and husbands die in dignity by giving them their full support. But it is also understandable that some of them were unable to withstand the almost daily pressure exerted on them by Father Faul and their local parish priest to intervene to save the life of their loved ones. After five relatives had intervened, allowing nourishment to be given to their loved ones after they lapsed into a coma, it became easier for others to give notice they would do the same when the time came. This is what finally stopped the hunger strike.

In their press statement announcing the end of the hunger strike on 3 October 1981, the prisoners said: 'We, the protesting republican prisoners in the H-Blocks, being faced with the reality of sustained family intervention, are forced by this circumstance, over which we have no control at the moment, to end the hunger strike.'

The hunger strikers won all of their demands but one (restoration of remission lost during their protest). The government, however, held out for the ultimate public relations victory: the concessions were granted, but in such a piecemeal fashion that the fact the hunger strikers had won was overlooked.

After Patsy O'Hara died, his father was told that the family would be notified where to claim the body. At 4 am the RUC telephoned an IRSP member, Tommy McCourt, in Derry and said, 'If you want to collect this piece of garbage you better do so before daylight, otherwise we're going to drop it from a helicopter on the O'Hara doorstep.' Tommy contacted the local undertaker and they drove to the town of Omagh, 55 miles away, where they claimed Patsy's body. At some point between the time his parents left him in hospital and the time he was picked up some six hours later, Patsy's nose had been broken in two place. On his eyelids, face and body were nearly 50 burn marks which appeared to have been made by cigarettes.

Shannon Town Commissioner

In the autumn of 1981, the Shannon Town Alliance persuaded the Clare County Council to establish town boundaries for Shannon. As the IRSP representative on the Alliance I had argued forcefully that the boundaries should include the Shannon Industrial Estate. Predictably, the argument was lost when the County Council established boundaries that excluded this tax base; revenue collected from this source would remain under council control and it would continue to decide what portion Shannon would receive.

The IRSP campaigned actively against voter acceptance of the proposal arguing that failure to include the industrial estate meant we would continue to live in the 'Cinderella' town of County Clare. But the boundaries were accepted by a narrow margin based on a turnout of roughly 50 per cent of the eligible voters. The date of 10 March 1982 was established for the election of nine Town Commissioners and I decided to become a candidate.

Just as I had made my mind up to run it was announced that the Fine Gael/Labour coalition, after only six months in office, had received a vote of no-confidence over its proposed budget and a general election was scheduled for 18 February. Having served as the election agent for Tom McAllister, an IRSP prisoner at Long Kesh, who had run as an H-Block/Armagh candidate during the previous election, I recognised the value of the public forum provided by a Dail election, and so decided to become one of five IRSP candidates running in various constituencies.

My campaign was conducted on a shoestring budget during a whirlwind three weeks. Tom McDonagh, my election agent, and I located a headquarters overlooking the market square in Ennis, the Clare County seat. One advantage of being a candidate for Dail Eireann was to have free franking privileges which allowed us to mail our campaign brochure to every voter in the constituency. In line with IRSP policy I addressed Ireland's major economic and political issues in my campaign:

- *Economic crisis*: The RI had an unemployment rate of 16 per cent, almost no job creation and 20,000 new entrants into the job market each year. We called for full employment, the guarantee of a week's work or a week's pay, and nationalisation without compensation for firms threatening massive redundancies.
- *Foreign Debt*: Our foreign indebtedness was nearly US$9 billion (approximately £2,000 per capita), while multinational companies, banks and insurance companies were seeing their profits rise. We called for nationalisation of banks and financial companies, a massive injection of capital into the public sector, a price freeze on housing, food, clothing and public transportation.
- *Land and Fisheries*: Our policy of land ownership and the underdevelopment of our fishing industry had resulted in a disastrous waste of two of our greatest resources. We called for the establishment of a 200-mile fishing limit and a nationally owned fish processing industry, expansion of the fishing fleet, nationalisation of large estates with the establishment of farming cooperatives, and a minimum limit for private ownership of arable land.
- On the national question, we called for a united Ireland freed of British political and economic control.

We put together a small but dedicated group of volunteers who worked at least 15 hours a day addressing envelopes, putting up campaign posters and leafletting rallies in the various towns where I gave speeches. The most exciting period was when my sister Teresa, her husband Patsy Moore, and their oldest son Pearse, brought the Patsy O'Hara Memorial Flute Band from Derry for the last weekend before the election.

Patsy Moore had formed the band shortly after Patsy O'Hara's death and this was to be its first public appearance. For the two days they were available, we marched through nearly half the towns in the south of County Clare. They were magnificent as they marched, playing stirring traditional Irish tunes which brought people out of houses and shops to watch them pass by while volunteers handed out my campaign literature. Pearse acted as mentor to the band members (which included several of my nieces and nephews), dispensing first aid, ensuring they had plenty to eat, listening to their complaints of blisters and sore feet, and urging them to give their best performance in the next town, which they always did.

As expected, I lost the election, but the publicity I received helped my candidacy for the Shannon Town Commission election one month away. Fianna Fail won a majority of the seats in the Dail and Charles Haughey was elected the new head of government.

I was one of 22 candidates running for the nine seats on the Shannon Town Commission. The day of the vote count, two members of the Special Branch came into the hall and attempted to arrest Seamus Ruddy, my official observer at the count. I was on the other side of the room when they propelled Seamus out of the building but I managed to reach them before he was put into their car. As we were told later by those watching out the window, it was a comical sight as I attempted to stop his arrest – I had hold of one of Seamus's arms and the Special Branch person had the other and we both tried to pull Seamus in opposite directions. The Special Branch relented when I threatened to have the count called off because of their interference, but they let us know they would be waiting outside to arrest him when the count was finished.

I took the fourth seat on the Commission; the other eight were taken by five Fianna Fail candidates, two Fine Gael, and one Labour Party member. My first public act as a Shannon Town Commissioner was to help a wanted person escape the clutches of the law. Just before the count ended, I arranged for someone to be waiting with an automobile at a side entrance to the hall and we got Seamus out and away before the Special Branch knew what was happening.

On 23 March I received a call from Teresa telling me that Pearse and Terry Robson had been arrested in an early morning raid by the RUC and British army. Teresa also told me that Pearse's wife, Gabriel, who was expecting their third child, had been rushed to hospital where she was in labour. When I told Margie Bernard, who was staying at my house exploring the possibility of writing this book, she immediately offered to drive me to Derry.

When we arrived at Teresa and Patsy's house, they told us that Gabriel had given birth to a son, Michael, and that she wanted to come home from hospital. The doctor gaver her permission to sign herself out and Margie drove Teresa to Altnagelvin Hospital where they picked up Gabriel and her son, not yet 24 hours old, and brought them to Teresa's house. The following day, Gabriel took Michael to visit Pearse in Crumlin Road Jail in Belfast. Such is the stamina of, and support provided by, many wives. If not actively involved themselves, as many are, they suffer the hardship of having their husbands frequently in jail. Other women have had to leave their children in the care of husbands or relatives when they themselves have been jailed: several have given birth to their children in prison.[1]

Pearse and Terry Robson's arrest, and that of 20 others was solely on the word of a paid informer, Jackie Grimley, who claimed that they had been actively involved in INLA activities. This was Britain's latest 'internment by trial' ploy – using the testimony of paid informers who were given immunity or reduced sentences, promises of large sums of money, new identities and relocation in other countries, in exchange for naming names, many of which were provided by the RUC. By the end of 1982, over 300 people had been charged on the word of 25 informers, their word being the only evidence used to levy charges against those arrested. Only two people, one of whom was Sean Flynn, an IRSP member who was a Belfast City Councillor, were granted bail. All the others were held on remand awaiting massive show-trials in the one-judge Diplock courts.

Eleven of the 25 informers eventually retracted, resulting in the release of 83 people, although some of these were recharged under other informers. Of the 14 who did not retract, 5 were UVF, 6 were Provisional IRA and 3 were INLA members. Several of them, like Grimley, had been in the pay of the British army/RUC when they joined these organisations. Of the 22 named by Grimley, 12 were from Craigavon, County Armagh, and he alleged that he had sworn 8 of them into the INLA. The trial of Pearse and Terry Robson and the 20 others charged under Grimley was not scheduled to take place until the autumn of 1983; until then they would remain in jail.

My brother-in-law, Patsy Moore, had started another band, the Mickey Devine Memorial Flute Band. My nephew Patrick Collins, Eileen and Jim's second child, and his friend Stephen McConomy decided to become members even though neither knew how to play a note of music.[2] On 16 April, just after a practice session, Stephen was walking home when a British army patrol passed him in a saracen vehicle. Without warning, one of the soldiers fired a plastic bullet at Stephen, hitting him in the back of his head and taking away most of his skull. All Stephen was armed with was a tin whistle. He died three days later, the fourteenth victim of a plastic or rubber bullet since April 1972. Patrick was devastated by the sudden death of his 11 year-old friend, but the one most deeply affected was Patsy. Several years earlier Patsy, while attempting to quell a riotous situation, had been hit in the eye with a rubber bullet which had left him partially blind.

Rubber bullets had originally been used for riot control in NI but in 1973 were replaced by the more lethal plastic version. Both were banned from use in Britain.[3] The plastic bullet, a heavy PVC cylinder 4 inches by 1.5 inches, is fired at a velocity of about 160 mph and is supposed to be aimed at a person's leg or lower torso. The 14 who died had been struck either in the head or in the heart. Seven of the 14 were children ranging in age from 10 to 15. Like Patsy, many have been partially blinded; others have been totally blinded and still others permanently injured. In September the DPP stated the soldier who killed Stephen would not be charged with his death.

In December 1982, the RI Supreme Court granted an extradition request by the RUC for Dominic McGlinchey. It would be the first time in the history of the state that a Republican political activist was to be extradited to stand trial in NI. Under the 1965 Extradition Act, persons wanted in connection with a political offence committed in NI were granted immunity from extradition although they could be tried for the offence in the RI under the 1976 Criminal Law Jurisdiction Act, which grants joint jurisdiction between NI and RI for politically motivated offences.

McGlinchey, whom the RUC alleged was Chief of Staff of the INLA, was wanted in connection with the death of Hester McMullan in County Antrim, NI, in March 1977. McGlinchey fought the extradition request on the grounds that the RUC had offered no evidence connecting him with McMullen's death and that in reality they wanted him because of his political activities in NI. The RI Supreme Court, ignoring the no-evidence issue, ruled that it did not regard the offence McGlinchey was charged with as being politically motivated and ordered his extradition. McGlinchey resisted by going on the run.

The one joyous event of 1982, if not the decade, occurred in October. Leo and I were made grandparents when Stella and her husband Donal became parents of a son, Sean August Fean. For me, it felt like only yesterday that I had given birth to Stella.

The year of Stella's birth had coincided with the beginning of the 1956–62 IRA border campaign. As the eldest grandchild of my father and mother, she herself had become an activist in the effort to free Ireland from British rule. In December 1979, when she gave the commemoration address at the Derry gravesite of her friend, Colm McNutt, Stella summed up not only the reasons for Colm's involvement, but the meaning of the struggle for all of us – a united, socialist Ireland:

> Colm was nothing out of the ordinary as young men of eighteen go, except he was driven by an ideal which has been championed by others in former generations who placed the cause of freedom as the central aspect of their lives. Their dream and Colm's was the same, to break the connection with England by all and any means at their disposal because that cruel connection has robbed us of our nationhood, control of our political and economic affairs, and general social advancement as a people. Those who talk of peace do not seem to understand the reason for the present war. By peace they mean surrender to the forces of foreign aggression, the continuation of the profit-motive society, and the maintenance of a status quo which is riddled with contradictions that will again force young men and women into armed resistance. Those of us who have seen the inside of the interrogation centres, the jails, the H-Block, and walked behind our assassinated comrades know only too well that true peace can only be based on justice, and justice means national liberation and socialism. Towards that end we must reaffirm our personal pledges to that cause. To do otherwise would be to give our children, and their children's children the status of colonial slaves and second class natives in their own country. If we persist history will salute our efforts, for the age of colonialism is at an end and we can build a great new socialist future in which the horrors of this past ten years will be but a bitter memory.[4]

Epilogue

I am no longer a member of IRSP. I tendered my resignation in June 1985 when it became clear that the party was no longer committed to a broad-front strategy and had instead become a narrow Marxist-Leninist, politically sectarian organisation which had lost the socialist principles of James Connolly and Seamus Costello. As is sometimes the case, the younger generation is often quicker to make an accurate assessment than their battle-weary predecessors. Stella saw the hand-writing on the IRSP wall before I did and resigned in 1983. The party was in disarray; with few exceptions, the original founders were either dead, in jail or in exile, and there was an absence of leadership. IRSP involvement in the H-Block/Armagh committee during the hunger strike had sapped our energies and diverted us from party organisational matters. The paid-informers, Jackie Goodman, Jackie Grimley, Raymond Gilmour and Harry Kirkpatrick, had decimated the NI leadership of the IRSP and INLA, and allowed less politically principled members to come to the fore which in turn created internal friction and finally factional disputes. I began to suspect also that the organisations had been infiltrated by British intelligence.

Loath to confront the fact that another political party had fallen by the wayside and that once again I would have to search for a new one, I allowed myself to hope the situation would be resolved. In the year following the 1983 national convention, although I let it be known I was displeased with the IRSP's direction, I chose to focus on Shannon Town Commission matters. Then in 1984, I found myself again in the role of full-time mother when Leo and I assumed the guardianship of Dominic and Mary McGlinchey's two children, Declan, who was seven, and Dominic, who was six.

About a year after he went on the run to avoid extradition to NI, Dominic came to our house to ask if Leo and I would be willing to assume the care of his two sons. His wife Mary, also wanted by the authorities, had joined him on the run. To complicate matters, she was pregnant. The two boys had been staying in Dublin with friends but Dominic and Mary were looking for a better home for their children.

After talking it over with Leo, we agreed to take the two boys and they were brought to our house in February 1984. With only our teenage son Brian still at home, I now found much of my time once again taken up with supervising homework, packing school lunches, scheduling doctor and dentist appointments, arranging birthday parties, and all the other things that go with having two young children in the house. Leo and I developed a very great affection for the two boys and Leo supervised their chores and religious instruction as he had with his own children.[1]

A month after the boys came to live with us, Dominic came to see how they were getting on. He was staying at Newmarket-on-Fergus with three other men at the home of John and Marion Lyons. On St Patrick's morning they awoke to find the house surrounded by Special Branch and gardai. A shoot-out ensued and, fearful that members of the Lyons family might be injured or killed, Dominic and the three men surrendered after sending for a priest to guarantee their safety.[2]

That afternoon, McGlinchey's lawyers obtained an injunction to stay his extradition. None the less, on an appeal by Attorney General Peter Sutherland before a special sitting of the Supreme Court, Justice Tom O'Higgins signed the extradition order. McGlinchey was handed over to the RUC just before midnight.

McGlinchey's extradition to NI cleared the way for the RI to become a signatory to the 1977 European Convention on the Suppression of Terrorism. Previously the government had claimed that the extradition provision of the convention was repugnant to the RI constitution as defined by the 1965 Extradition Act.

McGlinchey was convicted for the murder of Hester McMullen based on nothing more than a fingerprint found on an automobile alleged to have been seen at the scene of the killing; the fingerprint had been 'found' on the car after his extradition. McGlinchey appealed his conviction and in December 1985 was acquitted. On Christmas Eve, he was re-extradited to the RI and ordered to stand trial for shooting at a gardai to avoid arrest on 17 March 1984. On 12 March 1986, McGlinchey was sentenced to serve ten years, with no right of appeal, and is currently at Portlaoise Prison. In July 1987, on an application by Bernadette Devlin McAliskey as to the legality of McGlinchey's detention, the RI Supreme Court ordered a judicial inquiry and granted him the right to apply for free legal aid to pursue the case.[3] In addition to being RI's first political extradition, Dominic may have a place in the Guinness Book of Records as the first re-extradition in world history.

In January 1985, five months after the birth of her daughter Marie, Mary McGlinchey surrendered herself to the gardai at Shannon. She was charged with being an accomplice to the kidnaping of the stepfather of Harry Kirkpatrick (one of the paid informers) and was granted bail. She took Declan and Dominic to live with her and Marie in Dundalk, County Louth, while awaiting trial, and in November Marie died of meningitis. Mary was acquitted at her trial but on 31 January 1987 she was assassinated when two masked men burst into her house and shot her in front of Declan and Dominic. Nothing can erase the devastation and the sorrow I feel for the two McGlinchey boys.

Other close friends and political comrades have died. The beginning of a new RUC shoot-to-kill policy was exposed when INLA members Seamus Grew and Roderick (Roddy) Carroll were killed by an undercover RUC unit, known as E4A, on 12 December 1982. They were shot after their car was stopped by the unit which opened fire on the two, who were unarmed, killing them instantly. RUC Constable John Robinson was charged with the murder of Grew but was acquitted. During the trial it was:

> Revealed he [Robinson] was ordered under the Official Secrets Act not to reveal the true facts of the shooting. The revelations at the trial left little doubt that the deaths of Grew and Carroll were the results of a well-planned shoot-to-kill operation in which the RUC special branch and British army were involved.[4]

In May 1984, John Stalker, Deputy Chief Constable, Greater Manchester, was appointed to investigate charges of the RUC shoot-to-kill policy. The Stalker Interim Report was presented to the DPP in NI in 1985 where it gathered dust. The report recommended that 11 or 12 RUC officers be prosecuted over the shooting of 6 people in County Armagh in 1982. It has been alleged that forensic tests showed that one of the victims had been shot through the back of the head while kneeling. In May 1986, shortly before Stalker was to go to NI to interview RUC Chief Constable, John Hermon and his deputy, Mr Michael McAtamney, Stalker found himself under investigation for charges of misconduct. He appealed a decision to dismiss him and won reinstatement in August 1986. It was alleged the charges against him were the result of a conspiracy to prevent his full report being completed. Colin Sampson, Chief Constable of the West Yorkshire police, was appointed to complete the investigation. When the Stalker/

Sampson Report was completed in 1988, the British Attorney General, Sir Patrick Mayhew, announced in the House of Commons that the report would not be made public. Although there was evidence of misconduct by members of the security forces, there would be no prosecutions as it would not be in the 'national interest'.[5]

Neil McMonagle, an IRSP member, was shot by SAS in Derry in February 1983 while he was babysitting for a relative.[6] In December 1984, I learned of the death of Mickey Montgomery. Mickey never fully regained his old sense of self following the psychological torture he was subjected to as one of the Hooded Men in 1971, and his early death at the age of 47 can be directly attributed to that experience. Seamus Ruddy, who had been living and teaching English in Paris for about a year, disappeared under mysterious circumstances in April 1985 and is presumed to be dead.

But the saddest death was that of my nephew Pearse Moore, who died while trying to rescue his son Michael from a fire at his home in Derry on 15 December 1985. My daughter Margaret and her two-year-old daughter, Bláithín, were visiting Pearse and his wife Gabriel for the weekend. Margaret said later that if she had taken her other daughter, Fionnuala, with her they would never have got out of the house. Gabriel and her two older children managed to escape with help from Pearse, as did Pearse's younger brother, Kevin. But instead of saving himself, Pearse stayed behind to look for his youngest son. They died in each other's arms underneath a window in an upstairs bedroom and were buried together in the same coffin. We are still waiting for an inquiry to be held into the causes of the early morning fire.[7]

Only two years earlier, in November 1983, Pearse, along with Terry Robson and other IRSP members charged on the word of the paid informer, Jackie Grimley, had been released from jail when the judge rejected Grimley's evidence. In throwing out the case, Lord Justice Gibson said of Grimley:

> He is a man who lived in a sort of half world between reality and charade. I think he is a man who has little or no propensity for the truth. His whole life is characterised by instability. Looking at the whole picture, one unavoidably comes to the conclusion that his evidence is such that one can place absolutely no reliance on it.[8]

Upon his release, Pearse stated at a press conference held in Derry:

> Justice was not done yesterday in court. It was just that Grimley had

embarrassed the whole system. If Justice Gibson had not taken a decision to throw the whole thing out, would the case have gone on, and would we have been convicted like the [35] people in the [Christopher] Black trial, the [10] people in the [Kevin] McGrady trial, or the [14] people in the [Joseph] Bennett trial? [9]

Pearse was right: he and Terry were fortunate, others were not. The paid informer trials resulted in over 100 convictions, although several have been reversed on appeal. The trial of those named by Raymond Gilmour, like that of Grimley, was also thrown out of court.[10] However, other cases continued. In December 1985, the uncorroborated testimony of Harry Kirkpatrick resulted in the conviction of 27 IRSP members. And Kirkpatrick continued to name names, including that of his sister, just as fast as his handlers could come up with them. In December 1986, however, all the people convicted under evidence supplied by Kirkpatrick were released on appeal.

Paid informers who give uncorroborated testimony about people who are then denied bail while waiting up to two years before their case is heard in mass show trials are Britain's latest judicial substitute for internment. Now that this solution is failing, with the reversal of convictions and adverse publicity, the government will have to find an alternative. One line of thought is that selective internment may be introduced simultaneously in NI and the RI.

Another nephew, Jim Collins, Eileen and Jim's oldest son, was denied compassionate leave from Crumlin Road Jail to attend Pearse and Michael's funeral. Jim is a talented artist, the painter of many of the wall murals in Derry. Also a skilled photographer, he helped form the Derry Visual Arts Collective. Jim was arrested for suspicion of being involved in a bombing incident in Derry and spent nearly 18 months in jail awaiting trial only to be released in January 1986 when the charges against him were dropped. Holding people in jail without bail is also internment by other means.

The RI attempts to misapply the law in order to jail Republican activists were brought back to public attention in 1983-4 by the Release Nicky Kelly Committee and the untiring efforts of Siobhan Troddyn and Independent TD Tony Gregory. In May 1980, Brian McNally and Osgur Breatnach won the appeal against their conviction for the Sallins train robbery. Learning of this, Nicky returned from the US and voluntarily surrendered himself at Shannon Airport on 4 June 1980. The Special Criminal Court ordered that he serve his sentence and denied him the right to appeal on the grounds that he had waited

beyond the legal limit to lodge an appeal, a finding which was upheld
by the Supreme Court in July 1981. Nicky then sought an appeal
hearing on his original conviction. This was also rejected by the
Criminal Court and upheld by the Supreme Court in October 1982.

On 1 May 1983, Nicky went on hunger strike. He ended it on 7 June
when his lawyers filed an appeal to the European Commission on
Human Rights, but the ECHR rejected the application because it was
lodged more than six months after the Supreme Court decision in
October 1982. On the day he ended his hunger strike, Michael
Noonan, Minister for Justice, told Nicky he was free to take civil court
action on his charges of mistreatment by the Heavy Gang during his
interrogation. Then, unexpectedly, Noonan released Nicky for
'humanitarian reasons' on 17 July 1984. Nicky is now trying to hold a
public inquiry into the Heavy Gang's interrogation methods –
methods which led to his signing a 'confession' to a crime he never
committed, for which he was convicted in his absence and of which, in
the eyes of the law, he is still regarded as guilty.

In May 1985 I sought the endorsement of the IRSP national committee
for my re-election to the Shannon Town Commission in June. Endorsement was denied. My outspoken criticism of party policy had earned
me the enmity of the leadership. I tendered my resignation, ran as an
Independent Republican Socialist and was re-elected to the
commission.

The manner in which I was, in effect, 'purged' from IRSP was all too
reminiscent of the tactics used by Official Sinn Fein to stifle internal
criticism at the beginning of the 1970s, although our criticism has
proven to have been valid. In 1977 Official Sinn Fein renamed itself
Sinn Fein: the Workers' Party. In 1982 the Sinn Fein designation was
dropped; today the party is known simply as the Workers' Party. It sees
multinationals in Ireland as desirable, rejects the armed struggle in NI,
bends over backwards to accommodate Loyalists, has failed to support
the hunger strikers' demands, has turned its back on its political
prisoners still in jail in NI and Britain, and supports the RI's EEC
membership.

Provisional Sinn Fein is now entitled to sole use of the name Sinn
Fein and the Provisional IRA is the only IRA. They have earned the
right to be regarded as the inheritors of the Republican tradition. In
the 1980s, Sinn Fein is in the throes of change. Its newer and younger
leadership, products of the current national liberation struggle and

their 'university years' in NI and British prisons, are moving the party in the direction taken by IRSP in 1974. Provisional Sinn Fein is reexamining its former unwillingness to work in broad coalitions, and socialism is no longer a dirty word. At their national party convention in 1986, Sinn Fein delegates, having already decided to allow their elected members to take their seats on local government bodies, voted to abolish their policy of parliamentary abstentionism.

In line with the declaration by Provisional Sinn Fein chair Gerry Adams that independence will only be won by a 'ballot in one hand and an armalite in the other', the Provisional IRA has proven itself effective in undermining the efforts of the RUC and British army to intimidate and subjugate the Nationalist population in NI. The biggest hurdle Provisional Sinn Fein/IRA faces is whether or not they will lose the support of conservative, anti-communist Irish-Americans if they declare fully for an Irish socialist republic. Clan-na-Gael abandoned Sinn Fein in the 1960s on that issue; the question is what its current US supporter, Irish Northern Aid (NORAID) will do if Provisional Sinn Fein/IRA becomes socialist.

The past twenty years have seen no solution to the dilemma of a divided Ireland. British troops are still stationed in NI; the death toll rises; the injuries increase; as some political prisoners are released from prison, others take their place. Although it appears to have initial staying power, the current attempt at a 'solution', the Anglo-Irish Agreement, is ultimately doomed to failure – no British-imposed solution will ever be accepted by the Nationalist majority in Ireland or, in NI, by Loyalists. The long anticipated US foreign aid, initially $250 million, authorised by the US Congress to support the Anglo-Irish Agreement will only make it easier for CIA-channelled money to be used for covert activities to forestall the long-feared possibility that Ireland might become England's Cuba.

The real stumbling block, however, is Britain's need to maintain its presence in Ireland for national security purposes, particularly those centring on the issue of nuclear defence.[11] When the RI was declared in 1947, the government refused to join NATO so long as the country remained partitioned and the RI continues to maintain its position of neutrality, however lukewarm it may be.

The US has long had an interest in the RI joining NATO because of its strategic location at the edge of Europe.[12] The cruise missiles sited in Britain are under US control and some twenty of them are said to be slated for NI. This cannot happen until political stability is achieved.

Unemployment is worsening on both sides of the border – 22 per cent in NI and nearing 20 per cent in the RI – and emigration is again reaching the high levels of the 1950s. If asked to choose between constitutional neutrality and defence-related jobs that would keep their sons and daughters at home, how would the citizens of the RI vote? If the RI abandoned its neutrality and became a NATO member, would Britain begin a phased withdrawal from NI? If this happens will the US pick up the gauntlet from the British as they did from the French in Vietnam? These are questions the future will answer.

Ireland may become a united country before the end of the century but the price demanded may be too high to pay for those of us who want a united socialist democratic republic. The 800-year struggle for Irish sovereignty and independence may be only just beginning.

Notes

Chapter 1: Forces of Occupation

1. Founded in County Armagh in 1795, the Orange Order is similar to the Ku Klux Klan. Both organisations attempt to preserve the supremacy of their members in their respective communities over those they regard as inferior. Both groups are racist and use fundamentalist religious justification to provide the rationale for their privileged position. The patron saint of the Orange Order is William of Orange, refered to familiarly as 'King Billy'. Its rhetoric is fiercely anti-Catholic and anti-Nationalist. Through its ties with the majority Unionist Party, which has controlled the Northern Ireland Parliament since the inception of the state, it wields great influence over discriminatory employment in the policies, civil service and Loyalist-controlled industries.

2. The law regarding the issuing of gun permits discriminates against Nationalists. At the time of the 'Rape of the Falls', Loyalists owned 80 per cent of the 104,000 licensed guns in Northern Ireland.

Chapter 2: The Name of Freedom

1.
POBLACHT NA H EIREANN

THE PROVISIONAL GOVERNMENT

of the

IRISH REPUBLIC

TO THE PEOPLE OF IRELAND

IRISHMEN AND IRISHWOMEN: In the name of God and of the dead generations from which she receives her old tradition of nationhood, Ireland, through us, summons her children to her flag and strikes for her freedom.

Having organised and trained her manhood through her secret revolutionary organisation, the Irish Republican Brotherhood, and through her open military organisations, the Irish Volunteers and the Irish Citizen Army, having patiently perfected her discipline, having resolutely waited for the right moment to reveal itself, she now seizes that moment, and supported by her exiled children in America, and by gallant allies in Europe, but relying in the first on her own strength, she strikes in full confidence of victory.

We declare the right of the people of Ireland to the ownership of Ireland, and to the unfettered control of Irish destinies, to be sovereign and indefeasible. The long usurpation of that right by a foreign people and government has not extinguished the right, nor can it ever be extinguished except by the destruction of the Irish people. In every generation the Irish people have asserted their right to national freedom and sovereignty: six times during the past three hundred years they have asserted it in arms. Standing on that fundamental right and again asserting it in arms in the face of the world, we hereby proclaim the Irish Republic as a Sovereign Independent State, and we pledge our lives and the lives of our comrades-in-arms to the cause of its freedom, of its welfare, and of its exaltation among the nations.

The Irish Republic is entitled to, and hereby claims, the allegiance of every Irishman and Irishwoman. The Republic guarantees religious and civil liberty, equal rights and equal opportunities to all its citizens, and declares its resolve to pursue the happiness and prosperity of the whole nation and of all its parts, cherishing all the children of the nation equally, and oblivious of the differences carefully fostered by an alien government, which have divided a minority from the majority in the past.

Until our arms have brought the opportune moment for the establishment of a permanent National Government, representatives of the whole people of Ireland and elected by the suffrages of all her men and and women, the Provisional Government, hereby constituted, will administer the civil and military affairs of the Republic in trust for the people.

We place the cause of the Irish Republic under the protection of the Most High God, Whose blessing we invoke upon our arms, and we pray that no one who serves that cause will dishonour it by cowardice, inhumanity, or rapine. In this supreme hour the Irish nation must, by its valour and discipline and by the readiness of its children to sacrifice themselves for the common good, prove itself worthy of the august destiny to which it is called.

Signed on Behalf of the Provisional Government,

THOMAS J. CLARKE,
SEAN MacDIARMADA,   THOMAS MacDONAGH,
P. H. PEARSE,   EAMONN CEANNT,
JAMES CONNOLLY,   JOSEPH PLUNKETT.

2. This was the name given off-licence premises. 'Because of discrimination, the liquor trade was one of the few avenues of advancement open to Catholics and most pubs, spirit groceries ... [and] many hotels were Catholic owned.' Michael Farrell, *Northern Ireland: The Orange State*, London, Pluto Press, 1976, p. 367.
3. Nationalists never refer to Derry as Londonderry. That name was given to the city after 1609 when James I encouraged large-scale development of the Province of Ulster by English and Scottish farmers, labourers and landlords who were mostly Calvinists and fiercely loyal to the English throne. James awarded County Coleraine and the town of Derry to the City of London to 'rebuild, enlarge and fortify' and the county and town were renamed Londonderry.
4. The 1798 Rebellion, led by the Society of United Irishmen with the financial and

military assistance of the French Directory, was an attempt to free Ireland from England. Founded in 1791, the United Irishmen is considered to be the first Irish Republican organisation. Under the leadership of Theobald Wolfe Tone, the United Irishmen were greatly influenced by the ideas of liberty, equality and fraternity expressed by the US and French Revolutions. Tone and several other leaders of the United Irishmen were middle-class Presbyterian and Anglican descendants of English and Scottish colonists who settled in the Province of Ulster. The 1798 Rebellion was ill-timed, poorly planned and ended in disaster, but its boldness has continued to provide inspiration for the rebellions that followed.

5. James Connolly was a socialist and labour leader. For a time Connolly lived in the US, where he was an organiser for the Industrial Workers of the World (Wobblies) and the Socialist Party. After his return to Ireland, Connolly founded the Irish Socialist Republican Party in 1896. That he distrusted the class interests of the IRB leadership is clear in his statement to the men and women in his Irish Citizen Army the week before the Easter Rising. Connolly told those assembled that there would definitely be a rising, and that the odds were a thousand to one against them. 'If we win, we'll be great heros: but if we lose we'll be the greatest scoundrels the country every produced.' He then enjoined his troops, 'In the event of victory, hold on to your rifles, as those with whom we are fighting may stop before our gaol is reached. We are out for economic as well as political liberty.' Samuel Levenson, *James Connolly*, London, Martin Brian & O'Keeffe, 1973, p. 292.

6. David Hogan, *The Four Glorious Years*, Dublin, Irish Press, 1953, p. 183.
7. Ibid., pp. 189–90.
8. Farrell put the number of British troops at 1,500 for a population of 40,780. (Farrell, *Northern Ireland: The Orange State*, p. 26.)
9. Eamonn McCann, *War and an Irish Town*, London, Pluto Press, 1980, p. 10.

Chapter 3: Number Six Union Street

1. For centuries the native Irish were denied the right to live inside the walled tow Derry. As a result they settled in the boglands just outside (on the 'bog side' of the walls), hence the name Bogside.
2. The Coyle's were the grandparents of Marion Coyle who, in October 1975, along with Eddie Gallagher, kidnapped Dr Tide Herrema, the managing director of Ferenka Limited, the subsidiary of a Dutch multinational. Coyle and Gallagher demanded as ransom the release of Dr Rose Dugdale, an English heiress, who had been sentenced to Limerick Jail for smuggling arms and explosives to Northern Ireland. Herrema was released unharmed and Coyle and Gallagher were sentenced to prison in the Republic of Ireland where the kidnapping occurred. Marion Coyle was released from Limerick Jail in 1985.
3. Republicans refer to Northern Ireland as the 'Six Counties'. The original Province of Ulster contained nine counties – Antrim, Armagh, Cavan, Coleraine (Derry), Donegal, Down, Fermanagh, Monaghan and Tyrone. When Ireland was partitioned in 1920, 6 of the 9 counties of Ulster were retained by England and renamed Northern Ireland. The other 3 counties – Cavan, Monaghan and Donegal – formed part of the 26-county Irish Free State. Thus Donegal, the northern most county in Ireland, is referred to as part of the south of Ireland.

Chapter 4: Eleven Plus

1. During the debate over the Northern Ireland Education Act, Captain Terence O'Neill gave his maiden speech in the Northern Ireland Parliament, speaking in favour of the legislation. As the irony of history would have it, O'Neill became Prime Minister for Northern Ireland (1963–9), only to have his government brought down by the articulate and well-educated Nationalist products of this legislation.

Chapter 5: Emigration, Marriage, Culture Shock

1. During the ten-year period 1951–61, 12.5 per cent of Derry's population emigrated – mainly Nationalists who went elsewhere seeking employment denied them in NI. In that same period the Republic of Ireland lost 81,800 people to other countries.
2. A West Brit is an Irish citizen who identifies with England rather than Ireland. These people generally reside in the Dublin area which is west of England – hence a 'West Brit'.

Chapter 6: Clan-na-Gael

1. Major John MacBride was one of those executed for his part in the 1916 Easter Rebellion. He was married to Maude Gonne with whom W.B. Yeats was once in love. The MacBrides had one son, the late Sean, a winner of the Nobel Peace Prize and one of the founders of Amnesty International.
2. Commodore John Barry was the founder of the US Navy.
3. *United Irishman*, July 1962.

Chapter 7: Transitions

1. Peter Berresford Ellis (ed.), *James Connolly: Selected Writings*, London, Pluto Press, 1988, p. 37.
2. Patrick Marrinan, *Paisley: Man of Wrath*, Tralee, Anvil Books, 1973, p. 142.

Chapter 8: The Town I Love So Well

1. Every reference to the numbers that attended the march that day give the figure of 2,000 – except Eamonn McCann, one of the march organisers. Brigid agrees with McCann that the number was around 400 and even that may be too high. The 2,000 seems to include everyone who wishes they had been there or later claimed they were!
2. This film was later confiscated by the Special Branch from Brigid's home in Limerick and never returned to her.
3. When Westminster introduced the universal franchise in 1946, NI opted in favour of its own Representation of the People Act. This legislation limited voting rights to those who either owned their own home or lived in public housing; the vote was denied to people who rented. In addition, directors of limited corporations were granted extra votes based on the amount of rates (taxes) they paid, which in some instances amounted to six extra votes per company. This legislation effectively disenfranchised large numbers of Nationalists who neither owned property nor, due to discrimination and lack of new construction, were allocated public housing units. What voting restrictions failed to achieve, gerrymandered election wards copper-fastened. Thus in 1966, 28 per cent of the potential Nationalist voters in Derry were ineligible as compared to only 15 per cent of Loyalists. Based on their numbers (66 per cent of the population), Nationalists had the potential to control 13 of the 20 seats on the Derry Corporation, instead they had only 8 elected representatives. The

odds were so overwhelmingly stacked against them that in many elections Nationalists didn't bother contesting them.

Chapter 9: Battle of the Bogside

1. Farrell, *Northern Ireland: The Orange State*, pp. 250–1.
2. Levenson, *James Connolly*, pp. 209–10.
3. What Goulding neglected to tell us was that the Official IRA had also received
   money from the Irish government. In an excellent series of articles written about the
   period, Vincent Browne states, '... there is a lot of evidence to show that whatever
   was going at the time, in terms of money and guns, went to the Officials as well as to
   those who later became Provisionals' (Vincent Brown, *Magill*, May 1980, p.40). Also
   see his articles in the June and July 1980 issues of *Magill*.

Chapter 11: Internment

1. *Ballad For Martin O'Leary* – Anonymous

   As time goes by and years roll onward
   Deep in my memory I will keep
   Of a dark July morning
   When all Cork City was asleep.

   A band of gallant Irish soldiers
   To Mogul Mines they made their way
   To strike a blow against the boss class
   Who exploit the wealth beneath our clay.

   So rally all you Irish workers
   The wealth of Ireland is your right
   The foreign interests shall exploit you
   Unless like Martin we all fight.

   The miners down in Tipperary
   A hard and bitter struggle waged
   Against the foreign mine owners
   And the anger of the native slave.

   Solidarity was their slogan
   Determination was their mood
   While poverty and deprivation
   O'er their families loomed.

   A member of the raiding party
   Before the dawn fought for his life
   For injured he was while in action
   Upholding Irish workers rights.

   The Free State vultures standing o'er him
   A cell and trial their concern

But God above knew he had plans for Martin
In that glorious spot he had reserved.

2. Incident and name of SDLP member related to Brigid and the author by the former OC of the Derry IRA. To identify the IRA source could result in a potential jail sentence of five to seven years for that person on the charge of membership in an illegal organisation.
3. John McGuffin, *Internment*, Tralee, Anvil Books, 1973, pp. 124–5.

Chapter 12: Even the Skies Wept

1. Raymond McClean, *The Road to Bloody Sunday*, Dublin, Ward River Pres pp. 130–2.
2. NICRA, *Massacre at Derry*, Belfast, 1972, pp. 8–9.
3. McClean, *Road to Bloody Sunday*, p. 142.
4. For a scathing attack on the Widgery Report see Samuel Dash, *Justice Denied*, New York, International League for the Rights of Man, 1972. Dash was the Democratic Majority Chief Counsel for the US Senate Watergate Committee which investigated the President Richard M. Nixon Administration following the break-in at the Democratic National Committee Offices on 17 June 1972.

Chapter 13: Green, Orange and Whitelaw

1. Ellis, *James Connolly*, p. 145.

Chapter 14: Bullets and Ballot Boxes

1. Quoted in Kevin Kelley, *The Longest War: Northern Ireland and the IRA*, London, Zed Press, 1982, p. 169.

Chapter 15: Treacherous Comrades

1. In Ireland it is permissible to hold more than one seat simultaneously. Thus a person can be a member of a Town Commission or Urban District Council and a member of Dail Eireann at one and the same time. Over 60 per cent of Dial Eireann members hold more than one elected office (1986). There is no requirement that a candidate for an office must live in the constituency.
2. Ronnie Bunting was the son of Major Ronald Bunting, Ian Paisley's right-hand man in the early days of the civil rights movement. As a Protestant who had 'defected' to the Republican/Nationalist cause, Ronnie was regarded by Loyalists as a traitor.
3. This incident was related to Brigid and the author by the person who confronted the member of the GHQ.
4. See Appendix II for the IRSP Manifesto.
5. *Take It Down From The Mast* — Traditional

   Take it down from the mast Irish traitors
   It's the flag we Republicans love
   It can never belong to Free Staters
   You have brought on it nothing but shame.

You have murdered our young Liam and Rory
You have butchered our Richard and Joe
On your hands our blood is still flowing
For you fill in the work of the foe.

Leave it to those who are willing
To uphold it in war and in peace
We're the men who intend to defend it
Until England's tyranny cease.

For we stand with Enright and Larkin
With Daly and Sullivan bold
We'll break down the English connection
And bring back the nation you sold.

6. Patsy McCardle, *The Secret War,* Cork, The Mercier Press 1984, p. 41.
7. Kelley, *The Longest War,* p. 215.

Chapter 16: The Heavy Gang

1. According to Tim Pat Coogan: 'O'Dalaigh took [Donnegan's statement] as a clear implication that the minister [was probably] voicing the cabinet's opinion ... that the President did not stand behind the state. He felt Donnegan's statement ... was an open affront to the dignity of the office of President in whom the constitution vests the supreme control of the defence forces ... Accordingly, following the utterance of Donnegan's statement in the presence of an army audience, O'Dalaigh felt that he had no way of preserving the dignity of the presidency save to resign.' (Tim Pat Coogan, *The I.R.A.*, London, Fontana Books, 1980, p. 529.)
2. For a full exposure of CIA involvement in Chile see John Dinges and Saul Landau, *Assassination on Embassy Row,* New York, McGraw-Hill Book Company 1981.

Chapter 17: Seamus is Dead

1. Quoted in *The Starry Plough*, December 1984.

Chapter 18: Justice Denied

1. Eamonn McCann, *War and an Irish Town,* London, Pluto Press, 1980, pp. 161–2.
2. United Nation Declaration Against Torture states in Article 9: 'Whenever there is reasonable grounds to believe that an act of torture as defined in Article 1 has been committed, the competent authorities of the State shall promptly proceed to an impartial investigation even if no formal complaint has been made.' Article 1 defines torture as: 'Any act by which severe pain or suffering, whether physical or mental is intentionally inflicted by or at the instigation of a public official on a person for such purpose as obtaining from him [sic] or a third person, information or confession, punishing him for an act he had committed or is suspected of having committed or intimidated him or other persons.'
3. *Amnesty International Report 1978,* London, Amnesty International Publications, 1979, p. 220.

4. Article 3 of the European Convention on Human Rights states: 'No on subjected to torture or to inhumane or degrading treatment, or punishment.'
5. Derek Dunne and Gene Kerrigan, *Round Up The Usual Suspects*, Dublin, Magill Publications, 1984, p. 201.
6. US Congress, Committee on the Judiciary, *Northern Ireland: A Role for the United States?*, Washington, US Government Printing Office, 1979, p. v.
7. Number of people picked up for questioning under Section 30, Offences Against the State Act:

1972	229
1973	271
1974	602
1975	607
1976	1,015
1977	1,144
1978	912
1979	1,431
1980	1,874
1981	2,303
1982	2,308
1983	2,234
1984	2,216

Chapter 19: Hunger For Justice

1. A fry consists of pan-fried bacon, sausage, eggs, tomatoes, potatoes and black pudding.
2. Report of the Commission to consider Legal Procedures to Deal with Terrorist Activities in Northern Ireland (Diplock Report), London, HMSO, 1972, p. 1.
3. Bobby Sands and three others were sentenced to 14 years each for possession of the same, one and only, handgun found in a car they were travelling in together.
4. Report of a Committee to Consider in the Context of Civil Liberties and Civil Rights, Measures to Deal with Terrorism in Northern Ireland (Gardiner Report), London, HMSO, 1975, pp. 53–4.
5. Ibid., p. 54.
6. Peter Taylor, *Beating the Terrorists?*, Harmondsworth, Penguin Books, 1980, p. 68.
7. Ibid., p. 151.
8. Bernadette Devlin McAliskey and her husband Michael were shot in front of their young children by members of the UDA who were convicted of the shooting in 1982. Bernadette and Michael survived only because a British army patrol had their house under surveillance and called in a helicopter to take them to hospital when the patrol found they were still alive. One wonders how the patrol missed seeing the UDA enter the house. Ronnie and Suzanne Bunting and Noel Little were shot in front of the Bunting children. A few weeks earlier Ronnie had been picked up and held for several hours by the RUC who told him there was a bullet waiting for him. Miriam Daly was also shot in front of her children in the hallway of her home in Belfast. The killers of Ronnie, Noel and Miriam have never been apprehended but they are presumed to be Loyalist paramilitaries.

9. *The Starry Plough*, June 1981.
10. Frantz Fanon, *Black Skin, White Masks*, London, Pluto Press, 1986. Also see Fanon's *The Wretched of the Earth* which describes neo-colonisation and provides insights into the reaction to events in NI by the Dublin government.

Chapter 20: Shannon Town Commissioner

1. In June 1984 Jacqueline Moore from Derry gave birth to a daughter, Dominique, while in Armagh Women's Prison where she was held awaiting trial. Jacqueline's mother Anna was also in Armagh Prison awaiting trial — three generations of Irish females serving time together, a historic first. Like her mother and grandmother, Dominique was constantly strip searched. This was done before and after her mother took her out into the exercise yard for a bit of fresh air — as often as 26 times a week. According to a NI Office spokesperson, 'In the interests of security, the baby is given a light rub-down search' (*Irish Press*, 26 July 1984).
2. The author gave Stephen and Patrick her tin whistle in March 1982. Delighted they went away and the next day came back, having each learned to play one tune. Stephen, as I recall him from an afternoon spent talking with him and Patrick at Mrs Sheil's home, was a very quiet, shy, polite and well-mannered young man.
3. *They Shoot Children*, London, Information on Ireland, 1982.
4. *The Starry Plough*, February 1980.

Epilogue

1. When I arrived at Brigid's and Leo's house in the Summer of 1984 to finish the writing of this book, I found Brigid's time considerably limited due to her care of the newest members of the household. I was even enlisted in helping Declan and Dominic with their homework on several occasions. There was a constant stream of the two boys' new friends for whom Brigid made popcorn daily — not to mention the story telling sessions in which she told them of the latest adventures of her invented characters the Chrushee Men! [M.B.]
2. John Lyons, who was out of the country at the time of McGlinchey's capture, was sentenced to 6 months at Portlaoise Prison for harbouring a fugitive.
3. *Irish Echo*, 8 August 1987.
4. Patsy McArdle, *The Secret War*, Cork, Mercier Press, 1984, p. 48.
5. For John Stalker's account of this see his book, *The Stalker Affair*, New York, Viking Penguin, 1988. Also see (under the same title), Frank Doherty, *The Stalker Affair*, Cork, The Mercier Press, 1986.
6. Doherty, *The Stalker Affair*, p. 27.
7. Having been the person who had brought Michael home from hospital when he was less than twenty-four hours old, I was devastated to learn of his tragic death. Only a few months earlier I had spent some time with Pearse and his family and took delight in their obvious care for one another and the great good humour I experienced in their company. I attended the funeral in Derry and although Pearse's father had gone to the RUC station to assure them that this was not to be a Republican funeral, the funeral procession was lined every step of the way with British soldiers and RUC who trained their guns on us. We were also followed by armoured vehicles and helicopters hovered overhead. At the graveside the noise of the helicopters completely drowned out the sound of the ceremony. [M.B.]

8. *Irish News*, 24 November 1983.
9. *Irish News*, 25 November 1983. As a born-again Christian, Kevin McGrady is the only paid-informer who can legitimately be regarded as a 'converted' terrorist, the euphemism the British use for these informers. McGrady was associated with 'Youth With a Mission' in Amsterdam and one of his spiritual advisers was a US citizen, Floyd McClung. During a prayer session with McClung and another person, McGrady was urged to return to NI and make a full confession of all his crimes, which he did. After a session at Castlereagh Interrogation Centre, he started naming names. Youth With a Mission was alleged during the McGrady informer trial to be a CIA front. Andrew Boyd, *The Informers,* Cork, The Mercier Press, 1984, p. 55.
10. For a moving account of how the Gilmour trial affected the Derry community see, 'The Accusing Finger of Raymond Gilmour' in Nell McCafferty, *The Best of Nell,* Dublin, Attic Press, 1985, pp. 102–14.
11. A British cabinet memo drafted in 1947 suggested that NI was so important to Britain's defence that it should not be allowed to leave the UK even if the majority there wanted to do so. The RI is a partner in the telecommunications satellite programme which can just as readily be used for military as civilian use and some hold the belief it is already linked into the NATO system.
12. For an in-depth look at how the US government has viewed RI neutrality see Sean Cronin, *Washington's Irish Policy, 1916–1986: Independence, Partition, Neutrality,* St Paul, Irish Books and Media, 1987.

Appendix I
The Catholic Church

The Church of Rome is not without historic blood on its hands due to its political intervention in the affairs of the Irish nation. This intervention originated with the *Bull Laudabiliter* issued by Pope Adrian IV which authorised the conquest of Ireland by England and paved the way for the first Anglo-Norman invasion of Ireland in 1169 by mercenaries loyal to Henry II. In exchange for this support Henry's task was to convince the non-conforming Irish bishops to abandon Irish Brehon Law and accept Roman Canon Law as legal authority, an endeavour in which Henry was successful. In the bargain Henry also obtained the bishop's pledge of loyalty to the English throne. When the Irish rebelled against this pledge, they were excommunicated by Pope Alexander III who in 1177 denied Irish rebels the right of sanctuary in church buildings.

In 1319, Irish chieftains invited Edward Bruce, brother of Robert the Bruce of Scotland, to help them in a war of independence and, in a joint effort, Irish and Scottish troops drove the English out of the Provinces of Ulster and Connaught. For this act of resistance against England, Pope John XXI ordered the Irish rebels excommunicated.

The Battle of the Boyne (1 July 1690 — 12 July in the new calendar), is regarded by Loyalists as their sacred national holiday. William of Orange led this battle in Ireland (where James II chose to make his stand to regain his throne), and defeated the forces loyal to James. But as history shows, the Pope sided with Protestant William against Catholic James as the result of:

> ... an alliance formed by Pope Innocent XI with William, Prince of Orange, against Louis, King of France. [When] King James of England joined with King Louis to obtain help to save his own throne ... the Pope joined in league with William to curb the power of France. When news of the defeat of the Irish [and James] at the Boyne reached Rome the Vatican was illuminated by order of the new Pope, Alexander VIII, and special masses were offered up in thanksgiving. (Berresford Ellis, editor, *Selected Writings of James Connolly*, p. 61)

However, kings can be as fickle as lovers in their loyalties. When King Henry VIII was denied by church doctrine the right to divorce Catherine of Aragon so he could marry Anne Boleyn, he forgot his debts to Rome and established the Church of England, which denied the supreme authority of the Pope. Henry not only declared himself to be head of both church and state in England, but in 1541 declared himself King of Ireland as well. This arbitrary act resulted in a new alliance between Irish Catholics, who continued to resist the authority of the English monarchy, and Irish Protestants, who dissented from the authority of the Church of England. When this alliance resulted in the 1798 Rebellion, led by

181

Wolfe Tone, which sought to establish an Irish Republic, the hierarchy of the Catholic Church in Ireland called upon its adherents to retain their loyalty to the British government.

In this same vein, the Irish bishops also supported the Act of Union with England in 1801 (which abolished the Irish Parliament), denounced the Home Rule Movement formed in 1870, condemned the 1916 Easter Rising and excommunicated members of the IRA during the Irish War of Independence in 1919. Then, in exchange for assurances that there would be no state interference with the requirement that Catholic children attend parochial schools, the church remained silent about discrimination and civil rights abuses by the Loyalist-controlled government in NI.

Appendix II
IRSP: The Way Forward

The Irish Republican Socialist Party was formed at a meeting held in Dublin on Sunday, 8 December 1974. The inaugural meeting was attended by approximately 80 delegates from Belfast, Armagh, Co. Derry, Derry City, Donegal, Wicklow, Cork, Clare, Dublin, Limerick and Tipperary.

It was unanimously agreed that the object of the party would be to 'End Imperialist Rule in Ireland and Establish a 32 County Democratic Socialist Republic, with the Working Class in control of the Means of Production, Distribution and Exchange'. To this end, it was agreed that the party would launch a vigorous campaign of political agitation and education, North and South, on the following issues:

Six Counties

1. Recognising that British Imperialist interference in Ireland constitutes the most immediate obstacle confronting the Irish people in their struggle for Democracy, National Liberation and Socialism, it shall be the policy of the IRSP to seek the formation of a broad front on the basis of the following demands.
   (a) That Britain must immediately renounce all claims to Sovereignty over any part of Ireland and its coastal waters and should immediately specify an early date for the total withdrawal of her military and political presence from Ireland.
   (b) Having specified the date for her total withdrawal from Ireland, Britain must immediately withdraw all troops to barracks; release all internees and sentenced political prisoners; grant a general amnesty for all offences arising from the military campaign against British Forces, or through involvement in the Civil Disobedience Campaign; abolish all represive legislation; grant a Bill of Rights, which will allow complete freedom of political action and outlaw all discrimination whether it be on the basis of class, creed, political opinion or sex. Britain must also agree to compensate the Irish people for the exploitation which has already occurred
   (c) It shall be the policy of the IRSP to seek an active working alliance of all radical forces, within the context of the Broad Front, in order to ensure the ultimate success of the Irish Working Class in their struggle for Socialism.
   (d) It will be an immediate objective of the party to launch an intensive campaign of opposition to EEC membership. We therefore, intend to play an active part in the EEC Referendum in the 6 county area and through our support groups in Britain.

(e) Recognising that sectarianism and the present campaign of sectarian assassinations arises as a result of British manipulation of the most reactionary elements of Irish society; we shall seek to end this campaign on the basis of united action by the Catholic and Protestant working class against British Imperialism in Ireland.

26 Counties

1. The IRSP shall seek to have an organised United Campaign of all democratic forces against repressive legislation in the South and against the policy of blatant collaboration with British Imperialism, which is now being pursued by the 26 County administration.
2. The IRSP is totally opposed to the exploitation of our natural resources by multinational corporations. It is, therefore, the policy of the party to give active and sustained support to the present campaign for the nationalisation of the resources.
3. Recognising that the rapidly increasing cost of living and rising unemployment are to a large extent a direct result of our EEC membership; it shall be the policy of the IRSP to actively support the formation of people's organisations to combat rising prices and unemployment.

Select Bibliography

Books

J. Bowyer Bell, *The Secret Army: The I.R.A. 1916–1979*, Cambridge: MIT Press, 1983.

Andrew Boyd, *The Informers: A Chilling Account of the Supergrasses in Northern Ireland*, Cork: Mercier Press, 1984.

Charles Carlton, *Bigotry and Blood: Documents on the Ulster Troubles*, Chicago: Nelson Hall, 1977.

Tom Collins, *The Centre Cannot Hold*, Dublin: Bookworks, 1983.

——*The Irish Hunger Strike*, Dublin: White Island Book Company, 1986.

Tim Pat Coogan, *On the Blanket: The H-Block Story*, Dublin: Ward River Press, 1980.

——*The I.R.A.*, London: Fontana Books, 1980.

Sean Cronin, *Irish Nationalism: A History of Its Roots and Ideology*, London: Pluto Press, 1983.

——*Washington's Irish Policy, 1916–1986: Independence, Partition, Neutrality*, St Paul: Irish Books and Media, 1987.

Raymond Crotty, *Ireland in Crisis: A Study in Capitalist Colonial Undevelopment*, Dingle: Brandon Book Publishers, 1986.

Liz Curtis, *Nothing but the Same Old Story: Roots of Anti-Irish Racism*, London: Information on Ireland, 1984.

——*The Propaganda War*, London: Pluto Press, 1984.

George Dangerfield, *The Damnable Question: One Hundred Years of Anglo-Irish Conflict*, Boston: Little, Brown & Company, 1976.

Bernadette Devlin, *The Price of My Soul*. London: André Deutsch, 1969.

Frank Doherty, *The Stalker Affair*, Cork: The Mercier Press, 1986.

Ruth Dudley Edwards, *An Atlas of Irish History*, London: Methuen & Company, 1981.

Derek Dunne and Gene Kerrigan, *Round Up the Usual Suspects*, Dublin: Magill Publishers, 1984.

P. Berresford Ellis, editor, *James Connolly: Selected Writings*, London: Pluto Press, 1988.

Roger Faligot, *Britain's Military Strategy in Ireland: The Kitson Experiment*, London: Zed Press.

Frantz Fanon, *Black Skin, White Masks*, London: Pluto Press, 1986.

——*The Wretched of the Earth*, New York: Grove Press, 1963.

Michael Farrell, *Northern Ireland: The Orange State*, London: Pluto Press, 1976.

Eric Gallagher and Stanley Worrall, *Christians in Ulster 1968–1980*, Oxford University Press, 1982.

Thomas Gallagher, *Paddy's Lament: Ireland 1846–1847*, New York: Harcourt, Brace, Jovanovich, 1987.

C. Desmond Greaves, *Liam Mellows and the Irish Revolution*, London: Lawrence & Wishart, 1971.

——*The Life and Times of James Connolly,* London: Lawrence & Wishart, 1976.

Max Hastings, *Barricades in Belfast,* New York: Taplinger Publishing Company, 1970.

Edward S. Herman, *The Real Terror Network: Terrorism in Fact and Propaganda,* Boston: South End Press, 1982.

'David Hogan' (pseudonym for Frank Gallagher), *The Four Glorious Years,* Dublin: Irish Press, 1953.

Jack Holland, *Too Long a Sacrifice,* Harmondsworth: Penguin Books, 1983.

——*The American Connection: U.S. Guns, Money, & Influence in Northern Ireland,* New York: Viking, 1987.

Joe Joyce and Peter Murtagh, *Blind Justice,* Swords: Poolbeg Press, 1984.

Robert Kee, *The Green Flag: A History of Irish Nationalism,* London: Weidenfield & Nicolson, 1972.

Kevin Kelley, *The Longest War: Northern Ireland and the IRA,* London: Zed Press, 1982.

Patsy McArdle, *The Secret War,* Cork: Mercier Press, 1984.

Eamonn McCann, *War and an Irish Town,* London: Pluto Press, 1980.

Nell McCafferty, *The Best of Nell,* Dublin: Attic Press, 1984.

Raymond McClean, *The Road to Bloody Sunday,* Dublin: Ward River Press, 1983.

John McGuffin, *Internment,* Tralee: Anvil Books, 1973.

——*The Guineapigs,* Harmondsworth: Penguin Books, 1974.

Patrick Marrinan, *Paisley: Man of Wrath,* Tralee: Anvil Books, 1973.

Ernie O'Malley, *On Another Man's Wounds,* Dublin: Anvil Books, 1979.

——*The Singing Flame,* Dublin: Anvil Books, 1978.

John Stalker, *The Stalker Affair,* New York: Viking Penguin, 1988.

Sunday Times (Insight Team), *Ulster,* Harmondsworth: Penguin Books, 1973.

Peter Taylor, *Beating the Terrorists?,* Harmondsworth: Penguin Books, 1980.

Government Publications

Republic of Ireland Parliament. *O'Briain Report*, Report of the Committee to Recommend Certain Safeguards for Persons in Custody and for Members of An Garda Siochana, Dublin: Stationery Office, 1978.

United Kingdom Parliament. *Bennett Report*, Report of the Committee of Enquiry into Police Interrogation Procedures in Northern Ireland, London: HMSO, 1979.

——*Compton Report*, Report of the Enquiry into Allegations Against the Security Forces of Physical Brutality in Northern Ireland Arising Out of Events on 9 August 1971, London: HMSO, 1971.

——*Diplock Report*, Report of the Commission to Consider Legal Procedures to Deal with Terrorist Activities in Northern Ireland, London: HMSO, 1972.

——*Gardiner Report*, Report of a Committee to Consider in the Context of Civil Liberties and Civil Rights, Measures to Deal with Terrorism in Northern Ireland, London: HMSO, 1975.

——*Widgery Report*, Report of the Tribunal Appointed to Enquire into the Events on Sunday, 30th January 1972 which Led to Loss of Life in Connection with the Procession in Londonderry on the Day, London: HMSO, 1972.

United States Congress. Committee on Foreign Affairs, *Northern Ireland Hearings before the Subcommittee on Europe,* Washington: US Government Printing Office, 1972.

———Committee on the Judiciary, Subcommittee on Immigration, Citizenship and International Law, *Northern Ireland: A Role for the United States?*, Washington: US Government Printing Office, 1979.

Magazines

Magill, Vincent Browne, 'Arms Crisis 1970', May 1980.
———Vincent Browne, 'The Barry File', June 1980.
———Vincent Browne, 'The Misconduct of the Arms Trial', July 1980.

Reports and Pamphlets

Amnesty International, *Report of an Amnesty International Mission to Northern Ireland,* London: Amnesty International Publications (AIP), 1977.
———*Report of an Amnesty International Mission to the Republic of Ireland,* London: AIP, 1977.
———*Amnesty International Report 1978,* London: AIP, 1979.
Information on Ireland, *They Shoot Children: The Use of Rubber and Plastic Bullets in the North of Ireland,* London, 1982.
Investor Responsibility Research Center, *U.S. Companies and Fair Employment Practices in Northern Ireland,* Washington, 1988.
Irish Republican Socialist Party, *Framed Through the Special Criminal Court,* Dublin: Starry Plough Publications, 1979.
Northern Ireland Civil Rights Association, *Massacre at Derry,* Belfast, 1972.

Newspapers

An Phoblacht (Provisional Sinn Fein 1970–9), Dublin.
An Phoblacht/Republican News (Provisional Sinn Fein), Dublin & Belfast.
Derry Journal, Derry.
Guardian, London.
Irish Echo, New York.
Irish News, Belfast.
Irish Press, Dublin.
Irish Times, Dublin.
The Starry Plough (Irish Republican Socialist Party), Dublin.
United Irishman (Sinn Fein and Official Sinn Fein), Dublin.

Index